Contents Table

I0009779

Hybrid Networking with AWS

Networking Automation and Optimization

Performance and Monitoring

Security Best Practices

Use Cases and Practical Applications

Emerging Trends and Future of AWS Networking

Appendices

- Appendix A: Glossary of AWS Networking Terms
- Appendix B: Key AWS Networking CLI Commands
- Appendix C: Comparison of AWS Networking Tools with Other Cloud Providers
- Appendix D: Troubleshooting Checklist for Common AWS Networking Issues

~ *Conclusion*

Introduction to AWS Networking

Welcome & What You'll Learn

Welcome to *AWS Networking: Building Robust Cloud Networks*! This book serves as a comprehensive guide to understanding, designing, and managing scalable, secure, and efficient cloud networks using AWS tools and services. Whether you're new to AWS or looking to deepen your expertise in AWS networking, this book will provide you with the foundational knowledge and advanced insights needed to harness the full potential of AWS networking.

Why AWS Networking Matters

In today's cloud-driven world, networking plays a critical role in ensuring seamless connectivity, scalability, and security. AWS provides a wide array of networking services designed to meet the diverse needs of modern enterprises, from startups to global organizations. Mastering AWS networking allows you to design cloud architectures that are not only robust and high-performing but also cost-effective and secure.

This book is tailored for professionals, developers, and IT teams who want to build resilient networks that support applications, services, and workloads of all sizes and complexities.

What You'll Learn in This Book

This book is divided into carefully structured sections to ensure a step-by-step learning experience. Here's a brief overview of what you'll explore:

1. **Introduction to AWS Networking Services**
   Gain an understanding of AWS's core networking offerings and the fundamental principles of cloud networking.
2. **Networking Foundations in AWS**
   Learn the basics of Virtual Private Cloud (VPC), subnets, IP addressing, routing, and AWS's regional architecture, which form the backbone of AWS networking.
3. **Security in AWS Networking**
   Dive into the security mechanisms, such as Security Groups, NACLs, and IAM, and discover how to secure your networks against modern threats while adhering to the AWS Shared Responsibility Model.
4. **Advanced Networking Components**
   Explore advanced tools and techniques like Transit Gateway, VPC peering, load balancing, and global networking solutions to enhance your AWS architecture.
5. **Networking Tools and Services**
   Get familiar with services like AWS Direct Connect, Amazon Route 53, and CloudFront for DNS management, private connectivity, and content delivery.
6. **Scalable and High-Availability Networking**
   Understand how to design fault-tolerant and scalable networks using auto-scaling groups, Elastic IPs, and other AWS capabilities.
7. **Hybrid Networking with AWS**
   Discover how to connect on-premise systems to AWS using VPNs, Direct Connect Gateway, and Outposts, enabling seamless hybrid architectures.

8. **Networking Automation and Optimization**
    Learn to automate networking tasks with AWS CLI, CloudFormation, and the AWS CDK, while optimizing costs and performance.
9. **Performance and Monitoring**
    Master tools like CloudWatch and AWS Network Manager to monitor and troubleshoot your networks effectively.
10. **Security Best Practices**
    Explore advanced security measures, such as DDoS protection, GuardDuty for threat detection, and automated network security configurations.
11. **Use Cases and Practical Applications**
    Dive into real-world scenarios, including multi-region architectures, IoT networking, and big data workloads, to see AWS networking in action.
12. **Emerging Trends and Future of AWS Networking**
    Learn about cutting-edge trends like edge networking, 5G integration, and AWS's evolving role in new technological paradigms.

Who This Book Is For

This book is ideal for:

- **Network Engineers and Cloud Architects**: Looking to design and optimize AWS cloud networks.
- **IT Professionals and System Administrators**: Seeking to secure and manage AWS network environments.
- **Developers**: Interested in building robust cloud applications with AWS networking tools.
- **Students and Enthusiasts**: Wanting to understand AWS networking from the ground up.

How to Use This Book

The book is designed to be both a learning resource and a practical reference.

- Beginners can follow the chapters sequentially for a structured learning path.
- Experienced professionals can focus on specific chapters to address particular challenges or deepen their expertise in advanced topics.
- Use the appendices for quick access to networking terminology, CLI commands, troubleshooting tips, and comparisons with other cloud providers.

A Journey Into Robust AWS Networking

By the end of this book, you'll have a deep understanding of AWS networking principles and be equipped with the knowledge to build secure, scalable, and high-performance networks in the cloud. You'll also be prepared to address emerging trends and future challenges in cloud networking with confidence.

Let's begin this exciting journey into the world of AWS networking!

Introduction to AWS Networking Services

AWS (Amazon Web Services) has revolutionized the way organizations build, deploy, and manage their IT infrastructure. Central to AWS's success is its robust suite of networking services that empower users to create secure, scalable, and high-performing networks tailored to a wide variety of use cases. In this chapter, we'll explore the foundational services and features that AWS provides for networking, their significance, and how they support modern cloud-based applications.

The Role of Networking in AWS

Networking in AWS is not just about connecting resources; it is about creating a highly adaptable infrastructure that allows businesses to:

- **Facilitate Communication**: Enable seamless interaction between services, applications, and users across the globe.
- **Ensure Security**: Protect sensitive data with multiple layers of security features and configurations.
- **Optimize Performance**: Deliver low-latency, high-throughput connections for demanding workloads.
- **Scale Efficiently**: Dynamically adapt to the demands of growing businesses and fluctuating workloads.

Overview of Key AWS Networking Services

AWS offers a comprehensive set of networking services designed to address various organizational needs. Below is an introduction to some of the core networking services and their primary functions:

1. **Amazon Virtual Private Cloud (VPC)**
   Amazon VPC allows users to create isolated networks within the AWS cloud. These virtual networks serve as the foundation for deploying and managing resources with complete control over IP addressing, routing, and security.
2. **Elastic Load Balancing (ELB)**
   ELB ensures high availability by distributing incoming application traffic across multiple targets, such as EC2 instances, containers, and IP addresses. It supports multiple types of load balancers, including Application Load Balancer (ALB) and Network Load Balancer (NLB).
3. **AWS Transit Gateway**
   This service simplifies the management of complex networks by connecting multiple VPCs, on-premise networks, and AWS accounts via a central hub.
4. **Amazon Route 53**
   A scalable and highly available Domain Name System (DNS) web service that translates human-readable domain names into IP addresses. It also enables routing traffic based on latency, geolocation, and other criteria.
5. **AWS Direct Connect**
   Direct Connect provides a dedicated, high-speed connection between on-premise infrastructure and AWS, improving performance and reducing latency compared to internet-based connections.
6. **AWS PrivateLink**
   PrivateLink allows users to securely access AWS services and third-party applications within their VPCs without exposing traffic to the public internet.
7. **Amazon CloudFront**
   This content delivery network (CDN) service accelerates the delivery of static and dynamic content to users around the globe while ensuring secure connections.

8. **AWS Global Accelerator**
   A networking service designed to optimize the performance of global applications by directing user traffic to the nearest edge location or AWS Region.

Core Features of AWS Networking Services

AWS networking services share several key features that set them apart:

- **Scalability**: Automatically adjust to meet the growing or fluctuating demands of your workloads.
- **Security**: Integrate with Security Groups, Network Access Control Lists (NACLs), and AWS Identity and Access Management (IAM) for robust protection.
- **Global Reach**: Leverage AWS's extensive network of data centers and edge locations for worldwide connectivity.
- **Integration**: Seamlessly work with other AWS services like EC2, S3, and RDS for comprehensive infrastructure management.
- **Cost Efficiency**: Provide flexible pricing models to meet diverse budgetary needs.

Key Use Cases of AWS Networking Services

AWS networking services cater to a variety of use cases, including:

- **Hosting Web Applications**: Deploy scalable, secure, and high-performance web applications with services like VPC, ELB, and Route 53.
- **Hybrid Cloud Architectures**: Bridge on-premise and cloud environments using AWS Direct Connect and VPN solutions.
- **Data Analytics**: Transfer large datasets quickly and securely across networks with tools like AWS DataSync and Elastic Fabric Adapter.
- **IoT Applications**: Build and manage IoT networks that require low latency and high throughput.
- **Global Content Delivery**: Deliver rich media and other content globally using Amazon CloudFront and Global Accelerator.

Advantages of Using AWS Networking Services

AWS networking services offer several advantages:

1. **Customization**: Build networks tailored to specific business requirements.
2. **Reliability**: AWS's global infrastructure ensures high availability and disaster recovery capabilities.
3. **Advanced Security**: Protect data in transit and at rest with encryption, private connectivity, and firewall rules.
4. **Ease of Use**: Simplify complex tasks with intuitive interfaces, APIs, and automation tools.
5. **Flexibility**: Support diverse workloads, from small-scale applications to enterprise-grade solutions.

A Glimpse Into What's Next

As we proceed through this book, we'll explore each of these services in detail, along with practical examples and advanced techniques to leverage their capabilities. By the end of this journey, you'll have the tools and knowledge to design robust, secure, and scalable networks in AWS.

The Basics of Cloud Networking

Cloud networking is the backbone of modern cloud computing, enabling communication between resources, services, and applications deployed in the cloud. In this chapter, we will delve into the fundamental concepts and principles of cloud networking, providing you with the essential knowledge to understand how networking works in a cloud environment, particularly within the AWS ecosystem.

What Is Cloud Networking?

Cloud networking refers to the use of cloud-based services and infrastructure to establish and manage networks that connect applications, users, and devices. Unlike traditional on-premise networks, cloud networks offer flexibility, scalability, and global accessibility. They rely on virtualized resources, software-defined networking (SDN), and automation to achieve these benefits.

In AWS, cloud networking focuses on providing secure, reliable, and high-performance connectivity between cloud resources and external networks, such as on-premise data centers or the internet.

Key Principles of Cloud Networking

To effectively understand cloud networking, it is crucial to grasp the following core principles:

1. **Virtualization**
   Cloud networks use virtualized components, such as Virtual Private Clouds (VPCs), virtual firewalls, and elastic load balancers, to provide the same functionalities as physical networking devices without hardware dependency.
2. **Scalability**
   Cloud networks can automatically scale up or down based on workload demands, ensuring optimal resource utilization and cost efficiency.
3. **Automation**
   Networking tasks, such as provisioning, configuration, and monitoring, are automated using tools like AWS CloudFormation and AWS Command Line Interface (CLI), reducing the complexity of managing networks.
4. **Global Reach**
   Cloud providers like AWS operate data centers worldwide, allowing users to deploy applications and services closer to their end users for improved performance and reduced latency.
5. **Security**
   Cloud networking incorporates robust security mechanisms, including encryption, firewalls, and identity-based access controls, to protect data and applications.

Components of Cloud Networking

Cloud networks comprise several essential components that work together to enable seamless communication. These include:

1. **Virtual Networks**
   - AWS offers Virtual Private Cloud (VPC), allowing users to create isolated networks for their resources.
   - Subnets divide VPCs into smaller network segments for better organization and traffic management.

2. **Routing**
   - Route tables define how traffic is directed within a network and between networks.
   - Internet Gateways and NAT Gateways facilitate internet access for resources in public and private subnets, respectively.
3. **DNS and IP Addressing**
   - Domain Name System (DNS) services like Amazon Route 53 convert domain names into IP addresses, enabling resource communication.
   - Elastic IPs provide static IP addresses that can be associated with instances for consistent connectivity.
4. **Load Balancing**
   - Elastic Load Balancing (ELB) distributes traffic across multiple resources to ensure high availability and reliability.
5. **Firewalls and Access Controls**
   - Security Groups and Network Access Control Lists (NACLs) act as virtual firewalls, controlling inbound and outbound traffic based on defined rules.
6. **Connectivity Options**
   - AWS Direct Connect and VPNs enable secure, low-latency connections between on-premise environments and the cloud.

Benefits of Cloud Networking

Cloud networking offers numerous advantages over traditional networking approaches:

1. **Cost Efficiency**
   Pay-as-you-go pricing models eliminate the need for upfront investments in networking hardware, making cloud networking more affordable.
2. **Flexibility**
   Users can quickly adapt their networks to changing business requirements, such as adding new regions or scaling resources.
3. **Reliability**
   Built-in redundancy and failover mechanisms ensure consistent performance and minimize downtime.
4. **Ease of Management**
   Centralized management tools, such as AWS Network Manager, simplify the administration of complex networks.
5. **Security**
   Advanced encryption and access control mechanisms protect sensitive data from unauthorized access and cyber threats.

The Role of AWS in Cloud Networking

AWS provides an extensive suite of networking services that align with the principles and components discussed above. These services enable organizations to:

- Build secure and scalable virtual networks with VPCs and subnets.
- Manage traffic flow using Route Tables, Internet Gateways, and NAT Gateways.
- Enhance performance with Elastic Load Balancing and Amazon CloudFront.
- Establish hybrid cloud architectures with Direct Connect and VPN solutions.
- Monitor and troubleshoot networks with tools like Amazon CloudWatch and AWS Flow Logs.

Challenges in Cloud Networking

While cloud networking offers significant benefits, it is not without challenges. Some common issues include:

1. **Complexity**: Managing large-scale networks with multiple interconnected components can be challenging.
2. **Security Risks**: Misconfigurations in security settings may lead to vulnerabilities.
3. **Cost Management**: Without proper monitoring, networking costs can escalate.

Understanding these challenges and adopting best practices, which we will explore throughout this book, can help you overcome these obstacles effectively.

In this chapter, we've laid the groundwork for understanding the basics of cloud networking. In the next chapter, *Benefits of AWS Networking for Modern Enterprises*, we'll explore how AWS's networking capabilities specifically cater to the needs of businesses, enabling them to achieve their operational and strategic goals.

Let's continue building your knowledge to create robust cloud networks!

Benefits of AWS Networking for Modern Enterprises

Modern enterprises are rapidly shifting to cloud-based infrastructure to achieve scalability, flexibility, and cost efficiency. AWS networking plays a pivotal role in enabling organizations to build robust, secure, and high-performance cloud environments that meet their operational and business needs. In this chapter, we will explore the key benefits of AWS networking and how it empowers enterprises to thrive in a dynamic digital landscape.

1. Scalability and Flexibility

One of the most significant advantages of AWS networking is its ability to scale seamlessly with business demands. Enterprises can:

- **Scale Resources Dynamically**: Automatically adjust network resources, such as Virtual Private Clouds (VPCs), subnets, and load balancers, to accommodate growing traffic or fluctuating workloads.
- **Customize Network Configurations**: Tailor networks to fit unique requirements, whether for small-scale applications or enterprise-grade solutions.
- **Expand Globally**: Leverage AWS's global infrastructure to deploy resources closer to end-users, ensuring better performance and reduced latency.

AWS tools like Elastic Load Balancing (ELB) and Auto Scaling Groups simplify the scaling process, enabling organizations to maintain optimal performance under varying loads.

2. Enhanced Security and Compliance

AWS networking is designed with security as a cornerstone, offering multiple layers of protection to safeguard enterprise data and applications. Key features include:

- **Security Groups and Network Access Control Lists (NACLs)**: Control inbound and outbound traffic at both the instance and subnet levels.
- **Encryption**: Protect data in transit and at rest using industry-standard encryption protocols.
- **Identity and Access Management (IAM)**: Implement fine-grained access controls to ensure that only authorized users and services have access to resources.
- **DDoS Protection**: Mitigate Distributed Denial-of-Service (DDoS) attacks using AWS Shield and Web Application Firewall (WAF).

AWS also adheres to various regulatory frameworks, such as GDPR, HIPAA, and ISO 27001, helping enterprises meet compliance requirements effortlessly.

3. Cost Efficiency

AWS networking offers a cost-effective solution for building and managing enterprise networks. Businesses can:

- **Avoid Upfront Costs**: Eliminate the need for expensive hardware by leveraging virtualized network components.
- **Pay-As-You-Go**: Pay only for the resources used, with no long-term commitments or hidden costs.

- **Optimize Costs**: Use tools like AWS Trusted Advisor and Cost Explorer to identify opportunities for cost savings and optimize network configurations.

Additionally, AWS Direct Connect and PrivateLink enable cost-efficient private connectivity options, reducing data transfer expenses compared to traditional methods.

---

4. High Availability and Reliability

AWS provides enterprises with a highly available and reliable networking infrastructure, minimizing downtime and ensuring business continuity. Key features include:

- **Redundant Architecture**: AWS regions and availability zones (AZs) are designed with redundancy to protect against single points of failure.
- **Elastic Load Balancing**: Automatically distributes traffic across multiple targets to prevent overloading and ensure application uptime.
- **Backup and Recovery**: Integrate networking services with disaster recovery solutions like AWS Backup and Amazon Route 53 to maintain data availability during unexpected events.

This reliability makes AWS an ideal choice for mission-critical applications and services.

---

5. Improved Performance

AWS networking is built to deliver low-latency, high-throughput connections for demanding workloads. Enterprises benefit from:

- **Global Infrastructure**: AWS's extensive network of data centers and edge locations ensures minimal latency for users worldwide.
- **Content Delivery Networks (CDNs)**: Services like Amazon CloudFront accelerate the delivery of static and dynamic content, improving user experience.
- **AWS Global Accelerator**: Optimizes traffic routing to improve application performance for globally distributed users.

These capabilities make AWS networking well-suited for applications requiring real-time processing, such as video streaming and IoT.

---

6. Seamless Integration with Hybrid Architectures

For enterprises operating in hybrid environments, AWS networking offers seamless connectivity between on-premise systems and cloud resources. Features like:

- **Direct Connect**: Provide dedicated, low-latency links to AWS.
- **VPN Connections**: Enable secure communication between on-premise data centers and AWS.
- **AWS Outposts**: Bring AWS services to on-premise locations for consistent hybrid workflows.

This flexibility allows enterprises to gradually transition to the cloud or maintain critical workloads on-premise.

---

7. Centralized Management and Automation

AWS networking services simplify network management through centralized tools and automation. Enterprises can:

- **Monitor Networks**: Use tools like Amazon CloudWatch and AWS Network Manager for real-time monitoring and performance analysis.
- **Automate Tasks**: Leverage AWS CloudFormation and AWS CLI to automate network provisioning, configuration, and scaling.
- **Streamline Operations**: Consolidate multi-region and multi-account networks using AWS Transit Gateway and AWS Global Network Manager.

These features enable IT teams to focus on strategic initiatives rather than manual administrative tasks.

8. Innovation and Future-Ready Networking

AWS continually innovates its networking services to stay ahead of industry trends. Modern enterprises can take advantage of:

- **Edge Networking**: Leverage AWS Wavelength for low-latency applications like 5G.
- **Machine Learning Integration**: Incorporate AI-driven insights into network management using AWS services.
- **Emerging Technologies**: Stay prepared for advancements like quantum networking and the metaverse with AWS's forward-thinking approach.

Conclusion

AWS networking offers a comprehensive suite of tools and features that empower enterprises to build secure, scalable, and cost-efficient networks. By leveraging these capabilities, organizations can improve performance, ensure reliability, and drive innovation while maintaining a competitive edge in the digital era.

Core Networking Terminology and Concepts

Networking is the backbone of cloud computing, and understanding its core terminology and concepts is crucial for designing and managing robust cloud networks. In this chapter, we will explore the fundamental networking terms and principles that underpin AWS networking. This foundational knowledge will prepare you to navigate more advanced topics later in the book.

1. Networking Basics

Before diving into AWS-specific concepts, let's establish a solid understanding of basic networking principles:

- **IP Address**: A unique identifier assigned to devices in a network, enabling them to communicate. AWS uses both IPv4 and IPv6 formats for addressing.
- **CIDR (Classless Inter-Domain Routing)**: A method for defining IP address ranges. AWS uses CIDR blocks to allocate IP addresses to Virtual Private Clouds (VPCs) and subnets.
- **DNS (Domain Name System)**: Translates human-readable domain names (e.g., `example.com`) into IP addresses. AWS provides DNS services through Amazon Route 53.
- **Subnet**: A segment within a network, created by dividing a larger network into smaller, more manageable pieces.
- **Routing Table**: Defines the rules for directing traffic within a network or between networks.

2. Core AWS Networking Terminology

AWS networking builds upon traditional networking concepts, introducing unique terms and services specific to its cloud environment:

- **Virtual Private Cloud (VPC)**: A logically isolated section of the AWS cloud where you can launch resources within a defined network.
- **Availability Zone (AZ)**: A physically distinct data center within an AWS Region. AWS networking services allow you to build fault-tolerant architectures by distributing resources across multiple AZs.
- **Internet Gateway (IGW)**: A component that enables resources in a VPC to access the internet.
- **NAT Gateway (Network Address Translation Gateway)**: Allows private resources to connect to the internet while keeping them inaccessible from the public internet.
- **Elastic IP (EIP)**: A static public IP address that can be associated with an instance to ensure consistent connectivity.
- **Elastic Network Interface (ENI)**: A virtual network interface that can be attached to an EC2 instance, providing flexible network configurations.

3. Key Concepts in AWS Networking

AWS networking is built on a few critical concepts that differentiate it from traditional networking:

- **Software-Defined Networking (SDN)**: AWS leverages SDN to provide flexibility in defining and managing network configurations. This enables users to create complex architectures with ease.
- **Shared Responsibility Model**: AWS ensures the security of the cloud infrastructure, while customers are responsible for securing their data and resources within the cloud.
- **Elasticity**: AWS networking services are designed to scale automatically with changing workloads, ensuring consistent performance and cost efficiency.

- **Private and Public Networks**: AWS allows you to define private subnets (for resources that don't require internet access) and public subnets (for resources that need to interact with the internet).

---

4. Common Networking Components

AWS networking integrates a variety of components to facilitate secure and efficient communication:

- **Load Balancers**: Distribute incoming traffic across multiple resources to enhance availability and performance. AWS offers several types of load balancers, including Application Load Balancer (ALB) and Network Load Balancer (NLB).
- **Peering Connections**: Allow direct communication between two VPCs without using the internet.
- **Transit Gateway**: A central hub for managing connectivity between multiple VPCs, on-premise networks, and AWS accounts.
- **Route 53**: AWS's scalable DNS service for routing user requests to applications based on latency, geolocation, and other criteria.

---

5. Traffic Management and Routing

Traffic management is a critical aspect of AWS networking, ensuring efficient communication between resources and external networks:

- **Routing Policies**: AWS supports various routing policies (e.g., failover, latency-based, weighted) to direct traffic intelligently.
- **Route Tables**: Each VPC contains one or more route tables that define how traffic is directed within the network and to external destinations.
- **BGP (Border Gateway Protocol)**: Used in advanced scenarios like AWS Direct Connect for routing traffic between AWS and on-premise networks.

---

6. Security Concepts in AWS Networking

Security is integral to AWS networking. Understanding the following concepts is essential for designing secure networks:

- **Security Groups**: Act as virtual firewalls at the instance level, controlling inbound and outbound traffic.
- **Network Access Control Lists (NACLs)**: Operate at the subnet level, providing an additional layer of security.
- **Encryption**: AWS supports encryption in transit (using protocols like HTTPS) and at rest (using services like AWS Key Management Service).

---

7. Monitoring and Optimization

Efficient network management requires continuous monitoring and optimization. Key tools and concepts include:

- **Amazon CloudWatch**: Monitors network performance metrics, such as bandwidth usage and latency.
- **Flow Logs**: Capture detailed information about IP traffic in your VPC for analysis and troubleshooting.

- **AWS Trusted Advisor**: Provides recommendations to optimize network configurations, improve performance, and reduce costs.

---

8. Common Use Cases for AWS Networking

AWS networking concepts are applied across a wide range of use cases, including:

- **Hosting Web Applications**: Building secure, scalable, and high-performing architectures for web and mobile apps.
- **Hybrid Cloud Architectures**: Connecting on-premise systems with AWS resources.
- **Big Data Workloads**: Transferring and processing large datasets efficiently across networks.
- **IoT Applications**: Supporting low-latency, high-throughput communication for IoT devices.

Conclusion

In this chapter, we've covered the core networking terminology and concepts that form the foundation of AWS networking. By understanding these principles, you are now equipped to dive deeper into the specifics of AWS's networking services and their applications in real-world scenarios.

Networking Foundations in AWS

Understanding Virtual Private Cloud (VPC)

The Virtual Private Cloud (VPC) is the cornerstone of AWS networking, providing users with an isolated, customizable environment to launch and manage their AWS resources. A VPC acts as your private network within the AWS cloud, giving you full control over IP addressing, subnets, routing, and security. This chapter explores the core concepts, components, and capabilities of VPCs, equipping you with the foundational knowledge needed to design secure and efficient networks in AWS.

---

1. What is a Virtual Private Cloud (VPC)?

A **Virtual Private Cloud (VPC)** is a logically isolated section of the AWS cloud where users can launch AWS resources, such as EC2 instances and databases, in a virtual network environment. VPCs provide:

- **Complete Isolation**: Ensures that your resources are securely separated from other users in the AWS cloud.
- **Customization**: Allows you to define your IP address range, create subnets, and configure routing tables.
- **Connectivity Options**: Enables secure connections to the internet, other VPCs, or on-premise data centers.

---

2. Key Components of a VPC

Several components work together to create a fully functional VPC. These include:

1. **CIDR Block**
   - A VPC requires an IP address range specified in **CIDR (Classless Inter-Domain Routing)** notation, such as 10.0.0.0/16.
   - This defines the size of the IP address space available for your subnets and resources.
2. **Subnets**
   - Subnets divide a VPC into smaller segments, each associated with a specific CIDR block.
   - Subnets can be public (accessible to the internet) or private (restricted to internal communication).
3. **Route Tables**
   - Each VPC contains one or more route tables that define how traffic is directed within the network and to external destinations.
4. **Internet Gateway (IGW)**
   - An IGW enables resources in public subnets to communicate with the internet.
5. **NAT Gateway**
   - A NAT (Network Address Translation) Gateway allows resources in private subnets to access the internet without exposing them to inbound traffic.
6. **Elastic IPs (EIPs)**
   - Static public IP addresses that can be associated with resources to ensure consistent connectivity.
7. **Security Groups and NACLs (Network Access Control Lists)**
   - Security groups act as virtual firewalls for resources, while NACLs provide subnet-level traffic filtering.
8. **Endpoints**

- ○ VPC Endpoints allow private communication between resources in a VPC and AWS services without traversing the public internet.

---

3. Benefits of Using a VPC

- **Security**: Complete control over inbound and outbound traffic using security groups, NACLs, and encryption.
- **Customization**: Tailor IP addressing, routing, and subnet configuration to meet specific requirements.
- **Scalability**: Easily expand IP address ranges, add new subnets, or connect multiple VPCs.
- **Cost-Efficiency**: Pay only for the resources you use within your VPC.
- **Integration**: Seamless connectivity with other AWS services, such as RDS, Lambda, and S3.

---

4. VPC Configuration Options

AWS provides several ways to configure and manage VPCs:

1. **Default VPC**
   - ○ AWS automatically creates a default VPC in each region.
   - ○ The default VPC includes a public subnet, an internet gateway, and a route table configured for internet access.
2. **Custom VPC**
   - ○ Users can create custom VPCs to define their own IP ranges, subnets, and routing configurations.
   - ○ Custom VPCs offer greater flexibility and control over network architecture.
3. **VPC Peering**
   - ○ Connect two VPCs in the same or different regions for direct communication without the need for an internet gateway or VPN.
4. **Transit Gateway**
   - ○ A central hub that connects multiple VPCs, on-premise networks, and AWS accounts, simplifying complex network architectures.

---

5. Use Cases for VPCs

1. **Hosting Applications**
   - ○ Deploy web applications with public-facing subnets for frontend servers and private subnets for backend resources.
2. **Hybrid Cloud Architectures**
   - ○ Extend on-premise networks to AWS using VPN or Direct Connect.
3. **Big Data Analytics**
   - ○ Use private subnets for data storage and processing while maintaining secure access to data analysis tools.
4. **Multi-Region Deployments**
   - ○ Use VPC peering or Transit Gateway to create resilient, multi-region architectures for disaster recovery.

---

6. Best Practices for VPC Design

1. **Plan Your IP Addressing**
    *   Choose CIDR blocks that accommodate future growth while avoiding overlaps with on-premise or other VPC networks.
2. **Use Multiple Subnets**
    *   Distribute resources across multiple subnets in different Availability Zones for fault tolerance.
3. **Implement Network Segmentation**
    *   Separate sensitive workloads into private subnets and restrict access using security groups and NACLs.
4. **Enable Flow Logs**
    *   Monitor network traffic using VPC Flow Logs to troubleshoot connectivity issues and detect security threats.
5. **Leverage Endpoints**
    *   Use VPC endpoints for secure and cost-effective access to AWS services without internet exposure.

---

7. Common Challenges and Solutions

1. **IP Address Exhaustion**
    *   **Challenge**: Running out of IP addresses in your VPC.
    *   **Solution**: Use a larger CIDR block during VPC creation or add secondary CIDR blocks.
2. **Misconfigured Route Tables**
    *   **Challenge**: Incorrect routing rules can cause connectivity issues.
    *   **Solution**: Regularly audit and test route tables for accuracy.
3. **Security Gaps**
    *   **Challenge**: Inadequate security configurations can expose resources to attacks.
    *   **Solution**: Apply least-privilege principles to security groups and regularly review access rules.

Conclusion

Virtual Private Cloud (VPC) is the foundation of networking in AWS, offering flexibility, security, and scalability for a wide range of use cases. By understanding its components and best practices, you can design efficient and secure cloud networks tailored to your business needs.

Subnets and IP Addressing in AWS

Subnets and IP addressing form the backbone of any network configuration within AWS. These components enable users to organize their Virtual Private Clouds (VPCs) into smaller, manageable segments while ensuring efficient communication and secure resource allocation. In this chapter, we will explore the concepts of subnets, the basics of IP addressing, and their practical implementation in AWS.

1. What Are Subnets?

A **subnet** is a subdivision of a Virtual Private Cloud (VPC) that allows you to group resources and manage traffic within your network. Subnets play a critical role in defining whether resources are publicly or privately accessible and in improving security and performance.

- **Public Subnets**: These subnets allow resources to communicate with the internet, typically through an Internet Gateway (IGW). Common use cases include hosting web servers or other public-facing applications.
- **Private Subnets**: Resources in private subnets cannot communicate directly with the internet. These are often used for backend systems, such as databases and application servers.
- **Isolated Subnets**: A type of private subnet with no external access, often used for highly sensitive workloads.

2. Understanding IP Addressing

Every device in a network needs an **IP address** to communicate with other devices. AWS supports both IPv4 and IPv6 addressing schemes. Here's a quick overview:

- **IPv4**: A 32-bit address written in decimal format (e.g., 192.168.1.1). AWS uses Classless Inter-Domain Routing (CIDR) to allocate IPv4 address ranges for VPCs and subnets.
- **IPv6**: A 128-bit address written in hexadecimal format (e.g., 2001:db8::1). IPv6 is used for larger address spaces and better scalability.

3. CIDR Blocks in AWS

CIDR blocks are used to define the IP address range for a VPC and its subnets.

- **VPC CIDR Block**: When creating a VPC, you must assign a primary CIDR block (e.g., 10.0.0.0/16). This defines the IP address range for all resources within the VPC.
- **Subnet CIDR Block**: Each subnet in the VPC is assigned a smaller CIDR block (e.g., 10.0.1.0/24) that falls within the VPC's range.

CIDR Notation Breakdown:

- The 10.0.0.0 part represents the network address.
- The /16 or /24 specifies the subnet mask, defining the number of IP addresses in the block. For example:
    - /16: Provides 65,536 IP addresses.
    - /24: Provides 256 IP addresses.

4. Subnet Configuration in AWS

Subnets are a critical part of VPC configuration. Here's how they work:

1. **Subnet Placement**
   - Subnets are mapped to individual Availability Zones (AZs).
   - You can create multiple subnets in different AZs to improve redundancy and fault tolerance.
2. **Subnet Types**
   - **Public Subnet**: Configured with a route to the Internet Gateway.
   - **Private Subnet**: Configured with a NAT Gateway or NAT Instance for outbound internet access, with no direct inbound access.
   - **Dual-Stack Subnet**: Supports both IPv4 and IPv6 traffic.
3. **IP Address Allocation**
   - AWS reserves a small number of IP addresses in every subnet for internal use:
     - `.0`: Network address.
     - `.1`: VPC router.
     - `.2`: AWS-provided DNS server.
     - `.3`: Reserved for future use.
     - `.255`: Broadcast address (not supported in AWS).

5. Routing in Subnets

Each subnet must be associated with a **route table** that defines how traffic flows in and out of the subnet.

- **Public Subnet Routing**: Contains a route to the Internet Gateway for outbound traffic.
- **Private Subnet Routing**: Contains a route to the NAT Gateway for secure outbound traffic.
- **Local Routing**: Every subnet automatically has a local route for communication within the VPC.

6. Best Practices for Subnets and IP Addressing

1. **Plan IP Addressing Carefully**
   - Choose CIDR blocks that provide enough addresses for current and future needs. Avoid overlapping ranges with other VPCs or on-premise networks.
2. **Use Separate Subnets for Different Workloads**
   - Isolate web servers, databases, and application servers into separate subnets for better security and performance.
3. **Distribute Subnets Across Availability Zones**
   - Ensure fault tolerance by creating subnets in multiple AZs within the same region.
4. **Enable IPv6 for Scalability**
   - Use IPv6 addresses for applications requiring global scalability and connectivity.
5. **Monitor IP Address Usage**
   - Use Amazon VPC IP Address Manager (IPAM) to track and manage IP address usage across your VPCs.

7. Common Challenges and Solutions

1. **IP Address Exhaustion**
   - **Challenge**: Running out of IP addresses in a subnet or VPC.
   - **Solution**: Add a secondary CIDR block to the VPC or create additional subnets.

2. **Misconfigured Subnets**
   - **Challenge**: Incorrect subnet CIDR blocks or routing configurations can lead to connectivity issues.
   - **Solution**: Validate CIDR block assignments and ensure subnets have the correct route tables.
3. **Overlapping CIDR Blocks**
   - **Challenge**: Using overlapping CIDR ranges can cause conflicts when connecting VPCs or hybrid networks.
   - **Solution**: Plan CIDR blocks carefully during network design.

---

8. Practical Use Cases for Subnets in AWS

- **Web Hosting**: Place web servers in public subnets and databases in private subnets for a secure, scalable architecture.
- **Hybrid Cloud Environments**: Use private subnets to host resources accessible via VPN or Direct Connect.
- **Data Analytics**: Segment big data processing workloads into isolated subnets for better organization and security.

Conclusion

Subnets and IP addressing are fundamental elements of AWS networking that allow you to design secure, scalable, and efficient architectures. By understanding how to allocate IP addresses, configure subnets, and manage routing, you can build VPCs that meet your application and organizational needs.

Elastic Network Interfaces (ENIs)

Elastic Network Interfaces (ENIs) are a crucial component of AWS networking that provides flexibility, scalability, and redundancy for networked resources within a Virtual Private Cloud (VPC). An ENI is a virtual network interface that can be attached to Amazon EC2 instances, enabling efficient communication and advanced networking configurations. This chapter dives into the purpose, functionality, and best practices for using ENIs in AWS.

1. What Is an Elastic Network Interface (ENI)?

An **Elastic Network Interface (ENI)** is a logical networking component in a VPC that represents a virtual network card. Each ENI is attached to an EC2 instance and serves as a gateway for the instance to communicate with other resources within the VPC or external networks.

Key attributes of an ENI include:

- **Primary Private IP Address**: The main IP address assigned to the ENI.
- **Secondary IP Addresses**: Optional additional IPs for advanced configurations.
- **Elastic IP Addresses (EIPs)**: Public IP addresses mapped to private IPs for internet access.
- **Security Groups**: Firewall rules that govern the ENI's traffic.
- **MAC Address**: A unique identifier for the ENI.
- **Network Interface ID**: A unique identifier for managing the ENI in AWS.

2. Types of ENIs

AWS provides several types of ENIs to support different use cases:

1. **Primary ENI**
   - The default ENI automatically created and attached to an EC2 instance when it is launched.
   - It cannot be detached or reassigned to another instance.
2. **Secondary ENI**
   - Additional ENIs that can be created and attached to an instance.
   - These ENIs are detachable and can be reassigned to other instances.
3. **Trunk ENI**
   - Used in scenarios like AWS Direct Connect and virtual network appliances to support VLANs (Virtual Local Area Networks).
4. **Elastic Fabric Adapter (EFA)**
   - Specialized ENIs designed for high-performance computing and low-latency networking applications.

3. Use Cases for ENIs

ENIs are versatile and applicable to various scenarios:

1. **High Availability and Failover**
   - Attach multiple ENIs to an instance to enable seamless failover. If one interface fails, traffic can be rerouted to the backup ENI.
2. **Network Segmentation**
   - Assign different ENIs to manage traffic for distinct applications or environments, such as separating development and production traffic.

3. **Multi-Homed Instances**
   - Use multiple ENIs to connect an instance to different subnets, VPCs, or even on-premise networks.
4. **Custom Networking**
   - Host applications that require multiple IP addresses, such as web servers hosting multiple sites or applications requiring dedicated IPs.
5. **Virtual Appliances**
   - Configure ENIs to work with virtual appliances like firewalls, load balancers, and NAT devices.

---

4. Managing ENIs

AWS provides tools and options to manage ENIs effectively:

1. **Creating ENIs**
   - ENIs can be created in the AWS Management Console, AWS CLI, or using AWS SDKs.
   - When creating an ENI, you define its associated subnet, IP addresses, security groups, and description.
2. **Attaching ENIs**
   - ENIs can be attached to running EC2 instances without stopping them.
   - Use cases include adding additional IPs or network paths dynamically.
3. **Detaching and Reattaching ENIs**
   - Secondary ENIs can be detached from one instance and reattached to another instance, facilitating resource migration or failover.
4. **Deleting ENIs**
   - Unused ENIs can be deleted to free up resources, provided they are not attached to any instance.

---

5. Networking Features with ENIs

ENIs support several advanced networking features, enhancing their utility in complex architectures:

1. **Source and Destination Checks**
   - By default, EC2 instances verify the source and destination of packets.
   - Disabling this check on an ENI allows it to act as a NAT device or router.
2. **Private IP Addressing**
   - Each ENI can have a primary private IP address and multiple secondary private IP addresses.
3. **Elastic IP Addressing**
   - Map Elastic IPs to ENIs to enable public internet access.
4. **Security Groups**
   - Attach up to five security groups to an ENI to manage its inbound and outbound traffic.
5. **Traffic Mirroring**
   - Duplicate network traffic from an ENI to a monitoring or analysis appliance for troubleshooting and security analysis.

---

6. Best Practices for Using ENIs

1. **Leverage Secondary ENIs for Flexibility**

        ○ Use secondary ENIs to implement failover strategies, resource migration, or traffic segmentation.

2. **Optimize Security Group Configurations**
   - ○ Assign appropriate security groups to ENIs to enforce least privilege and minimize exposure.
3. **Monitor IP Address Utilization**
   - ○ Avoid IP address exhaustion by regularly monitoring and auditing ENI configurations.
4. **Plan for Failover Scenarios**
   - ○ Preconfigure backup ENIs for critical workloads to minimize downtime during failures.
5. **Use Elastic IPs Strategically**
   - ○ Assign Elastic IPs to ENIs only when public internet access is necessary to avoid unnecessary costs.

---

7. Common Challenges and Solutions

1. **IP Address Exhaustion**
   - ○ **Challenge**: Running out of private IP addresses for ENIs in a subnet.
   - ○ **Solution**: Expand the VPC CIDR block or add secondary CIDR blocks.
2. **Traffic Bottlenecks**
   - ○ **Challenge**: Performance issues due to insufficient bandwidth.
   - ○ **Solution**: Use Enhanced Networking or Elastic Fabric Adapters for high-throughput workloads.
3. **Misconfigured Security Groups**
   - ○ **Challenge**: Overly permissive or restrictive security group rules can disrupt traffic.
   - ○ **Solution**: Regularly audit and refine security group settings.

Conclusion

Elastic Network Interfaces (ENIs) are a powerful feature of AWS networking, providing the flexibility to create robust, high-performing, and secure network configurations. By understanding their capabilities and best practices, you can enhance the scalability, availability, and reliability of your AWS-based applications.

The Role of AWS Regions and Availability Zones

AWS Regions and Availability Zones (AZs) form the backbone of Amazon Web Services' global infrastructure, offering unparalleled reliability, scalability, and low-latency connectivity for cloud networking. This chapter explores the significance of AWS Regions and AZs, how they influence network architecture, and how you can leverage them to design fault-tolerant and high-performing systems.

1. What Are AWS Regions?

An **AWS Region** is a geographically isolated area where AWS provides its services. Each Region consists of multiple Availability Zones and is designed to be independent and self-sufficient. AWS currently operates Regions around the world to ensure proximity to end users, legal compliance, and optimized performance.

Key Characteristics of AWS Regions:

- **Geographic Distribution**: Spread across continents to serve global customers. Examples include us-east-1 (North Virginia), eu-central-1 (Frankfurt), and ap-southeast-1 (Singapore).
- **Independence**: Each Region operates independently, providing full isolation for disaster recovery.
- **Data Residency**: Ensures compliance with data sovereignty requirements by keeping data within the chosen Region.
- **Service Availability**: Not all services are available in every Region; choosing the correct Region based on service availability is crucial.

2. What Are Availability Zones?

An **Availability Zone (AZ)** is a physically distinct data center within an AWS Region. Each AZ has independent power, cooling, and networking infrastructure but is interconnected with other AZs in the same Region using low-latency, high-throughput links.

Key Characteristics of AZs:

- **Fault Isolation**: AZs are designed to isolate failures, ensuring high availability for applications.
- **High Throughput**: The connectivity between AZs within a Region supports synchronous replication and low-latency operations.
- **Scalability**: Applications can be distributed across multiple AZs to scale horizontally.

3. Benefits of Using AWS Regions and AZs

1. **High Availability**
   Distribute workloads across multiple AZs to minimize downtime and ensure redundancy. For example:
   - Deploying EC2 instances in multiple AZs ensures that even if one AZ experiences a failure, your application remains operational.
2. **Disaster Recovery**
   Use AWS Regions for disaster recovery by replicating data and applications to a secondary Region. For example:
   - Store backups in a different Region using Amazon S3's cross-region replication.

3. **Low Latency**
   Choose the closest Region to your end users to reduce latency and improve application performance. For example:
   - Use ap-southeast-2 (Sydney) for applications targeting Australian users.

4. **Regulatory Compliance**
   Select Regions that comply with local laws and data residency requirements. For example:
   - Deploy workloads in eu-west-1 (Ireland) to meet GDPR compliance.

5. **Cost Optimization**
   Some Regions offer lower pricing than others. For example:
   - us-east-1 is often more cost-effective than other Regions.

---

4. Networking Between Regions and AZs

4.1 Inter-Region Connectivity

AWS Regions are connected via high-speed, redundant links to support data transfers and global applications. Key features include:

- **AWS Global Accelerator**: Improves performance by routing traffic to the optimal Region.
- **S3 Cross-Region Replication**: Automatically replicates objects between S3 buckets in different Regions.
- **Amazon Route 53**: Routes traffic to the best-performing Region based on latency.

4.2 Intra-Region Connectivity

Within a Region, AZs are interconnected with high-bandwidth, low-latency links. This allows for:

- **Synchronous Replication**: Services like Amazon RDS and Aurora use synchronous replication between AZs for high availability.
- **Load Balancing**: Elastic Load Balancing distributes traffic across instances in multiple AZs to enhance availability.

---

5. Best Practices for Using Regions and AZs

1. **Deploy Across Multiple AZs**
   - Use multi-AZ deployments for services like RDS and EC2 Auto Scaling groups to ensure fault tolerance.

2. **Leverage Multi-Region Architectures**
   - Use multiple Regions for disaster recovery, compliance, or proximity to users. For example:
     - Primary Region: us-east-1 (North Virginia).
     - Secondary Region: us-west-2 (Oregon) for disaster recovery.

3. **Consider Latency and Throughput**
   - Use AWS Direct Connect or Global Accelerator for low-latency connectivity between Regions or from on-premise networks.

4. **Plan for Data Residency**
   - Ensure that the Region chosen complies with local data sovereignty laws.

5. **Monitor Costs and Performance**
   - Use AWS Cost Explorer and CloudWatch to track and optimize costs and performance across Regions and AZs.

---

6. Common Challenges and Solutions

1. **Challenge: Region Selection**
   - **Problem**: Selecting a Region without considering latency, cost, or service availability.
   - **Solution**: Use the [AWS Regional Services List] (https://aws.amazon.com/about-aws/global-infrastructure/regional-product-services/) to identify the best Region for your application.
2. **Challenge: AZ Failure**
   - **Problem**: Downtime due to the unavailability of an AZ.
   - **Solution**: Distribute workloads across multiple AZs and use Elastic Load Balancing to reroute traffic.
3. **Challenge: Inter-Region Costs**
   - **Problem**: High data transfer costs between Regions.
   - **Solution**: Optimize data transfers and consider consolidating workloads into fewer Regions.

---

7. Practical Use Cases for Regions and AZs

1. **E-Commerce Platforms**
   - Deploy web servers in multiple AZs to handle traffic spikes and ensure uptime.
   - Use S3 cross-region replication for product catalogs to improve performance globally.
2. **Content Delivery**
   - Use Amazon CloudFront for global content delivery, with Regions acting as origins.
3. **Disaster Recovery**
   - Replicate databases and critical applications to a secondary Region for rapid failover.
4. **Big Data Analytics**
   - Process data in a Region close to where it's generated to minimize latency, then replicate results to a central Region.

Conclusion

AWS Regions and Availability Zones are foundational elements of the AWS infrastructure, enabling scalable, reliable, and geographically distributed applications. By understanding how to effectively leverage Regions and AZs, you can design cloud architectures that meet the demands of modern enterprises.

Internet Gateways and NAT Gateways

Internet Gateways (IGWs) and NAT Gateways (Network Address Translation Gateways) are fundamental components of AWS networking that enable secure and controlled internet connectivity for resources within a Virtual Private Cloud (VPC). These gateways ensure that instances in public and private subnets can communicate with external networks without compromising security or reliability. This chapter explores the functionality, configuration, and use cases of Internet Gateways and NAT Gateways.

1. Internet Gateways (IGWs)

An **Internet Gateway (IGW)** is a horizontally scaled, highly available component that allows resources in a VPC to connect to the internet. It acts as a bridge between the VPC and the internet, providing outbound internet access for public subnets and allowing inbound traffic for publicly accessible resources.

Key Characteristics of an Internet Gateway:

- **Scalability**: Automatically scales to accommodate varying levels of traffic.
- **High Availability**: Operates as a fully managed AWS service, ensuring no single point of failure.
- **Bidirectional Communication**: Supports both outbound and inbound traffic for resources in public subnets.

1.1 Configuring an Internet Gateway

To enable internet connectivity for your VPC, you need to attach an Internet Gateway to it. Here's the process:

1. **Create an Internet Gateway**
   - In the AWS Management Console, navigate to **VPC > Internet Gateways** and create a new IGW.
2. **Attach the IGW to a VPC**
   - Attach the IGW to the target VPC to establish connectivity.
3. **Update Route Tables**
   - Add a route in the VPC's route table pointing 0.0.0.0/0 (all traffic) to the Internet Gateway. This ensures that traffic destined for the internet is routed through the IGW.

1.2 Use Cases for Internet Gateways

- **Public-Facing Applications**: Host web servers, APIs, or applications accessible to the internet.
- **File Downloads and Updates**: Enable instances to download updates or connect to third-party services.
- **Remote Management**: Allow SSH or RDP access to instances for maintenance.

2. NAT Gateways (Network Address Translation Gateways)

A **NAT Gateway** enables instances in private subnets to connect to the internet or other external networks without exposing them to inbound internet traffic. It provides a secure method for instances to access resources outside the VPC, such as downloading updates or accessing APIs, while keeping them isolated from public access.

Key Characteristics of a NAT Gateway:

- **Outbound-Only Traffic**: Allows instances to send traffic to the internet but blocks unsolicited inbound connections.
- **Managed Service**: Fully managed by AWS, with built-in redundancy and scalability.
- **Elastic IP Address**: Uses an Elastic IP to provide a static public IP for outbound traffic.

2.1 Configuring a NAT Gateway

To set up a NAT Gateway, follow these steps:

1. **Create a NAT Gateway**
   - In the AWS Management Console, navigate to **VPC > NAT Gateways** and create a new NAT Gateway.
   - Specify the public subnet where the NAT Gateway will reside and associate an Elastic IP address with it.
2. **Update Route Tables**
   - Modify the route table of the private subnets to direct 0.0.0.0/0 traffic to the NAT Gateway.

2.2 Use Cases for NAT Gateways

- **Private Subnet Internet Access**: Allow instances in private subnets to access the internet securely.
- **Application Updates**: Enable private instances to download patches and updates.
- **API Access**: Connect private instances to external APIs or SaaS platforms.

---

3. Internet Gateway vs. NAT Gateway

Feature	Internet Gateway (IGW)	NAT Gateway (NAT)
Purpose	Bidirectional internet communication	Outbound-only internet access
Subnet Type	Public	Private
Traffic Allowed	Inbound and outbound	Outbound only
Elastic IP	Optional	Required
Security	Requires public IP assignment	Keeps private instances isolated
Management	Fully managed by AWS	Fully managed by AWS

---

4. Best Practices for Gateways

1. **Use IGWs for Public Resources Only**
   - Only associate public-facing resources with the Internet Gateway to minimize exposure.
2. **Implement NAT Gateways for Private Subnets**
   - Always use NAT Gateways for private subnets that require internet access to ensure isolation from inbound traffic.

3. **Enable High Availability**
   - Deploy NAT Gateways in multiple Availability Zones to avoid single points of failure.
4. **Monitor and Optimize Costs**
   - NAT Gateways incur per-hour and per-GB charges. Monitor usage with Amazon CloudWatch and optimize where necessary.
5. **Combine with Security Groups and NACLs**
   - Use Security Groups and Network Access Control Lists to enforce strict traffic filtering for both IGWs and NAT Gateways.

---

5. Common Challenges and Solutions

1. **Challenge: Misconfigured Route Tables**
   - **Problem**: Resources cannot access the internet due to missing or incorrect routes.
   - **Solution**: Ensure that the route table points `0.0.0.0/0` traffic to the correct gateway (IGW for public subnets or NAT Gateway for private subnets).
2. **Challenge: Single Point of Failure**
   - **Problem**: A single NAT Gateway in one AZ can fail, disrupting connectivity for private subnets.
   - **Solution**: Deploy NAT Gateways in multiple AZs and configure private subnets to use the nearest NAT Gateway.
3. **Challenge: Cost Overruns**
   - **Problem**: High NAT Gateway costs due to excessive data transfer.
   - **Solution**: Optimize data transfer usage and explore alternatives like NAT instances for specific use cases.

---

6. Practical Use Cases for Gateways

- **E-Commerce Platforms**: Use an IGW to host public-facing websites and a NAT Gateway for backend servers needing internet access.
- **Hybrid Cloud Architectures**: Use NAT Gateways to connect private workloads to external services securely.
- **Development Environments**: Allow private instances to fetch updates and dependencies from the internet using NAT Gateways.

Conclusion

Internet Gateways and NAT Gateways are essential tools for managing internet connectivity within AWS VPCs. By understanding their differences, use cases, and best practices, you can design secure and efficient network architectures that meet the demands of modern applications.

Route Tables and Their Configuration

Route tables are a fundamental part of AWS networking, serving as the blueprint for how traffic flows within and outside of a Virtual Private Cloud (VPC). By defining the rules for directing traffic, route tables play a pivotal role in ensuring connectivity, security, and efficiency in AWS network architectures. In this chapter, we will explore the structure of route tables, their configuration, and best practices for their implementation.

1. What Is a Route Table?

A **route table** is a set of rules, called routes, that determines the direction of network traffic within a VPC. Every subnet in a VPC is associated with a route table that dictates how traffic is forwarded to its destination, whether it's within the VPC, to another VPC, or to the internet.

Key Characteristics of Route Tables:

- **Default Route Table**: Every VPC is automatically created with a main route table. Subnets that aren't explicitly associated with a custom route table inherit the main route table.
- **Custom Route Tables**: Users can create additional route tables to define specific routing behaviors for subnets.
- **Local Route**: Each route table includes a default local route that allows communication within the VPC (e.g., between subnets).
- **Associations**: Each subnet can be associated with only one route table, but a route table can be associated with multiple subnets.

2. Components of a Route Table

A route table consists of the following key elements:

1. **Destination**: The IP address range that traffic is being directed to, defined in CIDR notation (e.g., `0.0.0.0/0` for all traffic or `10.0.1.0/24` for a specific subnet).
2. **Target**: The destination for the traffic, which could be:
   - An Internet Gateway (IGW) for internet-bound traffic.
   - A NAT Gateway for private subnet traffic accessing the internet.
   - A Virtual Private Gateway for VPN or Direct Connect traffic.
   - A VPC Peering Connection for traffic between VPCs.
   - A Network Interface for traffic directed to a specific instance.
3. **Propagated Routes**: Routes automatically learned through AWS Transit Gateway or Virtual Private Gateway (e.g., for hybrid or multi-VPC architectures).

3. Route Table Configuration

3.1 Default Route Table

- The main route table is automatically created with your VPC and includes a local route for communication within the VPC.
- You can modify the main route table to include additional routes or associate subnets with custom route tables.

3.2 Creating a Custom Route Table

1. **Navigate to the VPC Console**: Go to **VPC > Route Tables** and click on "Create route table."
2. **Select the VPC**: Choose the VPC where the route table will reside.
3. **Add Routes**: Define the destination and target for the traffic.
4. **Associate Subnets**: Assign one or more subnets to the custom route table.

3.3 Adding Routes

To define how traffic is routed:

- Add a route for all traffic (0.0.0.0/0) to an Internet Gateway for public subnets.
- Add a route for private subnets to a NAT Gateway for outbound internet access.

---

4. Use Cases for Route Tables

4.1 Public Subnets

- Use route tables to direct internet-bound traffic to an Internet Gateway.
- Example: A public subnet hosting web servers or APIs needs a route directing 0.0.0.0/0 to the IGW.

4.2 Private Subnets

- Configure route tables to direct internet-bound traffic to a NAT Gateway.
- Example: Backend servers and databases in private subnets require secure outbound access for updates or API calls.

4.3 VPC Peering

- Define routes to enable communication between peered VPCs.
- Example: Add a route to the CIDR range of the peered VPC and specify the VPC Peering Connection as the target.

4.4 Hybrid Architectures

- Use route tables to direct traffic to on-premise networks through a Virtual Private Gateway.
- Example: Add a route for the on-premise CIDR range and specify the Virtual Private Gateway as the target.

---

5. Best Practices for Route Tables

1. **Use Separate Route Tables for Public and Private Subnets**
   - Assign dedicated route tables for public subnets (with IGW routes) and private subnets (with NAT Gateway routes) to maintain clear separation of traffic flows.
2. **Keep Route Tables Simple**
   - Avoid overly complex route tables by minimizing the number of overlapping CIDR blocks and consolidating routes where possible.
3. **Leverage Prefix Lists**
   - Use AWS-managed prefix lists for common destinations (e.g., Amazon S3) to simplify route management and reduce the risk of misconfiguration.
4. **Monitor Route Table Changes**

      ○ Use AWS Config and CloudTrail to track changes to route tables and ensure compliance with organizational policies.
5. **Plan CIDR Blocks Carefully**
      ○ Prevent route conflicts by choosing non-overlapping CIDR ranges for VPCs, subnets, and on-premise networks.

---

6. Common Challenges and Solutions

1. **Challenge: Misconfigured Routes**
      ○ **Problem**: Resources cannot communicate due to incorrect destination or target in the route table.
      ○ **Solution**: Verify that the destination CIDR and target match the intended traffic flow. Use VPC Flow Logs to troubleshoot connectivity issues.
2. **Challenge: Route Overlaps**
      ○ **Problem**: Conflicting CIDR ranges can cause unpredictable routing behavior.
      ○ **Solution**: Plan non-overlapping CIDR ranges and validate route configurations during design.
3. **Challenge: Single Points of Failure**
      ○ **Problem**: Using a single NAT Gateway or Virtual Private Gateway in a route table can create a bottleneck or failure point.
      ○ **Solution**: Deploy gateways across multiple Availability Zones and update route tables to distribute traffic.

---

7. Practical Use Cases for Route Tables

- **E-Commerce Platforms**: Use separate route tables for web servers (public subnets) and backend databases (private subnets) to ensure secure traffic routing.
- **Hybrid Environments**: Configure route tables to direct traffic between AWS and on-premise networks for seamless integration.
- **Multi-VPC Architectures**: Use VPC Peering and Transit Gateway with custom route tables to manage communication between multiple VPCs.

Conclusion

Route tables are a critical element of AWS networking that define how traffic is directed within a VPC and beyond. By understanding their structure, configuration, and use cases, you can design efficient and secure routing strategies for your cloud networks.

Security in AWS Networking

Introduction to Security Groups and NACLs

Security Groups and Network Access Control Lists (NACLs) are essential components of AWS networking that provide layered protection for your cloud resources. These tools allow you to define rules for inbound and outbound traffic, helping you build secure, well-managed network architectures. In this chapter, we will explore the functionality, differences, and best practices for using Security Groups and NACLs effectively.

1. The Importance of Network Security in AWS

AWS follows a **shared responsibility model** for security, where AWS manages the security of the cloud infrastructure, while users are responsible for securing their applications and data. Security Groups and NACLs are critical in fulfilling your part of this model, ensuring that network traffic is filtered appropriately.

Key aspects of AWS network security:

- **Traffic Filtering**: Control access to resources by allowing or denying specific traffic.
- **Least Privilege Principle**: Restrict permissions and access to only what is necessary.
- **Layered Defense**: Combine multiple security mechanisms to protect against threats.

2. What Are Security Groups?

A **Security Group** is a virtual firewall attached to an Amazon Elastic Compute Cloud (EC2) instance, Elastic Load Balancer (ELB), or other network interfaces. It controls inbound and outbound traffic at the instance level.

Key Features of Security Groups:

- **Stateful**: Responses to allowed inbound traffic are automatically permitted for outbound traffic and vice versa.
- **Allow Rules Only**: Security Groups allow traffic based on defined rules; they do not support deny rules.
- **Instance-Level Control**: Security Groups operate at the instance level, providing granular control over network access.

Security Group Rules:

1. **Inbound Rules**: Specify the types of traffic (e.g., HTTP, SSH) allowed to reach an instance.
2. **Outbound Rules**: Define the traffic that the instance is allowed to send.

2.1 Configuring Security Groups

1. **Create a Security Group**:
   - Go to **EC2 > Security Groups** in the AWS Management Console.
   - Define a name, description, and VPC.
2. **Add Inbound and Outbound Rules**:

       ○ Choose a protocol (e.g., TCP, UDP), port range, and source/destination (e.g., IP address, CIDR block, or another Security Group).

3. **Assign Security Groups**:
   - ○ Attach the Security Group to an EC2 instance or network interface.

2.2 Use Cases for Security Groups

- **Web Applications**: Allow HTTP (port 80) and HTTPS (port 443) traffic for public-facing web servers.
- **Database Servers**: Restrict access to specific instances by allowing only traffic from trusted Security Groups or IP ranges.
- **SSH Access**: Allow SSH (port 22) connections only from specific IP addresses or ranges.

---

3. What Are Network Access Control Lists (NACLs)?

A **Network Access Control List (NACL)** is a subnet-level firewall that controls inbound and outbound traffic for the entire subnet. It provides an additional layer of security to VPCs and complements Security Groups.

Key Features of NACLs:

- **Stateless**: Rules for inbound and outbound traffic are evaluated independently.
- **Allow and Deny Rules**: NACLs support both allow and deny rules, offering greater flexibility.
- **Subnet-Level Control**: Apply to all instances within a subnet, providing broader security coverage.

NACL Rules:

1. **Inbound Rules**: Define traffic allowed or denied to enter the subnet.
2. **Outbound Rules**: Specify traffic allowed or denied to leave the subnet.
3. **Rule Numbers**: Rules are evaluated in ascending order by rule number, with the first match determining the action.

3.1 Configuring NACLs

1. **Create a NACL**:
   - ○ Navigate to **VPC > Network ACLs** in the AWS Management Console.
   - ○ Specify the associated VPC and assign a name.
2. **Add Rules**:
   - ○ Define inbound and outbound rules with protocol, port range, source/destination, and allow/deny actions.
3. **Associate NACLs with Subnets**:
   - ○ Associate the NACL with one or more subnets to apply its rules.

3.2 Use Cases for NACLs

- **Subnet Segmentation**: Implement broader security controls for specific subnets, such as isolating private subnets.
- **Deny Rules**: Block unwanted traffic at the subnet level, such as known malicious IP ranges.
- **Public and Private Subnets**: Allow public traffic in public subnets and restrict access in private subnets.

4. Security Groups vs. NACLs

Feature	Security Groups	Network ACLs
Scope	Instance-level	Subnet-level
State	Stateful	Stateless
Rules	Allow only	Allow and deny
Evaluation	Applied to instance traffic only	Applies to all subnet traffic
Use Cases	Fine-grained instance control	Broad subnet traffic filtering

5. Best Practices for Security Groups and NACLs

1. **Adopt a Layered Approach**
   - Use Security Groups for instance-specific rules and NACLs for subnet-wide policies.
2. **Follow the Principle of Least Privilege**
   - Restrict access to only what is necessary for both Security Groups and NACLs.
3. **Regularly Review and Update Rules**
   - Audit Security Group and NACL configurations to remove unused or overly permissive rules.
4. **Monitor Traffic**
   - Use VPC Flow Logs and Amazon CloudWatch to monitor and analyze network traffic.
5. **Combine Security Groups with NACLs**
   - Use Security Groups to allow required traffic and NACLs to block known threats or limit unwanted access.

6. Common Challenges and Solutions

1. **Challenge: Overly Permissive Rules**
   - **Problem**: Security Groups or NACLs allow unnecessary traffic, increasing attack surface.
   - **Solution**: Regularly audit and enforce stricter rules.
2. **Challenge: Rule Overlaps**
   - **Problem**: Conflicting rules between Security Groups and NACLs.
   - **Solution**: Prioritize Security Groups for specific controls and NACLs for broader policies.
3. **Challenge: Troubleshooting Connectivity**
   - **Problem**: Connectivity issues due to misconfigured rules.
   - **Solution**: Use AWS tools like Reachability Analyzer and VPC Flow Logs to identify and resolve issues.

7. Practical Use Cases

- **E-Commerce Platforms**: Use Security Groups to control instance-level access and NACLs to segment public and private subnets.
- **Hybrid Environments**: Combine NACLs with Virtual Private Gateways for secure communication between AWS and on-premise systems.
- **Big Data Workloads**: Secure data processing clusters with NACLs while using Security Groups to restrict access to specific nodes.

Conclusion

Security Groups and Network Access Control Lists are powerful tools for managing network security in AWS. By understanding their functionality and best practices, you can build robust, secure, and scalable cloud network architectures.

Configuring Firewalls for AWS Networks

Firewalls are a cornerstone of network security in AWS, ensuring controlled and monitored access to resources. AWS offers a range of firewall tools, including Security Groups, Network Access Control Lists (NACLs), and AWS Network Firewall, to help you protect your network and enforce security policies. This chapter focuses on configuring firewalls in AWS networks, covering their setup, best practices, and advanced configurations.

1. Introduction to AWS Firewalls

AWS provides multiple layers of security through its firewall solutions, enabling users to implement tailored security measures. These solutions address traffic filtering, monitoring, and management at both the instance and network levels.

Key Firewall Solutions in AWS:

- **Security Groups**: Instance-level firewalls that control inbound and outbound traffic.
- **Network Access Control Lists (NACLs)**: Subnet-level firewalls that filter traffic based on rules.
- **AWS Network Firewall**: A managed service for advanced network protection, including intrusion prevention and content filtering.

2. Configuring Security Groups as Firewalls

Security Groups act as virtual firewalls for EC2 instances and other resources. They are stateful, meaning they automatically allow return traffic for an allowed request.

Steps to Configure a Security Group:

1. **Create a Security Group**:
   - Navigate to **EC2 > Security Groups** in the AWS Management Console.
   - Specify a name, description, and associated VPC.
2. **Define Inbound Rules**:
   - Allow specific types of traffic (e.g., HTTP on port 80, SSH on port 22).
   - Specify the source (e.g., an IP range, CIDR block, or another Security Group).
3. **Define Outbound Rules**:
   - Configure outbound traffic to destinations, such as the internet or private networks.
4. **Attach the Security Group**:
   - Assign the Security Group to EC2 instances, Elastic Load Balancers, or other resources.

3. Configuring NACLs as Firewalls

Network Access Control Lists (NACLs) provide subnet-level traffic filtering. Unlike Security Groups, NACLs are stateless, requiring explicit rules for both inbound and outbound traffic.

Steps to Configure a NACL:

1. **Create a NACL**:
   - Go to **VPC > Network ACLs** in the AWS Management Console.
   - Specify a name and associated VPC.
2. **Add Rules**:

- o Define rules for inbound and outbound traffic.
- o Include the protocol, port range, source/destination, and allow/deny action.
- o Use rule numbers to control the order of rule evaluation (lower numbers are evaluated first).
3. **Associate Subnets**:
   - o Associate the NACL with one or more subnets in the VPC.
4. **Test Traffic**:
   - o Use tools like VPC Flow Logs to verify that traffic is being filtered as intended.

---

4. Advanced Configuration with AWS Network Firewall

AWS Network Firewall is a managed service designed for advanced network security needs, including intrusion detection, intrusion prevention, and centralized policy management.

Key Features of AWS Network Firewall:

- **Layer 7 Filtering**: Supports deep packet inspection and application-layer filtering.
- **Threat Intelligence**: Integrates with threat intelligence feeds for proactive defense.
- **Centralized Management**: Allows for consistent policies across multiple accounts and VPCs.

Steps to Deploy AWS Network Firewall:

1. **Create a Firewall**:
   - o Navigate to **AWS Network Firewall** in the Management Console.
   - o Specify a name, VPC, and associated subnets (for ingress and egress traffic).
2. **Define Firewall Policies**:
   - o Create policies that include rules for traffic filtering, intrusion detection, and prevention.
   - o Use rule groups for reusable configurations.
3. **Deploy Firewall Endpoints**:
   - o Deploy endpoints in the desired subnets to route traffic through the firewall.
4. **Monitor and Adjust**:
   - o Use Amazon CloudWatch for monitoring and AWS Firewall Manager for centralized policy enforcement.

---

5. Combining Firewalls for Layered Security

AWS encourages a **defense-in-depth approach**, using multiple firewall solutions to provide comprehensive protection.

Example Architecture:

- **Security Groups**: Restrict traffic at the instance level (e.g., allowing only HTTP/HTTPS traffic to a web server).
- **NACLs**: Enforce broader subnet-level policies (e.g., blocking all traffic from specific IP ranges).
- **AWS Network Firewall**: Add intrusion prevention and threat intelligence for enhanced protection.

---

6. Best Practices for Firewall Configuration

1. **Follow the Principle of Least Privilege**:
   - o Only allow traffic that is explicitly required for your application.
2. **Use Multiple Layers of Firewalls**:
   - o Combine Security Groups, NACLs, and AWS Network Firewall for layered security.

3. **Regularly Audit Rules**:
   - Review and update firewall rules periodically to ensure compliance and remove unnecessary entries.
4. **Enable Logging and Monitoring**:
   - Use VPC Flow Logs, AWS CloudWatch, and AWS Config to monitor firewall activity and detect anomalies.
5. **Plan for High Availability**:
   - Deploy firewalls across multiple Availability Zones to avoid single points of failure.

---

7. Common Challenges and Solutions

1. **Challenge: Overly Permissive Rules**
   - **Problem**: Allowing broad access can expose resources to attacks.
   - **Solution**: Use specific IP ranges and limit ports to reduce the attack surface.
2. **Challenge: Rule Conflicts**
   - **Problem**: Conflicting rules between NACLs and Security Groups can cause unexpected behavior.
   - **Solution**: Document and test rules to ensure consistency.
3. **Challenge: Misconfigured Logging**
   - **Problem**: Lack of visibility into firewall activity can hinder troubleshooting.
   - **Solution**: Enable logging for Security Groups, NACLs, and AWS Network Firewall.

---

8. Practical Use Cases for Firewalls in AWS

- **E-Commerce Platforms**:
  - Use Security Groups to allow web traffic and NACLs to block malicious IPs.
  - Employ AWS Network Firewall for threat detection and content filtering.
- **Hybrid Environments**:
  - Use NACLs to control traffic between on-premise networks and AWS through a VPN or Direct Connect.
- **Big Data Analytics**:
  - Secure data processing environments with fine-grained Security Group rules and subnet-level NACLs.

Conclusion

Configuring firewalls is an integral part of securing AWS networks. By leveraging Security Groups, NACLs, and AWS Network Firewall, you can build robust, scalable, and secure architectures tailored to your application's needs.

The Shared Responsibility Model in AWS Networking

In the realm of cloud computing, security is a paramount concern. AWS addresses this through the **Shared Responsibility Model**, a foundational concept that delineates the security obligations of AWS and its customers. Understanding this model is crucial for effectively securing your AWS network infrastructure. This chapter delves into the intricacies of the Shared Responsibility Model as it pertains to AWS networking, highlighting the division of responsibilities and offering guidance on how to fulfill your role in maintaining a secure environment.

1. Overview of the Shared Responsibility Model

The **Shared Responsibility Model** is a framework that defines the security responsibilities of AWS and its customers. It ensures that both parties are clear about their roles in securing the cloud environment.

AWS Responsibilities:

- **Security *of* the Cloud**: AWS is responsible for protecting the infrastructure that runs all the services offered in the AWS Cloud. This includes hardware, software, networking, and facilities that run AWS services.

Customer Responsibilities:

- **Security *in* the Cloud**: Customers are responsible for securing the applications, data, and configurations they deploy on AWS services. This includes network configurations, operating systems, and access controls.

2. AWS's Role in Networking Security

AWS takes on significant responsibilities to ensure the underlying cloud infrastructure is secure and reliable.

Key AWS Responsibilities:

1. **Physical Security**: Protection of data centers through access control, surveillance, and environmental safeguards.
2. **Network Infrastructure Security**:
    - **Hardware Maintenance**: Ensuring that routers, switches, and other network devices are securely configured and updated.
    - **DDoS Mitigation**: Providing services like AWS Shield to protect against Distributed Denial of Service attacks at the infrastructure level.
    - **Isolation**: Utilizing technologies like VPC to ensure customer networks are isolated from each other.
3. **Compliance and Audits**:
    - AWS adheres to various compliance standards (e.g., ISO 27001, SOC 1/2/3, PCI DSS).
    - Regular third-party audits to validate security controls.

3. Customer's Role in Networking Security

Customers bear the responsibility for securing their data, applications, and network configurations within the AWS environment.

Key Customer Responsibilities:

1. **Network Configuration**:
   - **VPC Design**: Creating secure Virtual Private Clouds with appropriate CIDR blocks.
   - **Subnet Segmentation**: Dividing networks into public and private subnets for security and efficiency.
2. **Access Management**:
   - **Security Groups and NACLs**: Configuring inbound and outbound traffic rules.
   - **Identity and Access Management (IAM)**: Defining user permissions and roles to control access to resources.
3. **Data Protection**:
   - **Encryption**: Implementing encryption for data at rest and in transit using AWS tools like KMS and SSL/TLS.
   - **Backup and Recovery**: Establishing data backup routines and disaster recovery plans.
4. **Monitoring and Logging**:
   - **CloudTrail and CloudWatch**: Monitoring network activity and logging API calls.
   - **VPC Flow Logs**: Capturing information about IP traffic going to and from network interfaces.
5. **Application Security**:
   - **Patch Management**: Keeping operating systems and applications up to date.
   - **Secure Coding Practices**: Developing applications with security in mind to prevent vulnerabilities.

---

4. Division of Responsibilities in Networking Services

Understanding which networking services fall under AWS's responsibility and which are the customer's is vital for maintaining security.

Services Managed by AWS:

- **Physical Network Devices**: Routers, switches, and cabling.
- **Managed Networking Services**: AWS handles the security of services like AWS Global Accelerator and AWS Transit Gateway infrastructure.

Services Managed by the Customer:

- **Virtual Networking Components**:
   - **VPC Configuration**: Setting up VPCs, subnets, route tables, and gateways.
   - **Network Security Controls**: Managing Security Groups, NACLs, and AWS Network Firewall.
- **DNS Management**:
   - **Amazon Route 53**: Configuring DNS settings and ensuring DNS security.
- **Load Balancing**:
   - **Elastic Load Balancing**: Securing configurations and SSL/TLS settings.

---

5. Shared Controls

Some controls are considered shared between AWS and the customer, meaning both parties have a role to play.

Examples of Shared Controls:

1. **Patch Management**:
   - ○ **AWS**: Patches and maintains the infrastructure and managed services.
   - ○ **Customer**: Responsible for patching guest operating systems and applications.
2. **Configuration Management**:
   - ○ **AWS**: Manages the configuration of infrastructure devices.
   - ○ **Customer**: Configures their own resources, such as EC2 instances and network settings.
3. **Awareness and Training**:
   - ○ **AWS**: Provides documentation and best practices.
   - ○ **Customer**: Ensures their team is trained in security protocols and AWS services.

---

6. Best Practices for Fulfilling Customer Responsibilities

1. **Implement the Principle of Least Privilege**:
   - ○ Use IAM policies to grant minimal required permissions.
   - ○ Regularly review and adjust permissions as needed.
2. **Secure Network Architecture**:
   - ○ Design VPCs with multiple layers of security, including public and private subnets.
   - ○ Utilize AWS Network Firewall for advanced threat protection.
3. **Regularly Update and Patch Systems**:
   - ○ Establish a routine for updating operating systems, applications, and security tools.
4. **Encrypt Data**:
   - ○ Use AWS Key Management Service (KMS) for managing encryption keys.
   - ○ Encrypt data at rest (e.g., EBS volumes, S3 buckets) and in transit (SSL/TLS).
5. **Monitor and Audit Activities**:
   - ○ Enable AWS CloudTrail and VPC Flow Logs for auditing.
   - ○ Set up Amazon CloudWatch alarms for unusual activities.
6. **Implement Multi-Factor Authentication (MFA)**:
   - ○ Require MFA for IAM users, especially those with privileged access.
7. **Use AWS Trusted Advisor**:
   - ○ Leverage Trusted Advisor to identify security gaps and optimize configurations.

---

7. Compliance and Regulatory Considerations

Customers are responsible for ensuring that their use of AWS services complies with relevant laws and regulations.

Steps to Achieve Compliance:

- **Understand Regulatory Requirements**: Identify which regulations apply to your organization (e.g., GDPR, HIPAA).
- **Map AWS Services to Compliance Needs**: Use AWS Compliance Programs and resources to align services with regulatory requirements.
- **Implement Necessary Controls**: Configure network settings, encryption, and access controls to meet compliance standards.
- **Document and Report**: Maintain documentation and evidence of compliance efforts for audits.

---

8. Common Pitfalls and How to Avoid Them

1. **Misconfigured Security Groups and NACLs**:
   - ○ **Pitfall**: Overly permissive rules expose resources to threats.

- ○ **Solution**: Regularly audit and tighten security rules; use AWS Config to monitor changes.
2. **Neglecting Encryption**:
   - ○ **Pitfall**: Unencrypted data is vulnerable to interception and breaches.
   - ○ **Solution**: Implement encryption for data at rest and in transit using AWS-provided tools.
3. **Ignoring Monitoring and Logs**:
   - ○ **Pitfall**: Lack of visibility hinders threat detection and response.
   - ○ **Solution**: Enable comprehensive logging and set up alerts for suspicious activities.
4. **Inadequate Access Management**:
   - ○ **Pitfall**: Shared accounts and weak credentials increase risk.
   - ○ **Solution**: Use IAM best practices, enforce strong passwords, and enable MFA.

9. Leveraging AWS Tools for Enhanced Security

AWS offers a suite of tools to help customers meet their security responsibilities.

Key Tools:

- **AWS Identity and Access Management (IAM)**: Manage user access and permissions.
- **AWS Key Management Service (KMS)**: Create and control encryption keys.
- **AWS Config**: Assess, audit, and evaluate configurations of AWS resources.
- **Amazon GuardDuty**: Continuous threat detection service monitoring malicious activities.
- **AWS Security Hub**: Provides a comprehensive view of security alerts and compliance status.

10. Case Study: Applying the Shared Responsibility Model

Scenario: A fintech company needs to deploy a secure application on AWS while complying with financial regulations.

Steps Taken:

1. **AWS Responsibilities**:
   - ○ AWS secures the infrastructure, data centers, and managed services.
   - ○ Provides compliance certifications relevant to the financial industry.
2. **Customer Responsibilities**:
   - ○ **Network Configuration**: Set up VPC with private subnets for sensitive data.
   - ○ **Access Control**: Implement strict IAM policies and Security Groups.
   - ○ **Encryption**: Use KMS for key management and encrypt all data.
   - ○ **Monitoring**: Enable CloudTrail and GuardDuty for real-time monitoring.
   - ○ **Compliance**: Map AWS services to regulatory requirements and document configurations.

Outcome: The company successfully deployed a secure application that met compliance standards by effectively fulfilling its responsibilities under the Shared Responsibility Model.

Conclusion

The Shared Responsibility Model is a foundational concept in AWS networking security. By clearly understanding and acting upon your responsibilities, you can build a secure, compliant, and robust network infrastructure on AWS. Remember that while AWS provides a secure foundation, it is up to you to secure your applications, data, and configurations within the cloud. Leveraging AWS tools and adhering to best practices will enable you to fulfill your role effectively, ensuring that your network is protected against threats and aligned with organizational and regulatory requirements.

Secure Communication with Virtual Private Gateways

Establishing secure communication between your on-premises network and AWS is a critical requirement for hybrid cloud architectures. Virtual Private Gateways (VGWs) are a key component in AWS networking that enable secure, private communication between your AWS Virtual Private Cloud (VPC) and external networks. This chapter explores the functionality, configuration, and best practices for using Virtual Private Gateways to ensure secure connectivity.

1. What is a Virtual Private Gateway?

A **Virtual Private Gateway (VGW)** is a VPN concentrator on the Amazon side of a VPN connection. It allows your VPC to connect securely to an external network, such as an on-premises data center, over an encrypted VPN connection.

Key Characteristics of Virtual Private Gateways:

- **Secure Communication**: Supports IPsec VPN connections for encrypted communication.
- **High Availability**: VGWs are designed with built-in redundancy to ensure consistent connectivity.
- **Simplified Integration**: Works seamlessly with other AWS services, such as Direct Connect, to establish hybrid networks.

2. Use Cases for Virtual Private Gateways

1. **Hybrid Cloud Architectures**:
   - Connect your on-premises data center to AWS VPCs for a seamless hybrid cloud environment.
2. **Disaster Recovery**:
   - Use VGWs to replicate critical data from on-premises infrastructure to AWS for backup and recovery.
3. **Secure Data Transfers**:
   - Encrypt sensitive data in transit between AWS and external networks.
4. **Global Business Operations**:
   - Enable secure connectivity between AWS VPCs and branch offices around the world.

3. How Virtual Private Gateways Work

A VGW acts as a gateway on the AWS side of a VPN or Direct Connect connection. Here's how it facilitates secure communication:

1. **VPN Connection**:
   - VGW establishes an encrypted IPsec tunnel between your on-premises environment and your VPC.
2. **Routing**:
   - VGW routes traffic between the on-premises network and the VPC using static or dynamic routing protocols such as BGP (Border Gateway Protocol).
3. **Integration with AWS Direct Connect**:

- VGW can work with AWS Direct Connect for high-throughput, low-latency communication, combining private connectivity with encryption.

---

4. Configuring a Virtual Private Gateway

Follow these steps to configure a VGW for secure communication:

Step 1: Create a Virtual Private Gateway

1. Go to the **VPC Console** in the AWS Management Console.
2. Navigate to **Virtual Private Gateways** and click "Create Virtual Private Gateway."
3. Assign a name and Autonomous System Number (ASN) to the VGW.
4. Attach the VGW to your VPC.

Step 2: Configure a VPN Connection

1. Navigate to **VPN Connections** in the VPC Console and click "Create VPN Connection."
2. Select the VGW and provide the following:
   - Customer Gateway details (IP address of your on-premises VPN device).
   - Routing type (static or dynamic).
3. Download the configuration file for your VPN device.

Step 3: Configure the Customer Gateway

1. Set up your on-premises VPN device using the configuration file.
2. Establish the IPsec VPN tunnel between the VGW and the Customer Gateway.

Step 4: Update Route Tables

1. Add routes in the VPC's route table to direct traffic destined for the on-premises network through the VGW.
2. Ensure that on-premises devices can route traffic back to the VPC.

---

5. Best Practices for Secure Communication with VGWs

1. **Use Redundant Connections**:
   - Establish multiple VPN tunnels to ensure failover in case of a connectivity issue.
2. **Enable BGP for Dynamic Routing**:
   - Use BGP to simplify routing and automatically adapt to changes in network topology.
3. **Monitor VPN Connections**:
   - Use Amazon CloudWatch to monitor tunnel status and set up alarms for connection failures.
4. **Use AWS Direct Connect for High Bandwidth**:
   - For high-bandwidth or latency-sensitive applications, combine VGWs with AWS Direct Connect.
5. **Encrypt Data in Transit**:
   - Ensure that all traffic between on-premises networks and AWS is encrypted using IPsec.
6. **Implement Network Segmentation**:
   - Use Security Groups and NACLs to control access to resources within the VPC.
7. **Regularly Audit Configurations**:
   - Use AWS Config to track changes in VGW settings and ensure compliance with security policies.

---

6. Common Challenges and Solutions

1. **Challenge: VPN Latency Issues**
   - **Problem**: High latency or inconsistent performance.
   - **Solution**: Use AWS Direct Connect for consistent, low-latency connections, or optimize VPN configurations.
2. **Challenge: Misconfigured Routing**
   - **Problem**: Traffic fails to reach the intended destination.
   - **Solution**: Verify routing tables on both the AWS and on-premises sides.
3. **Challenge: Single Point of Failure**
   - **Problem**: Loss of connectivity due to a single VPN tunnel.
   - **Solution**: Configure multiple VPN tunnels for redundancy and automatic failover.
4. **Challenge: Security Concerns**
   - **Problem**: Unencrypted traffic or overly permissive routing rules.
   - **Solution**: Use IPsec encryption and audit routing configurations to restrict access.

---

7. Practical Example: Connecting On-Premises to AWS Using a VGW

Scenario: A financial services company needs to securely connect its on-premises data center to AWS to run analytics on customer data.

Solution:

1. **Set Up the VGW**:
   - Create a VGW and attach it to the VPC hosting the analytics application.
2. **Establish a VPN Connection**:
   - Configure an IPsec VPN tunnel between the VGW and the on-premises firewall.
3. **Enable Dynamic Routing**:
   - Use BGP for efficient route management between the on-premises network and the VPC.
4. **Secure Data Transfers**:
   - Encrypt all data in transit using IPsec and implement strict routing policies.
5. **Monitor and Optimize**:
   - Use CloudWatch to monitor VPN connection health and optimize performance by fine-tuning the VPN configuration.

Conclusion

Virtual Private Gateways are an indispensable tool for enabling secure, private communication between AWS VPCs and external networks. By understanding their functionality and following best practices, you can build robust, secure, and high-performing hybrid cloud architectures.

Identity and Access Management (IAM) for Networking

Identity and Access Management (IAM) is a cornerstone of AWS security, providing robust mechanisms to manage access to AWS resources, including networking components. By implementing IAM effectively, you can enforce the principle of least privilege, control access to critical resources, and maintain the security of your cloud infrastructure. This chapter explores the role of IAM in AWS networking, covering key features, best practices, and configuration steps to secure your network resources.

1. Overview of IAM in Networking

AWS Identity and Access Management (IAM) enables you to control who can access your network resources, what actions they can perform, and under what conditions.

Key Features of IAM for Networking:

- **Granular Permissions**: Define fine-grained permissions for users, groups, and roles.
- **Policy-Based Access Control**: Manage access through JSON-based policies.
- **Conditional Access**: Enforce access conditions based on factors like IP addresses or request times.
- **Integration with AWS Networking Services**: Manage access to VPCs, Security Groups, Route Tables, and more.

2. Key IAM Concepts for Networking

Understanding IAM concepts is essential to managing networking resources securely.

IAM Users

- **Definition**: Represents individual accounts with long-term credentials.
- **Use Case**: Assign to administrators managing network configurations.

IAM Groups

- **Definition**: Collection of IAM users with shared permissions.
- **Use Case**: Group network administrators to apply uniform permissions.

IAM Roles

- **Definition**: Temporary credentials for AWS services or external users.
- **Use Case**: Grant EC2 instances permissions to manage network components.

IAM Policies

- **Definition**: JSON documents that define permissions.
- **Use Case**: Create policies to control access to VPCs, subnets, and other resources.

3. Managing Networking Permissions with IAM

IAM enables you to control access to key networking components.

3.1 VPC Permissions

- **Common Actions**: ec2:CreateVpc, ec2:DeleteVpc, ec2:DescribeVpcs.
- **Use Case**: Restrict who can create or modify VPCs to prevent misconfigurations.

3.2 Subnet Permissions

- **Common Actions**: ec2:CreateSubnet, ec2:DescribeSubnets.
- **Use Case**: Allow developers to view subnets but restrict creation to administrators.

3.3 Security Group Permissions

- **Common Actions**: ec2:AuthorizeSecurityGroupIngress, ec2:RevokeSecurityGroupIngress.
- **Use Case**: Allow only security engineers to modify Security Groups.

3.4 Route Table Permissions

- **Common Actions**: ec2:CreateRoute, ec2:DeleteRoute, ec2:DescribeRouteTables.
- **Use Case**: Permit network architects to manage route tables.

---

4. Creating and Assigning IAM Policies for Networking

Example 1: Policy to Restrict Access to a Specific VPC

```
{
  "Version": "2012-10-17",
  "Statement": [
    {
      "Effect": "Allow",
      "Action": "ec2:DescribeVpcs",
      "Resource": "*"
    },
    {
      "Effect": "Deny",
      "Action": "ec2:DeleteVpc",
      "Resource": "arn:aws:ec2:us-east-1:123456789012:vpc/vpc-abc12345"
    }
  ]
}
```

Purpose: Allows users to view VPCs but prevents deletion of a critical VPC.

Example 2: Policy for Managing Security Groups

```
{
  "Version": "2012-10-17",
  "Statement": [
    {
      "Effect": "Allow",
      "Action": [
        "ec2:DescribeSecurityGroups",
        "ec2:AuthorizeSecurityGroupIngress",
        "ec2:RevokeSecurityGroupIngress"
      ],
      "Resource": "*"
```

```
        }
    ]
}
```

Purpose: Grants permissions to manage Security Group rules.

---

5. Best Practices for Using IAM in Networking

1. **Implement the Principle of Least Privilege**:
   - Assign the minimal set of permissions required for a role or user.
2. **Use IAM Roles for Instances**:
   - Avoid hardcoding credentials in applications; assign roles to EC2 instances for accessing network resources.
3. **Enable Multi-Factor Authentication (MFA)**:
   - Require MFA for users with elevated privileges, such as network administrators.
4. **Regularly Audit IAM Policies**:
   - Use AWS IAM Access Analyzer and AWS Config to identify overly permissive policies.
5. **Leverage Service Control Policies (SCPs)**:
   - For organizations using AWS Organizations, apply SCPs to enforce governance across accounts.
6. **Enable Logging and Monitoring**:
   - Track IAM activity with AWS CloudTrail and set up alerts for unauthorized access attempts.
7. **Use Resource-Level Permissions**:
   - Restrict actions to specific resources (e.g., allow modifications to only certain subnets or route tables).

---

6. Common Challenges and Solutions

1. **Challenge: Overly Permissive Policies**
   - **Problem**: Allowing broad access increases security risks.
   - **Solution**: Use AWS IAM Policy Simulator to test and refine policies.
2. **Challenge: Managing Multiple Accounts**
   - **Problem**: Difficulties in maintaining consistent IAM policies across accounts.
   - **Solution**: Use AWS Organizations and SCPs for centralized management.
3. **Challenge: Credentials Mismanagement**
   - **Problem**: Hardcoded or leaked credentials compromise security.
   - **Solution**: Use IAM roles and rotate access keys regularly.
4. **Challenge: Lack of Monitoring**
   - **Problem**: Undetected unauthorized access or changes to network resources.
   - **Solution**: Enable CloudTrail for logging IAM activities and use CloudWatch for real-time alerts.

---

7. Practical Use Cases for IAM in Networking

1. **Secure API Gateway Access**:
   - Use IAM policies to control which users and applications can access or modify API Gateway configurations.
2. **Isolated Development Environments**:
   - Restrict development teams to specific subnets and Security Groups using IAM roles.
3. **Automated Network Management**:

- Assign roles to AWS Lambda functions for managing route tables dynamically.
4. **Cross-Account Networking**:
    - Use IAM roles to allow cross-account access to shared VPCs or network services.

Conclusion

IAM is an essential tool for securing networking resources in AWS. By leveraging its features, you can enforce access controls, ensure compliance, and protect your cloud network from unauthorized changes. Integrating IAM with best practices and AWS tools enables you to maintain a secure and well-managed networking environment.

Encryption and Data Protection in AWS Networks

In a world where data breaches and cyber threats are increasingly prevalent, securing sensitive information is a critical priority. AWS provides a comprehensive suite of encryption tools and best practices to ensure data remains protected both at rest and in transit. This chapter focuses on encryption methodologies, tools, and strategies to protect data within AWS networks.

---

1. Importance of Encryption in Networking

Encryption is a cornerstone of modern network security. It protects data from unauthorized access by converting it into an unreadable format, ensuring only authorized parties can decrypt and understand the information.

Key Reasons for Encryption:

- **Data Confidentiality**: Prevent unauthorized users from accessing sensitive data.
- **Compliance**: Meet regulatory requirements such as GDPR, HIPAA, and PCI DSS.
- **Trust**: Establish customer confidence by safeguarding their data.

---

2. AWS Encryption Services and Features

AWS provides several services to simplify encryption management and ensure robust data protection.

2.1 AWS Key Management Service (KMS)

- **Overview**: AWS KMS is a managed service for creating and controlling cryptographic keys.
- **Key Features**:
  - Generate and manage encryption keys.
  - Integrate with AWS services like S3, EBS, and RDS for seamless encryption.
  - Audit key usage with AWS CloudTrail.

2.2 AWS Certificate Manager (ACM)

- **Overview**: ACM simplifies the process of provisioning, managing, and deploying SSL/TLS certificates.
- **Key Features**:
  - Encrypt data in transit between clients and AWS resources.
  - Automatically renew certificates for continued protection.

2.3 Amazon Macie

- **Overview**: Amazon Macie leverages machine learning to discover, classify, and protect sensitive data.
- **Use Case**: Identify unencrypted sensitive data in S3 buckets.

2.4 AWS Secrets Manager

- **Overview**: Securely store, retrieve, and rotate credentials, API keys, and encryption keys.
- **Use Case**: Manage access to encrypted databases or networked applications.

---

3. Encryption for Data at Rest

Encrypting data at rest ensures that stored data remains secure, even if physical storage devices are compromised.

Key AWS Services Supporting Encryption at Rest:

1. **Amazon S3**:
   - Use server-side encryption (SSE-S3, SSE-KMS, or SSE-C) to automatically encrypt data at the storage layer.
   - Enable default bucket-level encryption for uniform protection.
2. **Amazon EBS**:
   - Encrypt data on EBS volumes and snapshots using KMS.
   - Automatically manage encryption keys to simplify operations.
3. **Amazon RDS**:
   - Encrypt databases at rest using KMS keys.
   - Ensure that automated backups, snapshots, and replicas are also encrypted.
4. **AWS Secrets Manager**:
   - Store secrets securely with automatic encryption.

---

4. Encryption for Data in Transit

Encrypting data in transit ensures that information is protected as it moves between systems, preventing interception or tampering.

Key Techniques for Data in Transit Encryption:

1. **SSL/TLS**:
   - Use AWS Certificate Manager (ACM) to provision and manage certificates for SSL/TLS encryption.
   - Encrypt traffic between web browsers and AWS services like CloudFront and Elastic Load Balancing.
2. **IPsec VPN**:
   - Use IPsec protocols to establish encrypted tunnels between AWS Virtual Private Gateways and on-premises networks.
3. **AWS Direct Connect**:
   - Encrypt traffic using MACsec or integrate with AWS Site-to-Site VPN for secure private connectivity.
4. **Application-Layer Encryption**:
   - Implement HTTPS for application-level communication security.
5. **AWS Network Load Balancer**:
   - Terminate SSL/TLS connections for secure data transfer to backend instances.

---

5. Best Practices for Encryption and Data Protection

1. **Enable Default Encryption**:
   - Automatically encrypt data in services like S3, EBS, and RDS using default settings.
2. **Use AWS KMS for Key Management**:
   - Centralize key management with AWS KMS.
   - Implement key rotation policies for enhanced security.
3. **Monitor and Audit Encryption Usage**:
   - Use AWS Config to ensure encryption is consistently applied across resources.
   - Enable AWS CloudTrail to track key usage and detect unauthorized access.
4. **Encrypt All Sensitive Data**:

- ○ Encrypt sensitive data both at rest and in transit to prevent accidental exposure.
5. **Leverage Multi-Factor Authentication (MFA)**:
   - ○ Require MFA for accessing encryption keys and sensitive resources.
6. **Classify and Tag Data**:
   - ○ Use Amazon Macie to identify sensitive data and ensure appropriate encryption measures.
7. **Test Encryption Implementations**:
   - ○ Regularly test encrypted connections, key rotations, and decryption processes to identify potential issues.

---

6. Common Challenges and Solutions

1. **Challenge: Managing Multiple Keys**
   - ○ **Problem**: Handling keys for various resources becomes complex.
   - ○ **Solution**: Use AWS KMS and IAM policies to centralize key management and simplify operations.
2. **Challenge: Overhead from Encryption**
   - ○ **Problem**: Encryption may impact performance in high-traffic environments.
   - ○ **Solution**: Use hardware-accelerated encryption options like Elastic Load Balancers or MACsec for Direct Connect.
3. **Challenge: Identifying Unencrypted Resources**
   - ○ **Problem**: Unencrypted resources may go unnoticed in large environments.
   - ○ **Solution**: Use AWS Config rules and Amazon Macie to identify and remediate unencrypted data.
4. **Challenge: Maintaining Compliance**
   - ○ **Problem**: Encryption configurations may not meet regulatory standards.
   - ○ **Solution**: Use AWS Artifact and AWS Audit Manager to ensure compliance with encryption requirements.

---

7. Practical Use Cases for Encryption in AWS Networking

1. **Secure Financial Transactions**:
   - ○ Encrypt transaction data at rest in Amazon RDS and in transit using SSL/TLS.
2. **Protect Healthcare Data**:
   - ○ Use AWS KMS and SSE-KMS to encrypt patient records stored in Amazon S3, ensuring HIPAA compliance.
3. **Hybrid Cloud Security**:
   - ○ Encrypt communication between on-premises networks and AWS using IPsec VPN.
4. **IoT Data Encryption**:
   - ○ Secure IoT traffic with application-layer encryption and S3 server-side encryption.

Conclusion

Encryption and data protection are essential to securing AWS networks. By leveraging AWS tools like KMS, ACM, and Secrets Manager, you can ensure robust protection for data at rest and in transit. Implementing encryption best practices and addressing common challenges will help you meet compliance requirements and safeguard sensitive information.

Advanced Networking Components

AWS Transit Gateway Overview

As cloud architectures grow in complexity, the need for scalable, efficient, and centralized connectivity solutions becomes paramount. AWS Transit Gateway is designed to address these challenges by enabling seamless communication between multiple Amazon VPCs, on-premises networks, and AWS accounts. In this chapter, we will explore the core features, architecture, use cases, and best practices for AWS Transit Gateway.

---

1. What is AWS Transit Gateway?

AWS Transit Gateway (TGW) is a highly scalable, managed service that acts as a hub for interconnecting VPCs, on-premises networks, and third-party services. It simplifies network architecture by replacing complex, point-to-point peering connections with a hub-and-spoke model.

Key Features:

- **Centralized Connectivity**: Acts as a single gateway for managing multiple network connections.
- **Scalability**: Supports thousands of VPCs and on-premises connections.
- **High Availability**: Designed with built-in redundancy across Availability Zones.
- **Routing Control**: Provides centralized route management with dynamic and static routing.

---

2. Benefits of AWS Transit Gateway

AWS Transit Gateway offers several advantages for modern network architectures:

1. **Simplified Network Management**:
    - Replaces the need for VPC peering and reduces operational complexity.
    - Centralizes routing policies, making it easier to manage connections.
2. **Improved Scalability**:
    - Scales to support up to 5,000 attachments, accommodating even the largest organizations.
3. **Cost-Effective**:
    - Reduces the number of data transfer charges by optimizing traffic flows through a single gateway.
4. **Enhanced Security**:
    - Integrates with AWS services like Network Firewall, enabling centralized security policies.
5. **Global Reach**:
    - Supports global network connectivity, enabling seamless communication across AWS Regions using Transit Gateway Inter-Region Peering.

---

3. How AWS Transit Gateway Works

AWS Transit Gateway operates as a hub-and-spoke model, connecting various network resources through attachments.

Key Components:

1. **Attachments**:
   - VPCs, VPNs, AWS Direct Connect, and other networks are connected to the Transit Gateway using attachments.
2. **Route Tables**:
   - Control the flow of traffic between attachments.
   - Support segmentation by associating specific attachments with dedicated route tables.
3. **Inter-Region Peering**:
   - Establishes secure communication between Transit Gateways in different AWS Regions.
4. **High Throughput**:
   - Offers up to 50 Gbps per VPC connection.

---

4. Use Cases for AWS Transit Gateway

1. **Enterprise Multi-VPC Architectures**:
   - Simplifies connectivity for organizations with multiple VPCs spread across accounts and Regions.
2. **Hybrid Cloud Deployments**:
   - Enables secure connections between on-premises data centers and AWS.
3. **Global Network Connectivity**:
   - Facilitates low-latency communication between VPCs in different AWS Regions using Inter-Region Peering.
4. **Segmentation and Security**:
   - Segregates traffic between departments or applications using route table associations and security policies.

---

5. Steps to Set Up AWS Transit Gateway

Step 1: Create a Transit Gateway

1. Go to the **VPC Console** and select **Transit Gateways**.
2. Click "Create Transit Gateway."
3. Specify the following:
   - **Name**: A descriptive name for the gateway.
   - **Amazon ASN**: Autonomous System Number for dynamic routing.
   - Enable **DNS Support**, **Multicast**, or **VPN ECMP** as needed.

Step 2: Attach VPCs to the Transit Gateway

1. Select the Transit Gateway and choose **Create Attachment**.
2. Specify the VPC and associated subnets.
3. Repeat for all VPCs to be connected.

Step 3: Configure Route Tables

1. Create and associate route tables with each attachment.
2. Define routes to direct traffic between attachments or to an on-premises network.

Step 4: Connect On-Premises Networks

1. Establish a VPN or Direct Connect connection.
2. Attach the connection to the Transit Gateway.
3. Update on-premises routing tables to direct traffic through the VPN or Direct Connect.

Step 5: Monitor and Test Connectivity

1. Use Amazon CloudWatch to monitor traffic flows and performance.
2. Test connectivity between VPCs, on-premises networks, and Regions.

---

6. Best Practices for Using AWS Transit Gateway

1. **Plan Route Table Segmentation**:
   - Use separate route tables for different environments (e.g., production, development) to enhance security and manageability.
2. **Enable DNS Support**:
   - Allow DNS queries to resolve seamlessly between connected VPCs.
3. **Optimize Costs**:
   - Minimize inter-Region data transfer costs by strategically placing resources.
4. **Leverage Monitoring Tools**:
   - Use AWS Transit Gateway Network Manager to visualize and troubleshoot your network.
5. **Use Tags**:
   - Tag attachments and route tables to simplify resource identification and management.
6. **Integrate with Security Services**:
   - Combine Transit Gateway with AWS Network Firewall for centralized security enforcement.

---

7. Common Challenges and Solutions

1. **Challenge: Complex Route Management**
   - **Problem**: Multiple route tables can become difficult to manage.
   - **Solution**: Use AWS Transit Gateway Network Manager to centralize route visualization and management.
2. **Challenge: Latency in Inter-Region Peering**
   - **Problem**: Increased latency due to physical distance between Regions.
   - **Solution**: Optimize resource placement and use AWS Direct Connect where possible.
3. **Challenge: Scaling Beyond Attachment Limits**
   - **Problem**: Exceeding the maximum number of allowed attachments.
   - **Solution**: Aggregate connections using AWS Transit Gateway Connect or additional Transit Gateways.
4. **Challenge: Security Misconfigurations**
   - **Problem**: Unrestricted routes may expose sensitive data.
   - **Solution**: Regularly audit route tables and enforce least-privilege access.

---

8. Practical Example: Enterprise Multi-VPC Architecture

Scenario: A global retail company operates multiple VPCs across AWS Regions for its e-commerce platform and internal operations.

Solution:

1. **Set Up Transit Gateway**:
   - Deploy a Transit Gateway in each Region and enable Inter-Region Peering.
2. **Attach VPCs**:
   - Attach application VPCs (e-commerce, HR systems) and shared services VPCs (logging, monitoring) to the Transit Gateway.

3. **Configure Route Tables**:
   - ○ Segment traffic using route tables to restrict access between departments.
4. **Establish Hybrid Connectivity**:
   - ○ Connect on-premises data centers to the Transit Gateway via Direct Connect for low-latency access.
5. **Monitor Traffic**:
   - ○ Use CloudWatch and Transit Gateway Network Manager for performance monitoring.

Outcome: A scalable, secure, and centralized network architecture that supports seamless global connectivity and operational efficiency.

Conclusion

AWS Transit Gateway revolutionizes network connectivity by providing a scalable, centralized solution for managing complex architectures. With its hub-and-spoke model, integration capabilities, and robust security features, Transit Gateway is an essential component for modern cloud networking.

Connecting Multiple VPCs with Peering

As organizations scale their cloud infrastructure, the need to connect multiple Virtual Private Clouds (VPCs) becomes increasingly important. AWS VPC Peering offers a direct and efficient way to establish communication between VPCs, enabling resource sharing, data transfer, and multi-tier application setups. In this chapter, we will explore the fundamentals, use cases, and best practices of VPC Peering.

---

1. What is VPC Peering?

AWS VPC Peering is a networking connection that enables direct communication between two VPCs. It allows traffic to flow seamlessly across VPCs within the same AWS account or across different accounts, without passing through the public internet.

Key Features:

- **Private Communication**: Data is transferred securely over AWS's internal network.
- **Low Latency**: Offers high performance for VPC-to-VPC communication.
- **Flexible Topology**: Works across Regions and accounts.

---

2. Use Cases for VPC Peering

1. **Resource Sharing Across VPCs**:
   - Enable access to shared services, such as databases or logging systems, across VPCs.
2. **Multi-Tier Application Architectures**:
   - Connect frontend and backend tiers residing in separate VPCs for better isolation.
3. **Cross-Account Collaboration**:
   - Share resources between business units or partners while maintaining independent account management.
4. **Global Workloads**:
   - Use inter-Region VPC peering to connect workloads across different AWS Regions.

---

3. How VPC Peering Works

VPC Peering establishes a direct connection between two VPCs, creating a private route for communication.

Key Components:

1. **Peering Connection**:
   - A connection request must be initiated by one VPC (requester) and accepted by the other (accepter).
2. **Route Tables**:
   - Routes must be configured in both VPCs to enable traffic flow through the peering connection.
3. **DNS Resolution**:
   - Enable DNS resolution for private domain names across VPCs.

Limitations:

- VPC peering does not support transitive routing. If VPC A is peered with VPC B and VPC B is peered with VPC C, traffic cannot flow between VPC A and VPC C.

---

4. Steps to Configure VPC Peering

Step 1: Create a VPC Peering Connection

1. Navigate to the **VPC Console** and select **Peering Connections**.
2. Click "Create Peering Connection."
3. Specify:
   - The requester and accepter VPCs.
   - The account ID of the accepter if the VPC belongs to another account.

Step 2: Accept the Peering Connection

1. In the accepter VPC, navigate to the **Peering Connections** page.
2. Locate the pending request and click "Accept."

Step 3: Update Route Tables

1. Add routes in both VPCs' route tables to direct traffic to the peering connection.
2. For example:
   - In VPC A: Route traffic for VPC B's CIDR block through the peering connection.
   - In VPC B: Route traffic for VPC A's CIDR block through the peering connection.

Step 4: Update Security Groups

1. Update security group rules to allow inbound and outbound traffic between the peered VPCs.

Step 5: Test the Connection

1. Use tools like `ping` or `curl` to verify connectivity between resources in the two VPCs.

---

5. Best Practices for VPC Peering

1. **Plan CIDR Blocks Carefully**:
   - Ensure there is no overlap between the CIDR blocks of the VPCs to avoid routing conflicts.
2. **Enable DNS Resolution**:
   - Allow private domain name resolution across VPCs for seamless communication.
3. **Monitor Traffic**:
   - Use AWS CloudWatch and VPC Flow Logs to monitor traffic and identify anomalies.
4. **Use Tags for Organization**:
   - Tag peering connections to keep track of their purpose and ownership.
5. **Restrict Access with Security Groups**:
   - Apply least privilege principles to security group rules to limit access between VPCs.
6. **Leverage IAM for Cross-Account Peering**:
   - Use IAM policies to control who can create and accept peering connections.

---

6. Common Challenges and Solutions

1. **Challenge: Overlapping CIDR Blocks**

- ○ **Problem**: Traffic cannot route between VPCs with overlapping CIDR blocks.
- ○ **Solution**: Plan CIDR blocks in advance or use Network Address Translation (NAT).
2. **Challenge: DNS Resolution Issues**
    - ○ **Problem**: Private domain names do not resolve across VPCs.
    - ○ **Solution**: Enable DNS resolution in the peering connection settings.
3. **Challenge: Transitive Routing**
    - ○ **Problem**: Traffic cannot flow between indirectly connected VPCs.
    - ○ **Solution**: Use AWS Transit Gateway for complex network architectures.
4. **Challenge: Security Group Misconfigurations**
    - ○ **Problem**: Traffic is blocked despite a valid peering connection.
    - ○ **Solution**: Review and update security group rules to allow required traffic.

---

7. Practical Example: Connecting a Multi-Tier Application

Scenario: A company has separated its application into two VPCs: one for frontend services and another for backend services.

Solution:

1. **Create a VPC Peering Connection**:
    - ○ Establish a connection between the frontend VPC and the backend VPC.
2. **Update Route Tables**:
    - ○ Add routes to enable traffic between the VPCs.
3. **Configure Security Groups**:
    - ○ Allow traffic from the frontend subnet in the backend security group and vice versa.
4. **Test Connectivity**:
    - ○ Verify that the frontend servers can communicate with the backend database.

Outcome: A secure, scalable architecture that ensures the frontend and backend tiers can interact seamlessly.

Conclusion

AWS VPC Peering is a powerful solution for connecting multiple VPCs in a private and secure manner. By understanding its capabilities, limitations, and best practices, you can design scalable and efficient network architectures that meet your organization's needs.

Elastic Load Balancing for Network Traffic

In any scalable and reliable cloud architecture, distributing network traffic across multiple resources is a critical requirement. AWS Elastic Load Balancing (ELB) provides an efficient and automated way to handle incoming traffic by distributing it to the appropriate backend resources. This chapter delves into Elastic Load Balancing, its types, and how it plays a pivotal role in enhancing application performance and reliability.

---

1. What is Elastic Load Balancing?

AWS Elastic Load Balancing (ELB) is a managed service that automatically distributes incoming network or application traffic across multiple targets, such as Amazon EC2 instances, containers, IP addresses, and Lambda functions. It ensures high availability, scalability, and fault tolerance for your applications.

Key Features:

- **Traffic Distribution**: Balances traffic across multiple resources.
- **Automatic Scaling**: Scales seamlessly with your traffic demands.
- **Health Checks**: Monitors the health of registered targets and routes traffic only to healthy instances.
- **Security**: Supports integration with AWS Identity and Access Management (IAM), AWS WAF, and SSL/TLS for secure traffic.

---

2. Types of Elastic Load Balancers

AWS offers three primary types of load balancers, each designed for specific use cases:

2.1 Application Load Balancer (ALB)

- **Purpose**: Designed for HTTP and HTTPS traffic.
- **Features**:
    - Content-based routing (e.g., route based on URL path or host headers).
    - Integration with AWS Web Application Firewall (WAF).
    - WebSocket support.
- **Use Case**: Ideal for microservices and container-based applications.

2.2 Network Load Balancer (NLB)

- **Purpose**: Optimized for TCP, UDP, and TLS traffic at high performance.
- **Features**:
    - Handles millions of requests per second with ultra-low latency.
    - Supports static IP addresses and Elastic IPs.
    - TLS offloading for secure communication.
- **Use Case**: Best for latency-sensitive applications or when managing TCP/UDP traffic.

2.3 Gateway Load Balancer (GLB)

- **Purpose**: Simplifies the deployment, scaling, and management of third-party virtual appliances like firewalls and deep packet inspection systems.
- **Features**:
    - Operates at Layer 3 (network layer).
    - Routes traffic through virtual appliances for inspection or processing.

- **Use Case**: Ideal for security-focused architectures requiring third-party appliances.

---

3. Benefits of Elastic Load Balancing

1. **High Availability**:
   - Distributes traffic across multiple resources in one or more Availability Zones, ensuring uptime even during failures.
2. **Improved Performance**:
   - Optimizes resource utilization by directing traffic to the least-loaded or best-performing targets.
3. **Fault Tolerance**:
   - Routes traffic only to healthy instances, minimizing downtime.
4. **Enhanced Security**:
   - Provides SSL/TLS termination and integrates with AWS WAF for secure traffic management.
5. **Cost Efficiency**:
   - Reduces the need for over-provisioning resources by dynamically adjusting to traffic demands.

---

4. Configuring Elastic Load Balancers

Step 1: Choose the Load Balancer Type

1. Navigate to the **EC2 Console** and select **Load Balancers**.
2. Click "Create Load Balancer" and choose the appropriate type (ALB, NLB, or GLB) based on your use case.

Step 2: Configure Load Balancer Settings

1. Define basic settings, such as name, scheme (Internet-facing or internal), and VPC.
2. Select the required Availability Zones.

Step 3: Configure Listeners and Routing

1. **Listeners**:
   - Define the protocols and ports (e.g., HTTP, HTTPS, TCP).
2. **Target Groups**:
   - Create target groups and register your backend resources.

Step 4: Configure Security Settings

1. Enable SSL/TLS for secure communication.
2. Attach AWS WAF if necessary for additional security.

Step 5: Test the Configuration

1. Deploy traffic to the load balancer and verify distribution across targets.
2. Use tools like `curl` or AWS CloudWatch for monitoring.

---

5. Use Cases for Elastic Load Balancing

1. **Dynamic Web Applications**:

- Use ALB to distribute traffic between multiple EC2 instances running a web application.
2. **Real-Time Gaming Applications**:
   - Leverage NLB for low-latency, high-throughput gaming workloads.
3. **Security Inspection**:
   - Implement GLB to route traffic through third-party firewalls or intrusion detection systems.
4. **Hybrid Architectures**:
   - Use ELB to handle traffic between on-premises resources and AWS cloud resources.
5. **Microservices and Containers**:
   - Utilize ALB for routing traffic to services deployed in containers using Amazon ECS or Kubernetes.

6. Best Practices for Elastic Load Balancing

1. **Enable Cross-Zone Load Balancing**:
   - Distribute traffic evenly across targets in different Availability Zones.
2. **Perform Regular Health Checks**:
   - Configure health checks to monitor the status of your targets and avoid routing traffic to unhealthy instances.
3. **Use Security Groups**:
   - Restrict access to the load balancer by configuring security groups.
4. **Leverage Auto Scaling**:
   - Combine ELB with Auto Scaling to dynamically adjust capacity based on traffic patterns.
5. **Enable Logging and Monitoring**:
   - Use AWS CloudTrail and Elastic Load Balancing Access Logs for tracking requests and identifying potential issues.
6. **Optimize Costs**:
   - Use ALB for HTTP/HTTPS workloads and NLB for high-throughput, TCP-based workloads to match your application needs.

7. Common Challenges and Solutions

1. **Challenge: Overloading Targets**
   - **Problem**: Backend resources may become overwhelmed during traffic spikes.
   - **Solution**: Integrate ELB with Auto Scaling for automatic capacity adjustments.
2. **Challenge: Misconfigured Routing**
   - **Problem**: Traffic does not reach the intended targets.
   - **Solution**: Verify target group configurations and routing rules.
3. **Challenge: SSL Certificate Management**
   - **Problem**: Certificates may expire, leading to insecure traffic.
   - **Solution**: Use AWS Certificate Manager (ACM) for automated certificate renewal.
4. **Challenge: Monitoring and Debugging**
   - **Problem**: Lack of visibility into traffic patterns and errors.
   - **Solution**: Enable detailed monitoring in CloudWatch and use ELB access logs.

8. Practical Example: Deploying a Scalable Web Application

Scenario: A company wants to deploy a high-traffic e-commerce website with global reach.

Solution:

1. **Set Up an ALB**:
   - Create an ALB to handle HTTP/HTTPS traffic.
2. **Register Targets**:
   - Register EC2 instances running the e-commerce application in a target group.
3. **Configure Health Checks**:
   - Define health checks to monitor the status of the EC2 instances.
4. **Enable Auto Scaling**:
   - Automatically add or remove EC2 instances based on traffic demand.
5. **Enhance Security**:
   - Use AWS WAF to block malicious requests and enforce SSL/TLS for secure communication.

Outcome: A scalable, secure, and highly available web application that can handle varying traffic loads efficiently.

Conclusion

Elastic Load Balancing is an essential tool for distributing network traffic and ensuring high availability in AWS. By selecting the right type of load balancer and following best practices, you can optimize performance, improve fault tolerance, and secure your application traffic.

Application Load Balancer vs. Network Load Balancer

AWS Elastic Load Balancing (ELB) provides robust tools for distributing traffic to backend resources. Among its offerings, the **Application Load Balancer (ALB)** and **Network Load Balancer (NLB)** serve distinct purposes, optimized for specific workloads and protocols. This chapter explores the features, use cases, and differences between these two load balancer types to help you make informed architectural decisions.

1. Overview of ALB and NLB

Application Load Balancer (ALB): Designed for HTTP and HTTPS traffic, ALB operates at the **application layer (Layer 7)** of the OSI model. It enables advanced routing capabilities based on application-level information, such as hostnames, URLs, and HTTP headers.

Network Load Balancer (NLB): Optimized for TCP, UDP, and TLS traffic, NLB operates at the **transport layer (Layer 4)**. It provides ultra-low latency, handling millions of requests per second.

2. Key Features of ALB and NLB

Feature	Application Load Balancer (ALB)	Network Load Balancer (NLB)
Protocol Support	HTTP, HTTPS, WebSocket	TCP, UDP, TLS
Layer of Operation	Layer 7	Layer 4
Routing Capabilities	Content-based (path, host, headers)	Connection-based (IP address, port)
Performance	High, optimized for web applications	Ultra-low latency, optimized for high throughput
Static IP Support	Not supported	Supports Elastic IPs
TLS Termination	Supported	Supported
Target Types	EC2 instances, IPs, Lambda functions, containers	EC2 instances, IPs
Health Checks	Application-level (e.g., HTTP responses)	Connection-level (e.g., TCP connection status)

3. Use Cases

Application Load Balancer (ALB)

1. **Web Applications**:
    - Ideal for serving HTTP/HTTPS traffic with complex routing requirements.
    - Example: Route requests to /api to backend API servers and /admin to admin services.
2. **Microservices**:

- Enables path-based routing to direct traffic to different services within a microservices architecture.
3. **WebSocket Communication**:
   - Supports WebSocket for applications requiring real-time updates, such as chat applications.
4. **Secure Applications**:
   - Integrates with AWS Web Application Firewall (WAF) for enhanced security.

Network Load Balancer (NLB)

1. **Latency-Sensitive Applications**:
   - Optimized for low-latency workloads, such as real-time gaming or financial applications.
2. **High-Throughput Applications**:
   - Handles millions of requests per second, ideal for high-performance applications.
3. **Hybrid Cloud Architectures**:
   - Use Elastic IPs for predictable static IP addresses, simplifying on-premises connections.
4. **TLS Offloading**:
   - Offloads TLS decryption to reduce the burden on backend servers.

---

4. Configuring ALB and NLB

Application Load Balancer

1. **Create ALB**:
   - Go to the **EC2 Console**, select **Load Balancers**, and choose "Application Load Balancer."
2. **Configure Listeners**:
   - Specify HTTP/HTTPS protocols and port numbers.
3. **Define Target Groups**:
   - Register backend targets (EC2, Lambda, or IP addresses).
4. **Set Routing Rules**:
   - Configure path-based or host-based routing.
5. **Enable Security Features**:
   - Attach SSL/TLS certificates using AWS Certificate Manager (ACM).

Network Load Balancer

1. **Create NLB**:
   - Go to the **EC2 Console**, select **Load Balancers**, and choose "Network Load Balancer."
2. **Define Listeners**:
   - Specify TCP/UDP/TLS protocols and ports.
3. **Configure Target Groups**:
   - Register backend targets and set up health checks.
4. **Assign Elastic IPs**:
   - Allocate and attach static IPs for consistent routing.
5. **Integrate with Backend Services**:
   - Connect with AWS Direct Connect or hybrid architectures for seamless traffic flow.

---

5. When to Choose ALB vs. NLB

Requirement	Best Choice	Reason
Content-Based Routing	ALB	Supports path and host-based routing.

High Throughput	NLB	Handles millions of requests with low latency.
Static IP Addresses	NLB	Elastic IP support for predictable addressing.
Web Applications	ALB	Optimized for HTTP/HTTPS traffic.
Real-Time Applications	NLB	Designed for low-latency, real-time workloads.
WebSocket Support	ALB	Supports persistent WebSocket connections.
Hybrid Cloud Integration	NLB	Facilitates integration with on-premises networks.
Security with AWS WAF	ALB	Fully integrates with AWS WAF for Layer 7 protection.
Transport Layer Traffic	NLB	Optimized for Layer 4 traffic, such as TCP/UDP.

6. Best Practices

1. **Enable Cross-Zone Load Balancing**:
   - Distribute traffic across multiple Availability Zones for high availability.
2. **Monitor Performance**:
   - Use AWS CloudWatch to track metrics like latency, request count, and health status.
3. **Secure Traffic**:
   - For ALB: Use AWS WAF and SSL/TLS certificates.
   - For NLB: Enable TLS termination for encrypted communication.
4. **Optimize Costs**:
   - Choose the load balancer type based on specific application requirements to avoid over-provisioning.
5. **Test Health Checks**:
   - Configure health checks to ensure only healthy targets receive traffic.
6. **Leverage Auto Scaling**:
   - Pair load balancers with Auto Scaling groups for dynamic resource scaling.

7. Practical Example: Multi-Layer Load Balancing

Scenario: A company runs an e-commerce website with a frontend UI and a backend API.

Solution:

1. **Frontend**:
   - Deploy an ALB to handle HTTP/HTTPS traffic and route requests to web servers based on URL paths (e.g., /checkout).
2. **Backend**:
   - Use an NLB to manage TCP traffic to backend database servers.
3. **Security**:

○ Terminate SSL/TLS at both the ALB and NLB to ensure end-to-end encryption.

Outcome: A robust, scalable architecture optimized for user experience and backend performance.

Conclusion

Choosing between an Application Load Balancer and a Network Load Balancer depends on the specific needs of your application. ALB excels in application-layer routing for web applications, while NLB is best suited for high-performance, transport-layer traffic. By understanding their unique features and capabilities, you can design network architectures that meet your workload's demands.

Global Accelerator for Low-Latency Connections

AWS Global Accelerator is a managed service designed to optimize application performance by providing low-latency, highly available connections for global users. By leveraging the AWS global network infrastructure, Global Accelerator routes traffic through optimal pathways, bypassing internet congestion and enhancing application performance.

1. What is AWS Global Accelerator?

AWS Global Accelerator is a network service that improves the availability and performance of your applications by using the global AWS network. It directs user traffic to optimal endpoints based on health, geography, or routing policies, ensuring fast and secure connections.

Key Features:

- **Static IP Addresses**: Provides two static IP addresses for your application, simplifying DNS configuration.
- **Global Traffic Management**: Automatically routes traffic to the nearest healthy endpoint.
- **Health Checks**: Continuously monitors the health of your application endpoints.
- **Elasticity and Scalability**: Scales as your application grows without additional configuration.
- **DDoS Protection**: Integrates with AWS Shield to protect against Distributed Denial of Service (DDoS) attacks.

2. How Does AWS Global Accelerator Work?

Global Accelerator uses AWS edge locations and global network infrastructure to route traffic. Here's a simplified process:

1. **Static IP Allocation**:
   - Global Accelerator assigns two static IP addresses to serve as entry points for your application.
2. **Traffic Routing**:
   - Based on routing policies and health checks, traffic is routed to the closest and most optimal endpoint (e.g., an Application Load Balancer or EC2 instance).
3. **Failover and Health Monitoring**:
   - If an endpoint becomes unhealthy, traffic is redirected to a healthy endpoint, maintaining application availability.

3. Use Cases for Global Accelerator

3.1 Real-Time Applications

- **Example**: Online gaming platforms or financial trading applications.
- **Benefit**: Low-latency connections ensure real-time responsiveness.

3.2 Content Delivery

- **Example**: Media streaming services.
- **Benefit**: Provides consistent and fast delivery of large files or video streams.

3.3 Multi-Region Failover

- **Example**: E-commerce websites with global customer bases.
- **Benefit**: Automatically redirects users to the nearest healthy region in case of regional outages.

3.4 API Gateways

- **Example**: Applications with a global API user base.
- **Benefit**: Ensures low-latency API responses by routing users to the closest API endpoint.

---

4. Benefits of AWS Global Accelerator

1. **Improved Performance**:
   - Bypasses public internet congestion by routing traffic through AWS's high-speed global network.
2. **High Availability**:
   - Ensures application uptime by redirecting traffic to healthy endpoints during failures.
3. **Enhanced Security**:
   - Integrates with AWS Shield for advanced DDoS protection.
4. **Simplified Management**:
   - Static IP addresses reduce the complexity of DNS configurations during failovers.
5. **Seamless Integration**:
   - Works with various AWS services, including Elastic Load Balancers, EC2 instances, and S3 buckets.

---

5. Configuring AWS Global Accelerator

Step 1: Create a Global Accelerator

1. Open the **Global Accelerator Console**.
2. Click on "Create Accelerator."
3. Assign a name and choose whether it is standard or custom routing.

Step 2: Add Listeners

1. Define the protocols (TCP/UDP) and port ranges for your application.

Step 3: Configure Endpoint Groups

1. Add one or more endpoint groups (e.g., regions like US-East-1 or EU-West-1).
2. Set traffic weights to balance traffic among multiple endpoints.

Step 4: Add Endpoints

1. Register specific endpoints, such as Application Load Balancers, EC2 instances, or Elastic IPs.

Step 5: Test and Monitor

1. Verify connectivity using the provided static IPs.
2. Monitor performance and health metrics in the AWS Management Console.

---

6. Comparison: Global Accelerator vs. CloudFront

Feature	AWS Global Accelerator	AWS CloudFront
Purpose	Optimizes application performance.	Delivers static and dynamic content.
Layer of Operation	Operates at Layer 4 (network layer).	Operates at Layer 7 (application layer).
Use Case	Low-latency, high-availability apps.	Content delivery for websites and media.
Static IP Support	Provides static IPs.	Does not provide static IPs.
DDoS Protection	Integrated with AWS Shield.	Integrated with AWS Shield.
Health Checks	Endpoint-level health checks.	No direct health checks.

7. Best Practices for Using Global Accelerator

1. **Leverage Endpoint Weighting**:
   - Use traffic weights to distribute traffic evenly or prioritize specific regions.
2. **Enable Health Checks**:
   - Regularly monitor the health of your endpoints to avoid routing traffic to unresponsive instances.
3. **Optimize for Costs**:
   - Use traffic policies to route users only when necessary to reduce costs.
4. **Integrate with Auto Scaling**:
   - Combine Global Accelerator with Auto Scaling to handle sudden traffic spikes.
5. **Secure Traffic**:
   - Use Global Accelerator with AWS Shield and TLS for end-to-end encryption.

8. Practical Example: Multi-Region E-Commerce Application

Scenario: A global e-commerce platform wants to ensure low-latency connections and high availability for users in North America, Europe, and Asia.

Solution:

1. **Deploy Multi-Region Infrastructure**:
   - Host instances in US-East-1, EU-West-1, and AP-Southeast-1.
2. **Set Up Global Accelerator**:
   - Create an accelerator with endpoint groups for each region.
   - Assign traffic weights to distribute traffic evenly.
3. **Enable Health Checks**:
   - Monitor the health of each endpoint to ensure uninterrupted service.
4. **Static IP Configuration**:
   - Use static IPs for DNS and client connections.

Outcome: Users experience low latency and uninterrupted access, even during regional failures.

Conclusion

AWS Global Accelerator is a powerful tool for optimizing the performance and availability of global applications. By leveraging AWS's extensive network, it ensures low-latency connections and seamless failovers. As applications continue to grow in complexity and reach, Global Accelerator plays a crucial role in building robust and reliable architectures.

Traffic Mirroring for Network Monitoring

Traffic mirroring in AWS provides a powerful mechanism for replicating network traffic from Elastic Network Interfaces (ENIs) to monitoring and security appliances. By enabling deep packet inspection and real-time network analysis, traffic mirroring empowers organizations to gain visibility into their cloud networks and detect potential issues.

1. What is Traffic Mirroring?

Traffic mirroring in AWS allows you to capture and replicate network traffic from an ENI attached to an EC2 instance. The mirrored traffic is sent to a target, such as a network packet analyzer, intrusion detection system (IDS), or forensic analysis tool, for further inspection.

Key Features:

- **Packet-Level Analysis**:
  - Provides raw network packets for in-depth inspection.
- **Source Filtering**:
  - Supports filtering based on IP addresses, protocols, and ports.
- **Flexible Targets**:
  - Traffic can be sent to an ENI of a monitoring appliance, a VPC traffic mirroring service, or on-premises tools.
- **Integration with Security Tools**:
  - Works seamlessly with third-party tools like Wireshark or Zeek.

2. How Traffic Mirroring Works

1. **Source ENI**:
   - Identify the ENI attached to the EC2 instance where traffic needs to be mirrored.
2. **Target**:
   - Specify the destination where mirrored traffic will be analyzed. This can be another ENI, a network appliance, or a custom solution.
3. **Mirror Filter**:
   - Create filters to control what traffic is mirrored (e.g., specific IP ranges, TCP/UDP traffic).
4. **Session Configuration**:
   - Establish a traffic mirroring session to define the relationship between the source, target, and filter.

3. Use Cases for Traffic Mirroring

3.1 Intrusion Detection

- **Example**: Implement an intrusion detection system (IDS) to monitor for malicious activity.
- **Benefit**: Identifies threats in real-time by analyzing mirrored traffic.

3.2 Performance Analysis

- **Example**: Debug latency issues or network bottlenecks.
- **Benefit**: Provides granular insights into network performance.

3.3 Forensic Investigations

- **Example**: Capture network traffic for post-incident analysis.
- **Benefit**: Enables root cause analysis and compliance reporting.

3.4 Compliance Monitoring

- **Example**: Ensure adherence to regulatory requirements by logging network activity.
- **Benefit**: Provides an auditable trail of network communication.

---

4. Setting Up Traffic Mirroring

Step 1: Create a Mirror Filter

1. Open the **VPC Console** and navigate to "Traffic Mirroring."
2. Click on **Create Filter**.
3. Define rules for inbound and outbound traffic based on:
   - Protocols (e.g., TCP, UDP).
   - Ports (e.g., port 80 for HTTP traffic).
   - IP ranges (e.g., a specific CIDR block).

Step 2: Define a Mirror Target

1. Select "Create Target" in the Traffic Mirroring section.
2. Choose one of the following target types:
   - **Network Load Balancer** for scalable traffic distribution.
   - **Elastic Network Interface (ENI)** for direct capture on monitoring appliances.

Step 3: Configure a Traffic Mirroring Session

1. Go to **Traffic Mirroring Sessions** and select "Create Session."
2. Specify the following:
   - **Source**: The ENI of the instance to mirror.
   - **Target**: The previously configured target.
   - **Filter**: Apply the traffic mirror filter to capture specific traffic.
3. Set session parameters, such as packet encapsulation and maximum bandwidth.

Step 4: Deploy and Test

1. Validate that mirrored traffic reaches the target.
2. Use tools like Wireshark or AWS-native monitoring solutions for analysis.

---

5. Security and Best Practices

1. **Secure Traffic Mirroring Targets**:
   - Ensure that only authorized systems can access mirrored traffic to prevent unauthorized data exposure.
2. **Filter Traffic Efficiently**:
   - Use filters to capture only relevant traffic, reducing overhead and analysis complexity.
3. **Monitor Costs**:
   - Traffic mirroring can generate significant data transfer costs, especially for high-volume workloads.
4. **Leverage Automation**:

- Use AWS CloudFormation or the AWS CLI to automate traffic mirroring configurations for large-scale deployments.
5. **Integrate with Security Tools**:
   - Pair traffic mirroring with tools like Amazon GuardDuty for enhanced threat detection.

---

6. Comparing Traffic Mirroring to VPC Flow Logs

Feature	Traffic Mirroring	VPC Flow Logs
Data Granularity	Packet-level traffic	Metadata about network traffic
Use Case	Deep packet inspection	High-level traffic analysis
Impact on Network Performance	Higher due to packet duplication	Minimal
Target Audience	Security teams and network engineers	Compliance and cost optimization teams

---

7. Practical Example: Setting Up a Security Monitoring Solution

Scenario: A financial services company wants to monitor traffic for potential data breaches.

Solution:

1. Deploy an IDS (e.g., Suricata) on a monitoring instance.
2. Configure traffic mirroring on critical EC2 instances hosting sensitive data.
3. Use filters to mirror only inbound and outbound traffic from specific IP ranges.
4. Analyze mirrored traffic in real-time to detect anomalies.

Outcome: The company gains visibility into its network, identifying and mitigating potential threats before they escalate.

Conclusion

Traffic mirroring is a versatile feature for enhancing network visibility and security in AWS. By capturing and analyzing packet-level traffic, organizations can identify performance bottlenecks, detect threats, and ensure compliance.

Networking Tools and Services

AWS Direct Connect and Use Cases

AWS Direct Connect is a high-speed, private network connection that allows organizations to connect their on-premises environments directly to AWS. By bypassing the public internet, it provides enhanced performance, reliability, and security, making it an indispensable tool for organizations with demanding network requirements.

1. What is AWS Direct Connect?

AWS Direct Connect is a dedicated network service that establishes a private connection between your on-premises data center or office and AWS. Unlike internet-based connectivity, Direct Connect provides a secure, low-latency path to AWS resources, ensuring optimal network performance for mission-critical workloads.

Key Features:

- **High-Speed Connectivity**:
  - Supports bandwidths ranging from 50 Mbps to 100 Gbps.
- **Reduced Latency**:
  - Provides consistent and predictable performance.
- **Enhanced Security**:
  - Avoids public internet, reducing exposure to common threats.
- **Cost-Effective**:
  - Lowers data transfer costs compared to traditional internet connections.

2. How AWS Direct Connect Works

AWS Direct Connect involves setting up a dedicated network link between your on-premises environment and an AWS Direct Connect location. This connection integrates with your Virtual Private Cloud (VPC) via a Direct Connect Gateway or Virtual Private Gateway.

Steps to Set Up:

1. **Choose a Location**:
   - Identify the nearest AWS Direct Connect location.
2. **Request a Port**:
   - Work with an AWS partner or network provider to set up the connection.
3. **Configure a Virtual Interface**:
   - Establish a virtual interface (VIF) to connect to AWS services.
4. **Integrate with VPC**:
   - Use a Direct Connect Gateway to route traffic to one or more VPCs.
5. **Test and Optimize**:
   - Validate connectivity and monitor performance using tools like Amazon CloudWatch.

3. Use Cases for AWS Direct Connect

AWS Direct Connect is ideal for scenarios requiring high-performance, secure, and reliable network connectivity.

3.1 Data Center Migration

- **Scenario**: A company is migrating its workloads from an on-premises data center to AWS.
- **Benefit**: Direct Connect enables fast and secure data transfers, minimizing downtime and latency during migration.

3.2 Hybrid Cloud Architecture

- **Scenario**: An organization needs to extend its on-premises infrastructure into AWS.
- **Benefit**: Provides seamless connectivity for hybrid deployments, enabling resource sharing and workload distribution across environments.

3.3 High-Performance Applications

- **Scenario**: Applications with stringent latency or bandwidth requirements, such as video streaming or financial trading platforms.
- **Benefit**: Direct Connect ensures predictable network performance and minimal latency.

3.4 Backup and Disaster Recovery

- **Scenario**: Regularly backing up critical data to AWS or implementing a disaster recovery solution.
- **Benefit**: Facilitates efficient data transfers and quick recovery in case of system failures.

3.5 Compliance and Security

- **Scenario**: Industries like healthcare or finance require secure data exchanges to meet compliance standards.
- **Benefit**: Avoids public internet, ensuring data integrity and compliance with regulatory requirements.

---

4. Components of AWS Direct Connect

Direct Connect Location

A physical location where AWS provides access to its network. You connect your on-premises environment to this location via a dedicated line.

Virtual Interface (VIF)

A logical connection that allows you to:

- Access public AWS services (Public VIF).
- Connect to a VPC (Private VIF).
- Enable hybrid connectivity (Transit VIF).

Direct Connect Gateway

A gateway that enables you to connect multiple VPCs or AWS Regions to a single Direct Connect link.

Partner Network Providers

AWS collaborates with network providers to facilitate connectivity between your data center and AWS.

5. Benefits of Using AWS Direct Connect

1. **Improved Performance**:
   - Provides high-speed, low-latency connectivity for demanding workloads.
2. **Increased Reliability**:
   - Reduces the impact of network interruptions by bypassing the public internet.
3. **Enhanced Security**:
   - Protects data in transit by using private network paths.
4. **Cost Savings**:
   - Lowers data transfer costs compared to internet-based connections.
5. **Global Access**:
   - Allows connectivity to multiple AWS Regions through a Direct Connect Gateway.

6. Configuring AWS Direct Connect

Step 1: Request a Connection

- Log in to the AWS Management Console.
- Navigate to the **Direct Connect** service and request a port at your desired location.

Step 2: Establish a Physical Connection

- Collaborate with a network provider to establish the dedicated line to the Direct Connect location.

Step 3: Configure a Virtual Interface

- Set up a VIF in the AWS Console.
- Choose between:
  - **Public VIF** for accessing AWS services like S3 or DynamoDB.
  - **Private VIF** for connecting to a VPC.

Step 4: Integrate with AWS Services

- Attach the Direct Connect Gateway to one or more VPCs.
- Use routing tables to control traffic flow.

Step 5: Monitor and Optimize

- Use Amazon CloudWatch to monitor metrics like latency and bandwidth.
- Regularly review usage to optimize costs.

7. Real-World Example: Accelerating Data Transfers

Scenario: A media company needs to transfer petabytes of video content to AWS for storage and processing.

Solution:

- Set up a 10 Gbps Direct Connect link to the nearest AWS location.
- Use a Private VIF to connect to an S3 bucket.
- Schedule transfers during non-peak hours to maximize bandwidth usage.

Outcome: The company achieves faster data uploads, reduced costs, and improved content delivery to its customers.

Conclusion

AWS Direct Connect is a cornerstone of advanced cloud networking strategies, offering unparalleled performance, security, and reliability. Its ability to seamlessly bridge on-premises environments with AWS services makes it an invaluable tool for enterprises.

AWS PrivateLink for Secure Services Access

AWS PrivateLink is a robust networking solution designed to provide secure, private access to AWS services and custom applications hosted on AWS. By eliminating the need to expose services to the public internet, PrivateLink ensures enhanced security and reduces the risk of unauthorized access.

1. What is AWS PrivateLink?

AWS PrivateLink simplifies the process of connecting to AWS services by establishing private connectivity over a Virtual Private Cloud (VPC). It allows you to securely access services without routing traffic through the public internet, providing a seamless and secure communication channel.

Key Features:

- **Private Connectivity**:
  - Directly connects your VPC to AWS services via an elastic network interface (ENI).
- **Enhanced Security**:
  - Data does not traverse the public internet, reducing vulnerabilities.
- **Simplified Access**:
  - Provides a consistent and seamless connection to AWS services.
- **Support for Custom Services**:
  - Enables private access to custom applications hosted on AWS.

2. How AWS PrivateLink Works

AWS PrivateLink uses endpoint services to establish a secure and private connection between a consumer VPC and a service provider's VPC.

Components:

1. **Service Endpoint**:
   - Created by the service consumer to connect to an endpoint service.
2. **Endpoint Service**:
   - Hosted by the service provider, representing the service being accessed.
3. **Elastic Network Interface (ENI)**:
   - A private IP-based interface within the consumer's VPC used for connectivity.

Workflow:

1. The service provider creates an endpoint service.
2. The service consumer creates a VPC endpoint and establishes a connection to the endpoint service.
3. The ENI within the consumer's VPC enables secure communication with the service provider.

3. Benefits of AWS PrivateLink

3.1 Enhanced Security

- Traffic remains within the AWS network, reducing exposure to external threats.
- Avoids the need for public IP addresses, DNS configurations, or firewalls for accessing services.

3.2 Simplified Networking

- Eliminates the complexities of setting up VPNs or Direct Connect for private communication.
- Supports consistent and low-latency connections to services.

3.3 Scalable Design

- Scales to support multiple VPCs and AWS accounts without complex routing configurations.

3.4 Cost Efficiency

- Reduces the costs associated with maintaining public-facing resources and internet gateways.

---

4. Use Cases for AWS PrivateLink

4.1 Secure Access to AWS Services

- **Scenario**: Accessing AWS services like Amazon S3 or DynamoDB securely.
- **Benefit**: No public IP exposure; data remains within the AWS private network.

4.2 Connecting to Partner Services

- **Scenario**: Utilizing third-party applications hosted on AWS.
- **Benefit**: Securely connect to partner-hosted services via private endpoints.

4.3 Hosting Private Applications

- **Scenario**: Exposing custom applications to multiple VPCs or AWS accounts.
- **Benefit**: Simplifies sharing services without exposing them to the internet.

4.4 Hybrid Cloud Architecture

- **Scenario**: Integrating on-premises environments with AWS services.
- **Benefit**: Direct, private communication without internet dependencies.

---

5. Steps to Set Up AWS PrivateLink

Step 1: Create an Endpoint Service

- Service providers configure an endpoint service in their VPC.
- Use the AWS Management Console, AWS CLI, or SDK to set up the service.

Step 2: Configure Permissions

- Grant permissions to specific AWS accounts or organizations to connect to the endpoint service.

Step 3: Establish a VPC Endpoint

- Service consumers create a VPC endpoint to connect to the endpoint service.
- Select the appropriate AWS Region and endpoint type.

Step 4: Test Connectivity

- Use tools like ping or telnet to validate connectivity and ensure private access.

Step 5: Monitor and Optimize

- Monitor traffic using Amazon CloudWatch.
- Optimize endpoint configurations based on usage patterns.

---

6. Key Differences Between AWS PrivateLink and VPC Peering

Feature	AWS PrivateLink	VPC Peering
Scope	Service-specific access	Full VPC-to-VPC communication
Security	Traffic stays within AWS private network	Requires route table configurations
Setup	Simplified with service endpoints	More complex with route configurations
Cost	Endpoint-specific charges	Data transfer charges between VPCs

---

7. Real-World Example: Private Data Exchange

Scenario: A financial services company needs to access a partner's transaction processing system hosted on AWS securely.

Solution:

- The partner sets up an endpoint service in their VPC.
- The company creates a VPC endpoint to connect to the partner's service.
- PrivateLink ensures that sensitive financial data does not traverse the public internet.

Outcome: The company achieves secure and efficient communication with its partner, maintaining compliance with industry regulations.

Conclusion

AWS PrivateLink is a powerful tool for organizations prioritizing security and simplicity in their networking strategies. By enabling private access to services and applications, PrivateLink enhances security, reduces complexity, and fosters seamless integration between environments.

Understanding Amazon Route 53

Amazon Route 53 is a highly scalable, secure, and reliable Domain Name System (DNS) web service designed to route end users to internet applications by translating human-readable domain names into IP addresses. Beyond its basic DNS functions, Route 53 offers advanced features, such as traffic management, health checks, and domain registration, making it a comprehensive solution for managing application access.

---

1. What is Amazon Route 53?

Amazon Route 53 acts as a highly available and scalable DNS service integrated with other AWS services to provide seamless domain management and routing solutions. Its primary purpose is to connect user requests to resources hosted in AWS or external systems.

Key Features:

- **DNS Management**:
    - Hosts zones and resolves domain names into IP addresses.
- **Traffic Management**:
    - Directs user requests based on policies, such as geolocation or latency.
- **Health Checks**:
    - Monitors the health of resources and reroutes traffic during failures.
- **Domain Registration**:
    - Enables registration and management of custom domain names.

---

2. Core Functions of Route 53

2.1 DNS Management

Route 53 offers complete DNS functionality to manage the mapping between domain names and IP addresses.

- **Hosted Zones**:
    - A hosted zone is a container for records that define how traffic is routed to a domain.
    - Types:
        - **Public Hosted Zones**: Manage public-facing resources.
        - **Private Hosted Zones**: Used within a Virtual Private Cloud (VPC) for private DNS needs.
- **Record Types**:
    - **A (Address) Record**: Maps a domain name to an IPv4 address.
    - **AAAA Record**: Maps a domain name to an IPv6 address.
    - **CNAME Record**: Redirects one domain name to another.
    - **MX (Mail Exchange) Record**: Directs email traffic.
    - **TXT Record**: Stores text-based information for domains (e.g., SPF, DKIM).

2.2 Traffic Management

Amazon Route 53 enables intelligent traffic routing using advanced routing policies.

- **Simple Routing**:
    - Directs traffic to a single resource.
- **Weighted Routing**:

- ○ Splits traffic between multiple resources based on assigned weights.
- **Latency-Based Routing**:
  - ○ Routes traffic to the resource with the lowest latency for the user.
- **Geolocation Routing**:
  - ○ Directs traffic based on the geographic location of users.
- **Failover Routing**:
  - ○ Automatically redirects traffic to healthy endpoints during outages.
- **Multi-Value Answer Routing**:
  - ○ Returns multiple IP addresses for a DNS query, enhancing availability.

2.3 Health Checks and Monitoring

Route 53 health checks ensure that traffic is directed only to healthy resources.

- **Endpoint Health Checks**:
  - ○ Monitors the health of endpoints (e.g., EC2 instances, web servers).
- **CloudWatch Alarms**:
  - ○ Automatically triggers alarms based on health check metrics.

2.4 Domain Registration

Route 53 simplifies the process of registering and managing custom domain names.

- Supports popular domain extensions like `.com`, `.org`, and `.net`.
- Fully integrates with AWS services, reducing setup complexity.

---

3. Benefits of Using Amazon Route 53

3.1 High Availability

Route 53 leverages AWS's global infrastructure to ensure DNS queries are resolved quickly and reliably, with 100% uptime guaranteed by the Service Level Agreement (SLA).

3.2 Seamless AWS Integration

Fully integrates with AWS services such as Elastic Load Balancer (ELB), CloudFront, and S3, enabling streamlined configuration and management.

3.3 Scalability and Flexibility

Route 53 dynamically scales to handle millions of requests per second, adapting to sudden traffic spikes or growth.

3.4 Security

Provides enhanced security through features like AWS Identity and Access Management (IAM), ensuring DNS configuration changes are tightly controlled.

---

4. Configuring Amazon Route 53

Step 1: Create a Hosted Zone

- Navigate to the Route 53 Console and create a public or private hosted zone.
- Associate the hosted zone with your domain name.

Step 2: Add DNS Records

- Define DNS records like A, AAAA, or CNAME to map domain names to IP addresses or other domains.

Step 3: Set Routing Policies

- Choose a routing policy (e.g., latency-based, weighted) to optimize traffic flow.

Step 4: Configure Health Checks

- Set up health checks for critical endpoints.
- Use CloudWatch to monitor health metrics and respond to changes.

Step 5: Test and Validate

- Use tools like `dig` or `nslookup` to verify that DNS resolution and routing policies are working as expected.

---

5. Use Cases for Amazon Route 53

5.1 Hosting Scalable Web Applications

Route 53 routes user traffic to web applications hosted on AWS with minimal latency and high reliability.

5.2 Disaster Recovery and Failover

Incorporates failover routing policies to ensure continuous availability during resource failures.

5.3 Multi-Region Architectures

Route 53 enables latency-based routing for applications deployed across multiple AWS Regions, improving user experience.

5.4 Hybrid Cloud DNS

Manages DNS resolution for hybrid cloud architectures by using private hosted zones in VPCs.

---

6. Real-World Example: Multi-Region Web Application

Scenario: A global e-commerce platform requires low-latency connections for customers in North America, Europe, and Asia.

Solution:

1. Deploy application resources in three AWS Regions: US East (N. Virginia), EU (Ireland), and Asia Pacific (Tokyo).
2. Use Route 53's latency-based routing policy to direct traffic to the nearest Region.
3. Configure health checks for each Region to ensure traffic is routed only to healthy endpoints.

Outcome: The platform achieves optimal performance and uninterrupted availability for global users.

---

7. Pricing and Cost Management

Amazon Route 53 pricing is based on the following factors:

- Number of hosted zones.
- Number of queries received.
- Additional charges for routing policies and health checks.

To manage costs:

- Use private hosted zones for internal applications.
- Monitor usage metrics with Amazon CloudWatch.

Conclusion

Amazon Route 53 is a powerful and flexible DNS service that goes beyond traditional DNS capabilities. It provides the foundation for building scalable, secure, and high-performance network architectures. Its advanced features, such as intelligent routing, health checks, and AWS integration, make it an indispensable tool for modern cloud applications.

DNS Management with Route 53

Domain Name System (DNS) management is a fundamental aspect of networking, enabling the translation of human-readable domain names into machine-readable IP addresses. With Amazon Route 53, DNS management is not only simplified but also enhanced with advanced features for reliability, scalability, and flexibility. This chapter delves into the specifics of managing DNS records and configurations using Route 53.

1. Overview of DNS Management in Route 53

Amazon Route 53 provides robust DNS management capabilities, designed to seamlessly integrate with AWS services and external resources. It serves as a highly available and scalable DNS service, enabling users to manage both public and private DNS zones effectively.

Key Features:

- **Hosted Zones**:
  - Containers for DNS records, representing domains and subdomains.
- **Record Types**:
  - A variety of DNS record types (A, AAAA, CNAME, MX, TXT, and more) to meet different application needs.
- **Traffic Policies**:
  - Customizable routing policies for directing user traffic based on latency, geographic location, or weighted distribution.

2. Hosted Zones in Route 53

A hosted zone is a collection of records that defines how DNS queries are routed for a specific domain.

Types of Hosted Zones:

- **Public Hosted Zones**:
  - Used for domains accessible over the internet.
  - Example: Configuring DNS for a website hosted on Amazon S3 or EC2.
- **Private Hosted Zones**:
  - Used within a Virtual Private Cloud (VPC) for internal domain resolution.
  - Example: Resolving internal service names within a private network.

Creating a Hosted Zone:

1. Navigate to the **Route 53 Console**.
2. Select **Create Hosted Zone** and provide the domain name.
3. Choose either public or private hosted zone based on your requirements.

3. Managing DNS Records in Route 53

DNS records define how domain names are mapped to their respective resources. Route 53 supports a wide array of record types.

Common Record Types:

- **A (Address) Record**:
  - Maps a domain to an IPv4 address.
  - Example: `example.com → 192.0.2.1`
- **AAAA Record**:
  - Maps a domain to an IPv6 address.
  - Example: `example.com → 2001:db8::1`
- **CNAME Record**:
  - Maps a domain to another domain name.
  - Example: `www.example.com → example.com`
- **MX (Mail Exchange) Record**:
  - Directs email traffic to mail servers.
  - Example: `example.com → mail.example.com`
- **TXT Record**:
  - Used for text-based data, such as SPF or DKIM records for email validation.
- **NS (Name Server) Record**:
  - Specifies the authoritative name servers for the domain.
- **SRV Record**:
  - Provides information about specific services.

Adding a Record:

1. Open the hosted zone in the Route 53 console.
2. Select **Create Record**.
3. Specify the record type, name, value, and TTL (time-to-live).
4. Configure routing policies if applicable.

---

4. Advanced Routing Policies in DNS Management

Amazon Route 53 allows fine-grained control over DNS traffic through routing policies.

Types of Routing Policies:

- **Simple Routing**:
  - Directs traffic to a single resource.
  - Use Case: Single-region websites or applications.
- **Weighted Routing**:
  - Distributes traffic across multiple resources based on assigned weights.
  - Use Case: A/B testing or gradual deployments.
- **Latency-Based Routing**:
  - Routes traffic to the resource with the lowest latency.
  - Use Case: Multi-region applications requiring low latency.
- **Geolocation Routing**:
  - Directs traffic based on user location.
  - Use Case: Region-specific content delivery.
- **Failover Routing**:
  - Ensures high availability by rerouting traffic to a healthy endpoint in case of failure.
  - Use Case: Disaster recovery setups.
- **Multi-Value Answer Routing**:
  - Provides multiple IP addresses in response to a DNS query.
  - Use Case: Improving availability by distributing traffic across multiple endpoints.

---

5. DNS Management for Hybrid Architectures

Route 53 seamlessly integrates with hybrid cloud environments by using private hosted zones and conditional forwarding.

Use Case: Hybrid Cloud DNS

- **Scenario**: A company hosts part of its infrastructure in AWS and part in an on-premises data center.
- **Solution**:
    1. Create a private hosted zone for internal DNS resolution.
    2. Use a Route 53 Resolver to forward queries between the VPC and on-premises systems.

---

6. Monitoring and Logging DNS Activity

Monitoring DNS activity is crucial for identifying and resolving issues.

Tools for Monitoring:

- **Amazon CloudWatch**:
    - Tracks DNS queries and provides metrics for analysis.
- **Route 53 Resolver Query Logs**:
    - Logs DNS queries for auditing and troubleshooting.

Use Case: Analyzing Query Traffic

1. Enable query logging in Route 53.
2. Use CloudWatch Insights to filter and analyze DNS query logs.
3. Identify abnormal traffic patterns, such as DNS query floods or misconfigurations.

---

7. Security Best Practices for DNS Management

Route 53 incorporates security features to safeguard DNS configurations.

Key Practices:

- **Access Control**:
    - Use AWS Identity and Access Management (IAM) policies to restrict access to Route 53 resources.
- **DNSSEC (Domain Name System Security Extensions)**:
    - Protect against DNS spoofing and ensure data integrity.
- **Health Checks**:
    - Monitor resource availability and reroute traffic in case of failures.

---

8. Real-World Example: Configuring a Multi-Region Application

Scenario: A global e-commerce company wants to optimize user experience by deploying resources across multiple AWS Regions.

Steps:

1. Create a public hosted zone for the domain (e.g., `example.com`).

2. Add A and AAAA records for resources in each Region.
3. Use latency-based routing to direct users to the closest Region.
4. Configure health checks to ensure only healthy endpoints receive traffic.

Outcome: The application achieves low latency, high availability, and seamless performance for global users.

---

9. Cost Considerations for DNS Management

Amazon Route 53 pricing is based on:

- The number of hosted zones.
- DNS query volume.
- Additional costs for advanced features like health checks and traffic policies.

Cost Optimization Tips:

- Consolidate hosted zones where possible.
- Monitor query usage with CloudWatch to identify and eliminate unnecessary queries.

Conclusion

Effective DNS management is pivotal for ensuring seamless access to applications and services. With Amazon Route 53, organizations can leverage advanced routing, traffic management, and health check features to enhance availability, performance, and security. By adopting best practices and leveraging Route 53's robust capabilities, you can build a reliable foundation for scalable and secure cloud networking.

CloudFront and Content Delivery Networks (CDNs)

In today's globalized and digital-first environment, delivering content efficiently and securely is critical for businesses. Amazon CloudFront, a leading content delivery network (CDN) service offered by AWS, plays a vital role in achieving this goal. This chapter provides a detailed exploration of CloudFront's functionality, its integration with other AWS services, and best practices for optimizing content delivery using CDNs.

---

1. Introduction to Content Delivery Networks (CDNs)

A **Content Delivery Network (CDN)** is a distributed system of servers designed to deliver content—such as websites, videos, APIs, and applications—to users efficiently and with minimal latency.

Key Features of CDNs:

- **Caching**:
  - Stores copies of content in edge locations closer to users.
- **Global Reach**:
  - Ensures faster delivery by reducing the physical distance between the user and the content.
- **Traffic Load Balancing**:
  - Distributes traffic across multiple servers to prevent bottlenecks.
- **Enhanced Security**:
  - Provides mechanisms for DDoS protection, secure data transmission, and access control.

---

2. Overview of Amazon CloudFront

Amazon CloudFront is a fully managed CDN that integrates seamlessly with other AWS services to deliver content securely, quickly, and reliably.

Benefits of CloudFront:

- **Global Distribution**:
  - Operates through a network of edge locations around the world.
- **Seamless Integration**:
  - Works natively with services like S3, EC2, Lambda@Edge, and Elastic Load Balancing.
- **Dynamic and Static Content Delivery**:
  - Optimized for delivering both cached (static) and on-the-fly (dynamic) content.
- **Cost-Effectiveness**:
  - Offers flexible pricing models based on usage.

---

3. Key Components of CloudFront

a) Edge Locations:

- Physical data centers where content is cached.
- Requests are routed to the nearest edge location to minimize latency.

b) Distribution:

- The mechanism used to deliver content through CloudFront.
  - **Web Distributions**:

- Designed for static and dynamic web content.
  - ○ **RTMP Distributions**:
    - Used for streaming media.

c) Cache Behavior:

- Defines how CloudFront caches and serves content.
- Includes configuration settings for:
  - ○ Path patterns.
  - ○ Time-to-Live (TTL) for cached objects.
  - ○ Allowed HTTP methods.

d) Origin:

- The source of the content CloudFront delivers.
  - ○ Can be an AWS service (e.g., S3 bucket, EC2 instance) or a non-AWS HTTP server.

---

4. Configuring Amazon CloudFront

Setting up CloudFront involves the following steps:

Step 1: Define the Origin

- Specify the source of your content (e.g., an S3 bucket or EC2 instance).

Step 2: Create a Distribution

- Navigate to the **CloudFront Console**.
- Select the type of distribution (Web or RTMP).
- Configure the origin and cache settings.

Step 3: Configure Cache Behaviors

- Define caching rules for specific URL patterns.
- Set TTL values to control how long objects remain in cache.

Step 4: Enable Security Features

- Use **SSL/TLS** for secure communication.
- Configure access controls with **Origin Access Identity (OAI)** for S3.

Step 5: Deploy the Distribution

- Once deployed, the distribution provides a unique domain name (e.g., d1234.cloudfront.net) to serve your content.

---

5. Security Features in CloudFront

a) HTTPS Support:

- Ensures secure data transmission using SSL/TLS encryption.

b) AWS Shield Integration:

- Protects against Distributed Denial of Service (DDoS) attacks.

c) Custom SSL Certificates:

- Allows you to use your own domain and certificates for secure content delivery.

d) Access Controls:

- Use **Signed URLs** or **Signed Cookies** to restrict access to premium content.

e) Field-Level Encryption:

- Encrypts sensitive data in HTTP requests (e.g., credit card information).

---

6. Use Cases for CloudFront

a) Static Website Hosting:

- Host static assets such as HTML, CSS, and JavaScript with S3 and CloudFront for enhanced performance.

b) Streaming Media:

- Stream live or on-demand video content using WebRTC, RTMP, or adaptive bitrate technologies.

c) API Acceleration:

- Reduce latency for APIs by caching responses at edge locations.

d) E-Commerce Platforms:

- Accelerate page load times and ensure secure transactions for global customers.

e) IoT Applications:

- Provide reliable data delivery for IoT applications that require low latency.

---

7. Optimizing CloudFront Performance

a) Enable Compression:

- Use Gzip or Brotli compression to reduce the size of assets delivered to users.

b) Configure Cache TTL:

- Set appropriate TTL values to balance between fresh content and caching efficiency.

c) Lambda@Edge:

- Customize the behavior of CloudFront requests and responses at edge locations.

d) Multi-Origin Setup:

- Use multiple origins with routing rules for improved scalability and redundancy.

e) Monitoring and Logging:

- Enable **CloudFront Logs** to monitor request activity and troubleshoot performance issues.

8. Monitoring CloudFront Distributions

Tools for Monitoring:

- **Amazon CloudWatch**:
  - Provides metrics such as cache hit ratio, error rates, and request counts.
- **AWS CloudTrail**:
  - Tracks changes made to CloudFront configurations.
- **Real-Time Metrics**:
  - Monitor traffic patterns and performance in near real-time.

Common Metrics:

- **Cache Hit Ratio**:
  - Measures the percentage of requests served from the cache.
- **Latency**:
  - Tracks the time it takes to process requests.

9. Pricing Considerations for CloudFront

Key Pricing Factors:

- **Data Transfer**:
  - Outbound data transfer to end users.
- **Requests**:
  - Number of HTTP/HTTPS requests processed.
- **Invalidation Requests**:
  - Charges apply when removing cached objects.

Cost Optimization Tips:

- Use **Origin Shield** to reduce origin request costs.
- Cache frequently accessed content at edge locations.
- Monitor usage with **AWS Budgets** to avoid unexpected costs.

10. Real-World Example: Global Content Delivery

Scenario: A global news portal requires fast and secure content delivery for its readers worldwide.

Solution:

1. Store articles, images, and videos in an S3 bucket.
2. Create a CloudFront distribution with latency-based routing.
3. Configure a custom SSL certificate for secure communication.
4. Use Lambda@Edge to localize content based on user location.

Outcome: The portal achieves lower latency, higher availability, and enhanced user experience.

Conclusion

Amazon CloudFront is a powerful tool for delivering content efficiently and securely to users around the globe. Its integration with AWS services and advanced features like Lambda@Edge and Origin Shield make it ideal for a wide range of use cases. By leveraging CloudFront, organizations can improve application performance, enhance security, and optimize costs.

AWS Global Network Manager

Modern enterprises rely on geographically dispersed applications and services to cater to their global customer base. Managing a network infrastructure that spans multiple regions and availability zones can be a daunting challenge. **AWS Global Network Manager** simplifies this task by providing a centralized view and control of your global network. This chapter explores the functionality, benefits, and configuration of AWS Global Network Manager and its role in ensuring an efficient and robust networking environment.

1. Introduction to AWS Global Network Manager

AWS Global Network Manager is a tool designed for **centralized monitoring and management** of global networks. It provides network insights, health monitoring, and topology visualization, enabling organizations to optimize and manage their AWS and on-premises networks effectively.

Key Capabilities:

- **Centralized Visibility**:
  - Provides a unified dashboard to view global network resources and connections.
- **Network Insights**:
  - Offers real-time data on network health, performance, and traffic patterns.
- **Simplified Management**:
  - Allows the management of AWS Transit Gateway and Direct Connect Gateway resources.
- **Topology Maps**:
  - Displays an interactive network map for visualizing resource relationships and locations.

2. Benefits of Using AWS Global Network Manager

AWS Global Network Manager streamlines network operations by providing several critical benefits:

- **Simplified Network Operations**:
  - Centralized control reduces complexity in managing global network resources.
- **Enhanced Visibility**:
  - Provides a clear view of global resource connectivity, performance metrics, and potential bottlenecks.
- **Improved Troubleshooting**:
  - Faster identification of issues with detailed network health data.
- **Cost Optimization**:
  - Insights into data transfer and usage help in making cost-efficient networking decisions.
- **Seamless Integration**:
  - Integrates with other AWS services like Transit Gateway, CloudWatch, and Direct Connect.

3. Key Components of AWS Global Network Manager

a) Global Network:

- Represents your global network infrastructure.
- Includes all AWS and on-premises network resources connected via Transit Gateways and Direct Connect Gateways.

b) Transit Gateways:

- Provides connectivity between multiple VPCs, regions, and on-premises networks.
- Managed centrally through the Global Network Manager.

c) Direct Connect Gateways:

- Enables private connections between AWS and on-premises networks.
- Monitored for performance and usage within the Global Network Manager.

d) Network Insights:

- Offers detailed analytics, including latency, packet loss, and traffic patterns.

e) Topology Viewer:

- Displays an interactive map of your network connections and relationships across regions.

---

4. Configuring AWS Global Network Manager

Setting up AWS Global Network Manager involves the following steps:

Step 1: Enable Global Network Manager

- Go to the **AWS Management Console**.
- Navigate to the **Global Network Manager** service.
- Create a global network to begin monitoring resources.

Step 2: Add Resources

- Link existing AWS Transit Gateways and Direct Connect Gateways to the global network.

Step 3: Configure Monitoring

- Set up monitoring policies to track health and performance metrics.
- Enable **CloudWatch Metrics** for real-time visibility.

Step 4: Use the Topology Viewer

- Access the interactive map to visualize the global network structure and troubleshoot connectivity issues.

---

5. Monitoring and Troubleshooting with Global Network Manager

a) Real-Time Metrics:

- Monitor network traffic, latency, and health using CloudWatch integration.
- Access data on packet loss, jitter, and throughput for optimized performance.

b) Network Events:

- Automatically detect and alert for network issues, such as latency spikes or connection failures.

c) Performance Reports:

- Generate detailed reports on network performance to identify optimization opportunities.

d) Troubleshooting Workflow:

1. Use the topology viewer to identify affected areas.
2. Analyze performance metrics to pinpoint the root cause.
3. Apply fixes or optimize configurations via the Global Network Manager console.

---

6. Use Cases for AWS Global Network Manager

a) Enterprise Multi-Region Architecture:

- Companies with operations in multiple regions can ensure seamless connectivity and monitor traffic between their VPCs and data centers.

b) Disaster Recovery Planning:

- Centralized visibility helps organizations plan and implement robust disaster recovery solutions across regions.

c) IoT Applications:

- Manage IoT network traffic effectively, ensuring low-latency connections for devices across the globe.

d) Hybrid Cloud Environments:

- Simplifies management of hybrid infrastructures that use both AWS and on-premises networks.

---

7. Best Practices for Using Global Network Manager

a) Enable Monitoring Across All Regions:

- Ensure that all regions and connected resources are included in the Global Network.

b) Regularly Review Metrics:

- Monitor network usage patterns and performance to make informed scaling decisions.

c) Optimize Data Transfer:

- Use insights to reduce data transfer costs by optimizing routing between regions.

d) Leverage CloudWatch Alarms:

- Set up alarms for critical thresholds such as latency or packet loss.

e) Integrate with Security Tools:

- Combine Global Network Manager with AWS Firewall Manager and GuardDuty for enhanced security monitoring.

---

8. Cost Considerations

a) Pricing Model:

- Charges are based on the number of resources (Transit Gateways and Direct Connect Gateways) monitored.

- Additional costs apply for data transfer and CloudWatch logs.

b) Cost Optimization Tips:

- Monitor usage to identify underutilized resources.
- Consolidate resources where possible to reduce overhead.

---

9. Real-World Example: Managing a Global Retail Network

Scenario: A retail company with stores worldwide needs to manage connectivity between regional VPCs and on-premises warehouses.

Solution:

1. Deploy Transit Gateways in key regions to connect VPCs.
2. Use Direct Connect for secure and fast communication with on-premises locations.
3. Monitor the global network using AWS Global Network Manager to identify and address performance issues.

Outcome: The company achieves seamless global connectivity, improved troubleshooting capabilities, and reduced operational complexity.

Conclusion

AWS Global Network Manager provides a powerful solution for managing global network infrastructures. By centralizing visibility and control, it enables organizations to optimize performance, reduce costs, and enhance reliability. With its integration with other AWS services, Global Network Manager becomes an indispensable tool for modern network architects.

Scalable and High-Availability Networking

Designing High-Availability Architectures

In the realm of cloud computing, ensuring uninterrupted access to applications and services is critical for modern enterprises. High availability (HA) is the backbone of this reliability, enabling systems to withstand failures and minimize downtime. This chapter explores the principles, components, and best practices for designing **high-availability architectures** in AWS, emphasizing how to leverage AWS networking tools to meet business continuity requirements.

1. What is High Availability?

High availability refers to the ability of a system or application to operate continuously without interruptions, even in the face of component failures. AWS provides a robust set of tools and services to build architectures that achieve high availability through redundancy, fault tolerance, and automated failover mechanisms.

2. Key Principles of High-Availability Architectures

To design a highly available system, it is essential to follow these principles:

- **Redundancy**:
  - Deploy multiple instances of components to avoid single points of failure.
- **Failover Mechanisms**:
  - Automatically switch to backup systems during failures.
- **Scalability**:
  - Ensure the system can handle increased load without performance degradation.
- **Distributed Design**:
  - Spread resources across multiple availability zones (AZs) or regions to improve resilience.
- **Monitoring and Recovery**:
  - Use automated monitoring and recovery tools to detect and mitigate failures quickly.

3. AWS Services Supporting High Availability

AWS offers a variety of services and features to help build high-availability architectures:

a) Amazon Route 53:

- Provides highly available DNS routing for failover between regions or endpoints.

b) Elastic Load Balancers (ELBs):

- Distribute traffic across multiple instances in one or more AZs to prevent overloads.

c) Auto Scaling Groups:

- Automatically adjust the number of instances based on traffic demands.

4. Store application data in Amazon RDS with Multi-AZ deployment.
5. Use Amazon S3 for static content delivery and backup storage.

Outcome: The architecture ensures zero downtime even during AZ or regional failures while maintaining low latency for users worldwide.

Conclusion

Designing high-availability architectures is a cornerstone of AWS networking, enabling enterprises to achieve operational excellence and reliability. By leveraging AWS services like Auto Scaling, Elastic Load Balancers, and Route 53, you can build scalable and fault-tolerant systems tailored to business needs.

Implementing Fault Tolerance in AWS Networks

Fault tolerance is a critical design principle in cloud architecture, ensuring that systems can continue to function seamlessly despite failures in one or more components. AWS offers an extensive suite of tools and services to implement fault-tolerant designs, enabling enterprises to deliver high availability and reliability for their applications and networks.

This chapter delves into the strategies, AWS services, and best practices for implementing fault tolerance in AWS networks.

1. What is Fault Tolerance?

Fault tolerance refers to the ability of a system to continue functioning correctly in the event of component failures. A fault-tolerant network minimizes downtime, data loss, and performance degradation through redundancy, failover mechanisms, and proactive monitoring.

2. Key Components of Fault-Tolerant Networks

a) Redundant Resources

Deploying duplicate resources ensures that if one fails, another can take over.

b) Load Balancing

Distributes traffic across multiple resources to prevent overloading a single component.

c) Failover Mechanisms

Automatically redirect traffic to healthy resources during failures.

d) Monitoring and Alerts

Real-time monitoring and alerting tools to detect and resolve failures quickly.

e) Data Replication

Ensures data consistency and availability across multiple resources or locations.

3. AWS Services for Fault Tolerance

AWS provides a range of services specifically designed to build fault-tolerant networks:

a) Elastic Load Balancing (ELB)

Automatically distributes incoming application traffic across multiple targets, such as EC2 instances, containers, and IP addresses.

- **Features**:
  - Health checks to route traffic only to healthy targets.
  - Support for multi-AZ deployments to improve availability.

b) Amazon Route 53

A highly available DNS service that supports health checks and routing policies for fault tolerance.

- **Failover Routing**: Directs traffic to a secondary endpoint if the primary endpoint is unavailable.
- **Latency-Based Routing**: Routes users to the endpoint with the lowest latency.

c) Auto Scaling

Automatically adjusts the number of instances based on demand, ensuring availability even during peak loads.

- **Key Benefits**:
  - Replaces unhealthy instances automatically.
  - Works seamlessly with load balancers for scaling.

d) AWS Transit Gateway

Enables fault-tolerant interconnectivity between VPCs, on-premises networks, and other AWS services.

- **Resilience Features**:
  - Centralized routing and failover across multiple VPCs.
  - Multi-region support for disaster recovery scenarios.

e) Amazon S3 and Cross-Region Replication

Provides durable object storage with built-in redundancy across multiple AZs.

- **Cross-Region Replication**: Automatically replicates data to another AWS region to improve disaster recovery.

f) AWS Global Accelerator

Enhances fault tolerance by routing traffic to the closest available endpoint based on health and proximity.

g) Amazon RDS Multi-AZ Deployments

Provides automatic failover for database instances across multiple availability zones.

---

4. Designing Fault-Tolerant Architectures in AWS

a) Multi-AZ Deployments

Deploy resources across multiple availability zones to ensure that a failure in one AZ does not disrupt the entire system.

Example:
A web application using EC2 instances deployed across two AZs with an Application Load Balancer for traffic distribution.

b) Multi-Region Architectures

Extend fault tolerance by replicating resources across AWS regions. This approach ensures global availability even if an entire region becomes unavailable.

Example:

- Deploying Amazon RDS with cross-region read replicas.
- Using Route 53 for latency-based or failover routing.

c) Decoupling Components

Use AWS managed services like Amazon SQS and Amazon SNS to decouple application components, reducing dependency-related failures.

d) Data Backup and Replication

- Implement Amazon S3 Versioning and Lifecycle policies for data protection.
- Use AWS Backup to automate backup schedules for critical resources.

---

5. Fault Tolerance in Network Connectivity

a) VPC Design for Fault Tolerance

- Use multiple subnets across different AZs.
- Configure routing tables with backup routes.

b) Direct Connect with VPN Backup

- Combine AWS Direct Connect with a VPN connection to ensure network availability during Direct Connect outages.

c) AWS Transit Gateway

Centralizes network management and provides built-in failover mechanisms for VPC interconnectivity.

---

6. Monitoring and Recovery

a) Amazon CloudWatch

- Set up alarms and metrics for network components to detect and respond to failures.
- Use CloudWatch Logs for detailed diagnostics.

b) AWS Elastic Disaster Recovery

Provides automated failover and recovery capabilities for critical workloads across AZs or regions.

c) Health Checks

Use Route 53 health checks to monitor endpoint availability and trigger failover.

---

7. Real-World Use Case: Fault-Tolerant E-Commerce Application

Scenario:
An e-commerce platform requires 24/7 availability to handle global traffic and ensure seamless shopping experiences.

Architecture:

1. EC2 instances deployed across multiple AZs with Auto Scaling.
2. Application Load Balancer to distribute traffic.
3. Amazon RDS Multi-AZ for fault-tolerant databases.
4. Amazon S3 with cross-region replication for product images and backups.

5. Route 53 failover routing between regions.
6. Amazon CloudWatch for monitoring and alerting.

Outcome:
The architecture ensures minimal downtime and provides a seamless user experience even during AZ or regional outages.

---

8. Best Practices for Fault-Tolerant Designs

- **Avoid Single Points of Failure**: Distribute resources across multiple AZs and regions.
- **Automate Recovery**: Use Auto Scaling, AWS Backup, and Elastic Disaster Recovery for automated failover and recovery.
- **Regular Testing**: Simulate failures to validate the effectiveness of fault-tolerance mechanisms.
- **Leverage AWS Managed Services**: Reduce operational overhead by using services like ELB, RDS, and S3.
- **Implement Proactive Monitoring**: Continuously monitor key metrics and set up alerts to detect issues early.

Conclusion

Fault tolerance is a vital aspect of building resilient cloud networks. By leveraging AWS services such as Elastic Load Balancers, Auto Scaling, and Route 53, you can design systems that minimize downtime and ensure seamless user experiences.

Scaling with Auto Scaling Groups

Auto Scaling Groups (ASGs) in AWS are a cornerstone of scalable and highly available cloud architectures. They allow you to dynamically adjust the number of compute resources based on demand, ensuring applications remain performant and cost-efficient under varying workloads.

In this chapter, we explore the core concepts of AWS Auto Scaling Groups, their configuration, and best practices for implementing scalable networks.

1. What Are Auto Scaling Groups?

An **Auto Scaling Group** is a logical collection of Amazon EC2 instances managed together for automatic scaling and high availability. AWS monitors and adjusts the number of instances in the group based on predefined conditions such as CPU utilization, memory usage, or custom metrics.

2. Benefits of Using Auto Scaling Groups

- **Dynamic Scalability**: Automatically increases or decreases the number of instances in response to demand.
- **Cost Efficiency**: Ensures you only pay for the resources needed at any given time.
- **High Availability**: Distributes instances across multiple Availability Zones to minimize downtime.
- **Resilience**: Replaces unhealthy instances automatically, ensuring a consistent application performance.

3. Key Components of Auto Scaling Groups

a) Launch Template

Defines the instance configurations, including:

- AMI (Amazon Machine Image).
- Instance type (e.g., t2.micro, m5.large).
- Network settings (e.g., VPC and subnet).
- Key pair for SSH access.

b) Scaling Policies

Determine how the Auto Scaling Group adds or removes instances:

- **Target Tracking Scaling**: Adjusts capacity to maintain a target metric, such as average CPU utilization.
- **Step Scaling**: Adjusts capacity based on a set of thresholds and corresponding scaling adjustments.
- **Scheduled Scaling**: Adds or removes instances at specific times or intervals.

c) Health Checks

Monitors the health of instances:

- EC2 status checks.
- Elastic Load Balancer (ELB) health checks.

d) Desired, Minimum, and Maximum Capacities

Defines the range of instances that can exist in the group:

- **Desired Capacity**: The initial or target number of instances.
- **Minimum Capacity**: The minimum number of instances to maintain.
- **Maximum Capacity**: The upper limit on the number of instances.

---

4. Configuring an Auto Scaling Group

Follow these steps to create and configure an Auto Scaling Group:

Step 1: Define a Launch Template

1. Go to the **EC2 Dashboard**.
2. Create a launch template with your preferred configurations (e.g., AMI, instance type, and network settings).

Step 2: Create an Auto Scaling Group

1. Navigate to the **Auto Scaling Groups** section.
2. Click **Create Auto Scaling Group** and provide a name.
3. Attach the previously created launch template.

Step 3: Configure Group Settings

- Specify the **desired**, **minimum**, and **maximum** instance capacities.
- Select subnets across multiple Availability Zones for high availability.

Step 4: Attach Load Balancers (Optional)

Integrate an Elastic Load Balancer (ELB) to distribute traffic across the instances.

Step 5: Set Scaling Policies

- Define target tracking, step scaling, or scheduled scaling policies based on application needs.

Step 6: Configure Notifications

Set up Amazon SNS notifications for scaling events to stay informed about changes in capacity.

---

5. Use Cases for Auto Scaling Groups

a) E-Commerce Websites

Auto Scaling Groups handle sudden traffic spikes during events like sales or promotions by scaling out resources.

b) Batch Processing

Schedule scaling for predictable workloads, such as nightly data processing tasks.

c) Media Streaming

Ensure low latency and high availability by scaling resources dynamically based on the number of concurrent users.

d) IoT Applications

Support millions of IoT devices by scaling instances in response to fluctuating demand.

---

6. Best Practices for Auto Scaling Groups

a) Use Multiple Availability Zones

Distribute instances across multiple Availability Zones to improve fault tolerance and reduce latency.

b) Define Realistic Scaling Policies

Set appropriate thresholds to avoid over-scaling or under-scaling.

c) Monitor Performance Metrics

Use **Amazon CloudWatch** to monitor key metrics like CPU utilization and set alarms for scaling actions.

d) Test Scaling Configurations

Simulate scaling events in a staging environment to validate scaling policies and configurations.

e) Combine with Spot Instances

Integrate Spot Instances with On-Demand Instances for cost optimization while maintaining performance.

---

7. Monitoring Auto Scaling Groups

a) CloudWatch Metrics

- Monitor metrics such as:
    - `GroupInServiceInstances`: Number of healthy instances.
    - `GroupDesiredCapacity`: Target number of instances.
    - `GroupMaxSize` and `GroupMinSize`: Upper and lower limits of the group.

b) CloudTrail Logs

Audit scaling events and changes to Auto Scaling Group configurations.

c) Health Check Alarms

Set alarms to trigger actions if an instance becomes unhealthy.

---

8. Limitations of Auto Scaling Groups

- **Cold Start Latency**: Adding new instances may take time, affecting performance during sudden spikes.
- **Dependency on Metrics**: Misconfigured metrics can lead to ineffective scaling actions.
- **Application Readiness**: Instances must be properly configured to handle traffic immediately after launch.

9. Real-World Example: Scaling a Web Application

Scenario:
An organization runs a web application that experiences fluctuating traffic throughout the day. During peak hours, the application requires more resources, while off-peak hours see reduced traffic.

Solution:

1. Configure an Auto Scaling Group with a minimum capacity of 2 instances and a maximum capacity of 10.
2. Use target tracking scaling to maintain CPU utilization at 50%.
3. Distribute instances across two Availability Zones using an Application Load Balancer.
4. Enable health checks to replace unhealthy instances automatically.

Outcome:
The application scales seamlessly during high traffic and reduces costs by scaling in during off-peak hours, ensuring both availability and efficiency.

Conclusion

Auto Scaling Groups are an essential tool for creating dynamic, resilient, and cost-efficient AWS architectures. By automatically adjusting resources to meet changing demands, they enable businesses to maintain high availability and optimize costs.

Elastic IPs and Their Applications

Elastic IP (EIP) addresses are a critical component of AWS networking, providing a flexible and resilient way to manage public IP addresses in the cloud. Unlike traditional static IPs, Elastic IPs are designed specifically for dynamic cloud environments, enabling seamless failover, easy reassignment, and efficient management of public-facing network interfaces.

In this chapter, we will explore what Elastic IPs are, their use cases, best practices, and how they integrate into scalable and highly available AWS architectures.

1. What Are Elastic IPs?

An **Elastic IP (EIP)** is a static, public IPv4 address allocated to your AWS account. Unlike traditional static IP addresses, Elastic IPs can be dynamically reassigned to different EC2 instances or network interfaces within the same region.

This flexibility allows AWS customers to manage public IP addresses independently of specific instances, making it easier to design fault-tolerant and scalable applications.

2. Key Features of Elastic IPs

- **Static Nature**: EIPs remain constant even when instances are stopped, started, or terminated.
- **Reassignment**: You can reassign EIPs to another instance in the same region without requiring DNS changes.
- **Resilience**: EIPs enable seamless failover by quickly remapping to backup instances during instance failures.
- **Cost Efficiency**: AWS charges for EIPs only when they are allocated but not associated with a running instance, encouraging optimal usage.

3. Use Cases for Elastic IPs

a) Fault-Tolerant Architectures

In failover scenarios, Elastic IPs allow you to quickly switch the public-facing IP address from a failed instance to a backup instance without disrupting services.

b) Static IP Requirements

Certain applications, such as whitelisted IP configurations for APIs or firewalls, require static IPs. Elastic IPs fulfill this requirement while remaining flexible.

c) Testing and Development

Elastic IPs are useful in development environments where instances are frequently started, stopped, or replaced, as the public IP remains unchanged.

d) Load Balancing

Although Elastic Load Balancers (ELBs) are typically used for balancing traffic, Elastic IPs can also serve as public-facing IPs for instances in simpler architectures.

4. Configuring Elastic IPs in AWS

Step 1: Allocate an Elastic IP

1. Navigate to the **EC2 Dashboard** in the AWS Management Console.
2. Select **Elastic IPs** under the "Network & Security" section.
3. Click **Allocate Elastic IP address**.
4. Choose the allocation type (e.g., from AWS's pool or BYOIP).

Step 2: Associate the Elastic IP

1. Select the newly allocated Elastic IP.
2. Click **Actions > Associate Elastic IP address**.
3. Choose the resource to associate (e.g., an instance or a network interface).
4. Confirm the association.

Step 3: Manage Reassignment (If Needed)

1. If the current instance fails, disassociate the EIP from the failed instance.
2. Reassociate the EIP with a backup instance or network interface.
3. Update monitoring and alarms to reflect the new configuration.

5. Best Practices for Using Elastic IPs

a) Optimize Allocation

- Avoid allocating unnecessary Elastic IPs to reduce costs.
- Regularly audit EIP usage to identify unused addresses.

b) Automate Failover

Use AWS services such as **CloudWatch** and **Auto Scaling** to monitor instance health and automate Elastic IP reassignment during failover scenarios.

c) Combine with Elastic Load Balancers

For high-traffic applications, consider combining Elastic IPs with Elastic Load Balancers (ELBs) for robust traffic management.

d) Leverage Private IPs

Where possible, use private IPs for inter-instance communication and reserve Elastic IPs for public-facing endpoints.

e) Secure Access

Restrict inbound and outbound traffic to Elastic IPs using **Security Groups** and **Network ACLs** for enhanced security.

6. Monitoring and Troubleshooting Elastic IPs

a) Monitor Elastic IP Usage

- Use the **AWS Cost Explorer** to track Elastic IP costs.
- Monitor associated resources to ensure Elastic IPs are not underutilized.

b) Troubleshoot Connectivity

- Verify that the EIP is correctly associated with the intended resource.
- Check route tables and security group rules for misconfigurations.

c) Audit Elastic IP Allocation

Regularly review allocated EIPs to ensure they align with application needs.

---

7. Real-World Example: High Availability with Elastic IPs

Scenario:
A company runs a public-facing web application that requires a highly available architecture. To achieve fault tolerance, the company uses two EC2 instances in separate Availability Zones, one as the primary instance and the other as a backup.

Solution:

1. Allocate an Elastic IP for the application.
2. Associate the Elastic IP with the primary instance.
3. Set up **CloudWatch Alarms** to monitor the primary instance's health.
4. In case of failure, use a **Lambda Function** triggered by CloudWatch to disassociate the Elastic IP from the failed instance and reassign it to the backup instance.

Outcome:
The application remains accessible during instance failures, minimizing downtime and ensuring a seamless user experience.

---

8. Limitations of Elastic IPs

- **IPv6 Not Supported**: Elastic IPs are limited to IPv4; IPv6 addresses are allocated differently in AWS.
- **Region-Specific**: Elastic IPs cannot be transferred across AWS regions.
- **Cost Implications**: AWS charges for unused Elastic IPs to encourage efficient allocation.

Conclusion

Elastic IPs are a powerful tool for building scalable and resilient AWS networking architectures. By enabling static, public-facing IPs that can be dynamically reassigned, they offer the flexibility required for high-availability and fault-tolerant applications.

Configuring Elastic Fabric Adapter

The **Elastic Fabric Adapter (EFA)** is a high-performance network interface designed to accelerate high-performance computing (HPC) and machine learning (ML) workloads in AWS. Unlike standard Elastic Network Interfaces (ENIs), EFAs provide low-latency, high-throughput communication, enabling tightly-coupled parallel applications to scale effectively in the cloud. In this chapter, we will explore how to configure and utilize EFAs for scalable and high-availability networking.

---

1. Overview of Elastic Fabric Adapter (EFA)

Elastic Fabric Adapter is a network interface optimized for HPC and ML workloads that require consistent, low-latency network communication. EFA extends the capabilities of traditional ENIs by supporting protocols such as **Message Passing Interface (MPI)** and **NVIDIA Collective Communications Library (NCCL)**, essential for distributed computing.

Key benefits of EFA include:

- **Low Latency**: Delivers sub-millisecond latency for inter-node communication.
- **High Bandwidth**: Supports large-scale data transfer with minimal bottlenecks.
- **Enhanced Scalability**: Enables efficient scaling of tightly coupled applications.
- **Elasticity**: Dynamically attaches to supported EC2 instances without disrupting workloads.

---

2. Supported Instances and Operating Systems

Before configuring EFA, ensure compatibility with your chosen EC2 instance and operating system.

Supported EC2 Instances:

- Compute-optimized: C5n, C6gn
- Memory-optimized: R5n, R6gn
- Accelerated computing: P3dn, G4dn

Supported Operating Systems:

- Amazon Linux 2
- Ubuntu 18.04 or later
- Red Hat Enterprise Linux 8

For a full list of supported instances and OS versions, refer to the [AWS EFA documentation] (https://docs.aws.amazon.com).

---

3. Use Cases for Elastic Fabric Adapter

EFA is specifically designed for workloads requiring high-performance, low-latency networking:

- **High-Performance Computing (HPC)**: Applications like weather modeling, computational fluid dynamics, and seismic analysis.
- **Machine Learning (ML)**: Distributed training of ML models using TensorFlow, PyTorch, or MXNet.
- **Real-Time Simulations**: Tasks such as 3D rendering, gaming simulations, and scientific research.

---

4. Steps to Configure Elastic Fabric Adapter

Step 1: Launch a Supported EC2 Instance

1. Open the AWS Management Console.
2. Navigate to the **EC2 Dashboard**.
3. Launch a new instance using a supported instance type (e.g., `c5n.18xlarge`) and compatible AMI (e.g., Amazon Linux 2).

Step 2: Attach an EFA to the Instance

1. Select the instance from the EC2 dashboard.
2. Click **Actions** > **Networking** > **Attach Network Interface**.
3. Create or attach an EFA-enabled network interface to the instance.

Step 3: Install the EFA Software

To enable EFA capabilities, install the required software on your instance:

- For Amazon Linux 2:

```
sudo yum install -y aws-efa-installer
sudo /opt/amazon/efa/install.sh
```

- For Ubuntu:

```
sudo apt-get update
sudo apt-get install -y aws-efa-installer
sudo /opt/amazon/efa/install.sh
```

Step 4: Configure MPI or NCCL Libraries

1. Install MPI or NCCL on your instance:
   - For MPI:

     ```
     sudo yum install -y openmpi
     ```

   - For NCCL (used with ML frameworks):

     ```
     sudo yum install -y libnccl
     ```

2. Test the installation using sample MPI or NCCL programs provided by AWS.

Step 5: Test EFA Connectivity

Run a benchmark test or your application to ensure the EFA is functioning correctly. AWS provides tools like `efa_test` to verify setup:

```
/opt/amazon/efa/bin/efa_test
```

---

5. Best Practices for Configuring EFA

- **Use Placement Groups**: For optimal performance, place EFA-enabled instances in a **cluster placement group** to reduce latency.
- **Enable SRD**: Configure **Scalable Reliable Datagram (SRD)** to enhance reliability and throughput for HPC workloads.

- **Monitor Performance**: Use tools like **Amazon CloudWatch** to monitor EFA traffic and ensure optimal performance.
- **Update Software**: Regularly update the EFA driver and associated libraries to leverage the latest features and optimizations.

---

6. Monitoring and Troubleshooting EFA

Monitoring

- Use **CloudWatch Metrics** to monitor network throughput, packet loss, and instance-level metrics.
- Monitor application-specific metrics to ensure proper utilization of EFA features.

Troubleshooting

- Ensure the instance type and operating system are supported for EFA.
- Verify that the EFA software and libraries are correctly installed.
- Check the security group and network ACL settings to ensure they allow necessary traffic.

---

7. Real-World Example: Scaling Distributed Machine Learning

Scenario:
A company trains a large language model requiring distributed training across multiple EC2 instances.

Solution:

1. Launch p3dn.24xlarge instances in a cluster placement group.
2. Attach EFAs to each instance.
3. Install TensorFlow and NCCL libraries on all instances.
4. Use Horovod to orchestrate distributed training across the nodes, leveraging EFA's low-latency communication.

Outcome:
Training time is significantly reduced, enabling faster iterations and cost savings.

---

8. Limitations of Elastic Fabric Adapter

- **Regional Constraints**: EFA is supported only in certain AWS regions.
- **Instance-Specific**: Not all EC2 instance types support EFAs.
- **Complex Configuration**: Requires additional setup for software and placement groups.

Conclusion

Elastic Fabric Adapter is a powerful tool for enabling high-performance networking in AWS. By providing low-latency, high-throughput communication, it is ideal for workloads like HPC and ML that demand efficient inter-node communication. Integrating EFAs into your architecture ensures scalability, reliability, and optimal performance for complex applications.

Hybrid Networking with AWS

Building Hybrid Cloud Architectures

Hybrid cloud architectures combine on-premises infrastructure, private cloud, and public cloud environments to create a cohesive and scalable solution for businesses. AWS provides several tools and services to facilitate hybrid cloud connectivity, ensuring security, performance, and flexibility.

In this chapter, we will explore the principles of hybrid cloud architectures, discuss AWS services for hybrid solutions, and walk through the steps for building a hybrid environment using AWS.

1. Understanding Hybrid Cloud Architectures

A hybrid cloud architecture integrates on-premises resources and AWS cloud services to:

- **Enhance scalability**: Use AWS for burst capacity while maintaining critical workloads on-premises.
- **Improve disaster recovery**: Replicate on-premises workloads to AWS for failover and data recovery.
- **Enable flexibility**: Choose the optimal environment for specific workloads based on compliance, latency, or cost requirements.

Key components of hybrid cloud solutions include:

- **Network connectivity**: Secure and high-performance communication between on-premises and cloud resources.
- **Resource synchronization**: Data replication and consistent configurations across environments.
- **Unified management**: Centralized monitoring and control of hybrid resources.

2. AWS Services for Hybrid Cloud Architectures

AWS offers several services to support hybrid environments:

- **AWS Direct Connect**: Provides a dedicated, low-latency link between on-premises data centers and AWS regions.
- **AWS VPN**: Establishes secure tunnels for encrypted communication between on-premises infrastructure and AWS.
- **AWS Outposts**: Extends AWS services and infrastructure to on-premises data centers.
- **AWS Storage Gateway**: Enables seamless integration of on-premises applications with AWS storage services like S3 and Glacier.
- **Amazon RDS Custom**: Allows databases to run on-premises while integrating with AWS cloud databases.
- **Amazon ECS Anywhere and EKS Anywhere**: Extends container orchestration to on-premises environments.

3. Steps to Build a Hybrid Cloud Architecture

Follow these steps to build a hybrid cloud environment with AWS:

Step 1: Assess Requirements

1. Identify workloads and applications suitable for hybrid deployment.
2. Determine data residency, compliance, and latency requirements.
3. Evaluate on-premises resources and integration needs with AWS.

Step 2: Establish Network Connectivity

1. Choose a connectivity method:
   - Use **AWS Direct Connect** for high-performance, low-latency links.
   - Use **AWS VPN** for encrypted connections over the internet.
2. Configure the necessary network components:
   - Set up Virtual Private Cloud (VPC) with subnets and route tables.
   - Attach a **Virtual Private Gateway** or **Direct Connect Gateway** for hybrid connectivity.
3. Test connectivity to ensure seamless communication between environments.

Step 3: Extend Compute and Storage

1. Deploy **AWS Outposts** to run AWS services on-premises, if needed.
2. Use **AWS Storage Gateway** for hybrid storage access.
   - Configure file, volume, or tape gateways based on your use case.
3. Integrate **Amazon RDS Custom** for database workloads requiring on-premises operation.

Step 4: Synchronize Data and Workloads

1. Use **AWS DataSync** to automate data transfers between on-premises storage and AWS.
2. Configure replication and synchronization policies for hybrid databases.

Step 5: Monitor and Manage Resources

1. Use **AWS Systems Manager** for unified monitoring and automation.
2. Enable **Amazon CloudWatch** for hybrid workload monitoring.
3. Leverage **AWS Control Tower** for governance and compliance.

---

4. Use Case: Hybrid Cloud for Disaster Recovery

Scenario:
A financial services company requires a disaster recovery solution for its on-premises data center.

Solution:

1. Establish a **Direct Connect** link between the data center and AWS.
2. Replicate critical applications and databases using **AWS Storage Gateway** and **Amazon RDS Custom**.
3. Use **Route 53** for DNS failover to switch traffic to AWS in case of downtime.

Outcome:
The company achieves high availability and seamless failover capabilities with minimal operational overhead.

---

5. Best Practices for Hybrid Cloud Architectures

- **Plan for scalability**: Design the architecture to scale seamlessly with workload demands.
- **Prioritize security**: Use encryption, IAM policies, and security groups to protect hybrid resources.

- **Optimize costs**: Monitor and optimize connectivity, storage, and compute costs.
- **Test regularly**: Conduct failover and performance tests to ensure reliability.
- **Use automation**: Leverage AWS CloudFormation and Systems Manager for automated configuration and management.

---

6. Challenges and Considerations

- **Latency and Bandwidth**: Ensure that connectivity options meet application latency and bandwidth requirements.
- **Data Residency**: Comply with regulations governing where data can be stored and processed.
- **Integration Complexity**: Simplify integration by using AWS-managed hybrid services like Outposts and Storage Gateway.

Conclusion

Hybrid cloud architectures provide the flexibility to balance on-premises and cloud resources, enabling businesses to meet unique workload and compliance needs. AWS offers a robust suite of tools and services to build secure, scalable, and cost-efficient hybrid solutions.

Setting Up VPN Connections with AWS

Virtual Private Network (VPN) connections are a critical component of hybrid cloud architectures, enabling secure communication between on-premises networks and AWS cloud environments. AWS provides two primary VPN options: **AWS Site-to-Site VPN** and **Client VPN**, each designed to address specific networking requirements.

In this chapter, we will explore the key features of AWS VPN services, the steps to set up VPN connections, and best practices for configuring and managing these secure connections.

1. Overview of VPN in AWS Networking

A VPN extends a private network across a public network, such as the internet, enabling secure data transmission between on-premises resources and AWS environments. Key use cases for AWS VPN include:

- **Secure hybrid cloud connectivity**: Extend on-premises networks to AWS.
- **Remote user access**: Provide secure access to AWS resources for remote employees.
- **Backup and disaster recovery**: Ensure secure data transfer between environments.

AWS VPN options:

- **Site-to-Site VPN**: Connects on-premises networks to Amazon Virtual Private Clouds (VPCs) via an encrypted tunnel.
- **Client VPN**: Allows remote users to securely access AWS resources using a managed client-based VPN.

2. Key Components of AWS Site-to-Site VPN

AWS Site-to-Site VPN relies on the following components:

1. **Virtual Private Gateway (VGW)**: A gateway attached to an Amazon VPC that enables VPN connectivity.
2. **Customer Gateway (CGW)**: A physical or software-based device on the on-premises network that connects to the VGW.
3. **VPN Connection**: The encrypted tunnel between the VGW and CGW.

Features of Site-to-Site VPN:

- **IPsec encryption**: Provides secure communication.
- **Redundancy**: Supports two tunnels for high availability.
- **Dynamic routing**: Uses BGP for scalable and dynamic route management.

3. Steps to Set Up AWS Site-to-Site VPN

Step 1: Create a Customer Gateway

1. Identify the public IP address of the on-premises VPN device.
2. In the AWS Management Console:
   - Navigate to **VPC > Customer Gateways > Create Customer Gateway**.
   - Specify the name, IP address, and type of the VPN device.

Step 2: Configure a Virtual Private Gateway

1. In the AWS Management Console:
   - Navigate to **VPC** > **Virtual Private Gateways** > **Create Virtual Private Gateway**.
   - Attach the VGW to the target VPC.
2. Modify the VPC's route table to route traffic through the VGW.

Step 3: Establish a VPN Connection

1. In the AWS Management Console:
   - Navigate to **VPN Connections** > **Create VPN Connection**.
   - Select the VGW and CGW created earlier.
2. Download the configuration file for the on-premises VPN device.

Step 4: Configure the On-Premises Device

1. Use the downloaded configuration file to set up the VPN device.
2. Establish IPsec tunnels and configure routing.

Step 5: Verify the VPN Connection

1. Test connectivity by sending traffic between on-premises and AWS resources.
2. Monitor the connection status in the AWS Management Console.

---

4. AWS Client VPN for Remote Access

AWS Client VPN provides secure access to AWS resources for remote users. It is a fully managed service that supports OpenVPN-based clients.

Steps to Set Up AWS Client VPN:

1. **Create a Client VPN Endpoint**:
   - Define the CIDR range for client IP addresses.
   - Specify the authentication method (e.g., Active Directory, mutual authentication, or SAML-based).
2. **Associate the VPN Endpoint with a Target Network**:
   - Associate the endpoint with subnets in the target VPC.
3. **Authorize Access**:
   - Define rules to grant users access to specific AWS resources.
4. **Download and Distribute Client Configuration**:
   - Provide users with the OpenVPN configuration file and credentials.

---

5. Use Case: Site-to-Site VPN for Hybrid Workloads

Scenario:
A retail company wants to securely connect its on-premises inventory system with AWS to run analytics workloads on Amazon RDS.

Solution:

1. Create a Site-to-Site VPN connection between the on-premises network and AWS VPC.
2. Configure dynamic routing with BGP to manage failover and scalability.
3. Use IPsec encryption to secure data transfer.

Outcome:
The company achieves seamless connectivity and secure data exchange between its on-premises systems and AWS environment.

---

6. Best Practices for AWS VPN Connections

- **Enable redundancy**: Configure both tunnels in Site-to-Site VPN for high availability.
- **Monitor traffic**: Use Amazon CloudWatch to monitor VPN connection metrics.
- **Optimize latency**: Use AWS Direct Connect for latency-sensitive applications.
- **Secure access**: Use strong encryption protocols and regularly update VPN device firmware.
- **Test failover**: Regularly test failover scenarios to ensure business continuity.

---

7. Challenges and Considerations

- **Latency and bandwidth**: Ensure the VPN connection meets application performance requirements.
- **Complex routing**: Avoid route conflicts between on-premises and AWS networks.
- **Scalability**: For high data volumes, consider AWS Direct Connect as an alternative.

Conclusion

Setting up VPN connections with AWS is an essential step for creating secure and efficient hybrid cloud architectures. Whether connecting on-premises networks with Site-to-Site VPN or enabling remote user access with Client VPN, AWS provides reliable tools to meet diverse networking needs.

AWS Outposts for On-Premise Connectivity

AWS Outposts is a fully managed service that extends AWS infrastructure, services, and tools to on-premises environments. By enabling organizations to run AWS services locally while maintaining seamless integration with the AWS Cloud, Outposts provides a unified hybrid cloud experience. This chapter explores the architecture, benefits, use cases, and step-by-step guidance for deploying and managing AWS Outposts for on-premise connectivity.

1. Introduction to AWS Outposts

AWS Outposts is designed to bring the power of AWS to on-premises environments. It enables businesses to:

- **Run AWS services locally**: Host applications requiring low latency or local data processing.
- **Achieve hybrid consistency**: Use the same AWS APIs, tools, and infrastructure on-premises and in the cloud.
- **Simplify hybrid operations**: Manage on-premises workloads with familiar AWS tools like the AWS Management Console and AWS CLI.

Key components of AWS Outposts:

- **Outposts Rack**: Physical hardware deployed in your data center.
- **AWS Services**: Access to services such as EC2, EBS, S3, and RDS, locally.
- **Networking Integration**: Seamless connectivity between Outposts and the AWS Region for management and hybrid operations.

2. Benefits of AWS Outposts for On-Premise Connectivity

- **Low Latency**: Ideal for applications that require ultra-low latency by processing data locally.
- **Local Data Residency**: Ensures compliance with regulations requiring data to remain in a specific location.
- **Seamless Hybrid Operations**: Provides a consistent operating model for on-premises and cloud environments.
- **Scalability**: Easily integrate with AWS services in the cloud for scaling workloads as needed.
- **Managed Service**: AWS handles hardware provisioning, monitoring, patching, and maintenance.

3. Use Cases for AWS Outposts

- **Manufacturing and IoT**:
  - Real-time processing of IoT data at the edge.
  - Local machine learning inference for factory automation.
- **Healthcare and Life Sciences**:
  - Store and process sensitive patient data locally for compliance.
  - Support hybrid workloads such as imaging and genomic analysis.
- **Financial Services**:
  - Enable low-latency trading platforms.
  - Ensure local data processing for regulatory requirements.
- **Media and Entertainment**:
  - High-performance editing of video content on-premises.

- Local rendering workloads with cloud-scale burst capability.

---

4. Architecture of AWS Outposts Deployment

AWS Outposts architecture consists of:

1. **Outposts Rack**:
   - A physical rack installed in your data center.
   - Contains EC2 instances, EBS storage, and other AWS services.
2. **Networking**:
   - Requires a stable network connection to an AWS Region for service management and updates.
   - Supports VPN or Direct Connect for hybrid operations.
3. **Integration with AWS Services**:
   - Use AWS Identity and Access Management (IAM), CloudWatch, and other services for governance and monitoring.

---

5. Setting Up AWS Outposts

Step 1: Assess Your Requirements

- Determine your workloads and application requirements.
- Identify data residency or latency needs.
- Ensure adequate power, cooling, and network infrastructure for the Outposts rack.

Step 2: Order an Outposts Rack

- In the AWS Management Console, navigate to **AWS Outposts** and place an order.
- Specify your configuration (compute and storage capacity) and on-premises location.

Step 3: Install and Connect

- AWS delivers the Outposts rack to your site and assists with installation.
- Connect the rack to your on-premises network and power supply.
- Establish connectivity between the Outposts rack and the designated AWS Region.

Step 4: Configure Networking

- Configure a Virtual Private Cloud (VPC) for your Outposts.
- Set up subnets, route tables, and security groups.
- Use VPN or Direct Connect for hybrid connectivity if required.

Step 5: Launch and Manage Workloads

- Use the AWS Management Console, CLI, or SDK to launch and manage services on Outposts.
- Monitor workloads using AWS tools like CloudWatch and Trusted Advisor.

---

6. Managing Outposts for On-Premise Connectivity

- **Monitoring**:
   - Use Amazon CloudWatch for performance metrics and alerts.
   - Monitor network health between Outposts and the AWS Region.

- **Security**:
  - ○ Leverage IAM for access control.
  - ○ Use AWS Key Management Service (KMS) for encryption.
- **Patching and Maintenance**:
  - ○ AWS handles all hardware maintenance and software updates.
- **Integration**:
  - ○ Seamlessly integrate Outposts workloads with cloud services like S3, Lambda, and SageMaker.

---

7. Best Practices for AWS Outposts

- **Plan Networking**: Ensure sufficient bandwidth and low-latency connectivity to the AWS Region.
- **Optimize Costs**: Use cost calculators to select the right Outposts configuration for your needs.
- **Ensure Security**: Implement robust security measures, including IAM policies and encryption.
- **Test Workloads**: Validate the performance and compatibility of workloads before deployment.

---

8. Challenges and Considerations

- **Network Dependency**: Outposts requires a reliable connection to the AWS Region for management.
- **Physical Space**: Ensure your data center can accommodate the rack's size, power, and cooling needs.
- **Cost**: Evaluate whether the hybrid benefits outweigh the higher initial investment.

Conclusion

AWS Outposts bridges the gap between cloud and on-premises environments, enabling organizations to run AWS services wherever they are needed. By integrating seamlessly with AWS tools and services, Outposts simplifies hybrid cloud operations, making it a compelling choice for businesses with specific data residency, latency, or regulatory requirements.

Direct Connect Gateway for Hybrid Environments

As organizations increasingly adopt hybrid cloud strategies, seamless and secure connectivity between on-premises data centers and AWS becomes critical. The **Direct Connect Gateway** is a powerful tool that simplifies and scales hybrid cloud networking by providing a single, centralized gateway for managing multiple connections to AWS Regions and Virtual Private Clouds (VPCs). This chapter explores the architecture, benefits, use cases, and configuration steps for implementing AWS Direct Connect Gateway in hybrid environments.

---

1. Introduction to AWS Direct Connect Gateway

AWS Direct Connect Gateway is a networking feature that facilitates connectivity between:

- On-premises environments connected through **Direct Connect locations**.
- Multiple AWS VPCs across different Regions.

By consolidating connections, the Direct Connect Gateway simplifies hybrid networking, reduces complexity, and enhances scalability.

Key Features:

- **Inter-Region Connectivity**: Enables access to VPCs across multiple AWS Regions through a single Direct Connect connection.
- **Centralized Management**: Provides a centralized gateway for managing hybrid network connections.
- **High Performance**: Supports high-bandwidth, low-latency connections.
- **Enhanced Security**: Data does not traverse the public internet, ensuring secure communication.

---

2. Benefits of Direct Connect Gateway in Hybrid Environments

1. **Centralized Connectivity**:
   - Consolidates multiple Direct Connect connections and VPCs under a single gateway.
   - Simplifies network architecture and management.
2. **Global Reach**:
   - Facilitates cross-region communication, enabling hybrid workloads across different AWS Regions.
3. **Scalability**:
   - Connects multiple VPCs without the need for individual Direct Connect connections for each VPC.
4. **Cost Efficiency**:
   - Reduces the cost of maintaining multiple dedicated connections by centralizing traffic through a single gateway.
5. **Secure Data Transfers**:
   - Ensures data remains within the AWS private network without exposure to the internet.

---

3. Architecture of Direct Connect Gateway

AWS Direct Connect Gateway involves the following components:

- **Direct Connect Locations**:

- Physical locations where AWS Direct Connect connections are established.
- **Direct Connect Gateway**:
  - Serves as a centralized hub that connects Direct Connect connections to multiple VPCs.
- **Virtual Private Gateway (VGW)**:
  - The connection point between a VPC and the Direct Connect Gateway.
- **Transit Gateway** (optional):
  - Can be used alongside Direct Connect Gateway for advanced routing and multi-VPC connectivity.

---

4. Use Cases for Direct Connect Gateway

1. **Hybrid Cloud Workloads**:
   - Run applications with components hosted on-premises and in AWS for low-latency interaction.
2. **Multi-Region Architectures**:
   - Enable seamless communication between VPCs in different AWS Regions and on-premises systems.
3. **Disaster Recovery**:
   - Establish secure and reliable connections to AWS for backup and recovery operations.
4. **Data Processing**:
   - Transfer large datasets securely between on-premises environments and AWS.

---

5. Setting Up Direct Connect Gateway

Step 1: Create a Direct Connect Gateway

1. Navigate to the **AWS Management Console**.
2. Open the **Direct Connect** service.
3. Create a new Direct Connect Gateway and assign a name.
4. Specify the ASN (Autonomous System Number) for the gateway.

Step 2: Associate VPCs

1. Use the Direct Connect Gateway to associate one or more VPCs.
2. Specify the Virtual Private Gateways (VGWs) attached to the target VPCs.

Step 3: Establish a Direct Connect Connection

1. Set up a Direct Connect connection between your on-premises environment and an AWS Direct Connect location.
2. Configure the BGP (Border Gateway Protocol) sessions for routing traffic.

Step 4: Configure Routing

1. Define routes between on-premises environments and the associated VPCs.
2. Use AWS Transit Gateway, if necessary, for advanced routing scenarios.

Step 5: Test and Validate

1. Ensure data transfer between on-premises systems and AWS VPCs.
2. Monitor connectivity using **Amazon CloudWatch** and other AWS tools.

---

6. Best Practices for Using Direct Connect Gateway

- **Plan Connectivity**: Assess bandwidth requirements and choose appropriate Direct Connect port speeds (1 Gbps, 10 Gbps, etc.).
- **Use Transit Gateway**: For connecting multiple VPCs within a region, consider integrating with AWS Transit Gateway.
- **Monitor Traffic**: Leverage **AWS CloudWatch** for monitoring and optimizing network performance.
- **Optimize Routing**: Use route filters and BGP path selection to manage traffic effectively.
- **Implement Redundancy**: Establish redundant Direct Connect connections for high availability and failover.

---

7. Challenges and Considerations

- **Network Latency**:
  - Latency can vary based on the distance between your on-premises data center and the Direct Connect location.
- **Complex Routing**:
  - Complex routing configurations may arise when integrating multiple VPCs and Regions.
- **Cost**:
  - While cost-efficient for high-volume data transfers, the initial setup and management can be expensive.

Conclusion

AWS Direct Connect Gateway is a crucial component for organizations building robust hybrid cloud architectures. By providing secure, centralized, and scalable connectivity, it simplifies hybrid networking and ensures optimal performance for workloads spanning on-premises and AWS environments.

Hybrid Data Transfers Using AWS DataSync

In hybrid cloud environments, efficient and secure data transfers between on-premises systems and the AWS Cloud are crucial. AWS DataSync simplifies this process by automating data transfers at scale, ensuring fast, reliable, and secure data movement across diverse storage systems. This chapter provides an in-depth exploration of AWS DataSync, including its architecture, use cases, and step-by-step guidance on configuring and optimizing hybrid data transfers.

1. Introduction to AWS DataSync

AWS DataSync is a managed data transfer service designed to simplify, automate, and accelerate the movement of data between:

- On-premises storage systems and AWS.
- AWS storage services across Regions.

Key Features:

- **High-Performance Transfers**: Transfers data at speeds up to 10 times faster than traditional open-source tools.
- **Automated Processes**: Automates manual tasks such as scripting, scheduling, and monitoring.
- **Data Validation**: Ensures the integrity of transferred data through checksums.
- **Secure Transfers**: Encrypts data in transit and at rest, meeting stringent security standards.

2. Benefits of AWS DataSync for Hybrid Cloud Networking

1. **Simplified Data Transfers**:
   - Reduces complexity by automating workflows for large-scale data transfers.
2. **High Scalability**:
   - Handles terabytes or petabytes of data efficiently without manual intervention.
3. **Versatile Storage Integration**:
   - Supports a wide range of on-premises storage systems (e.g., NFS, SMB) and AWS services (e.g., Amazon S3, Amazon EFS, FSx).
4. **Cost-Effective**:
   - Pay-as-you-go pricing ensures no upfront costs, and you pay only for the transferred data.
5. **Enhanced Security**:
   - Provides end-to-end encryption and integrates with AWS Identity and Access Management (IAM).

3. Architecture of AWS DataSync

AWS DataSync consists of the following components:

- **DataSync Agent**:
  - A lightweight software agent installed on an on-premises server or virtual machine (VM) to access local storage.
- **DataSync Service**:
  - Fully managed by AWS, responsible for orchestrating, transferring, and monitoring data.
- **Destination Storage**:
  - AWS storage services such as Amazon S3, Amazon EFS, or Amazon FSx.

- **Management Console or APIs**:
  - Interfaces for configuring, managing, and monitoring data transfer tasks.

---

4. Use Cases for AWS DataSync

1. **Data Migration**:
   - Migrate on-premises workloads to the AWS Cloud for improved scalability and reliability.
2. **Disaster Recovery**:
   - Regularly replicate critical data to AWS for disaster recovery and business continuity.
3. **Hybrid Storage Architectures**:
   - Maintain synchronized storage between on-premises systems and AWS for hybrid operations.
4. **Big Data Processing**:
   - Transfer large datasets to AWS for processing with services like Amazon EMR, Redshift, or Athena.
5. **Backup and Archiving**:
   - Archive on-premises data to cost-effective AWS storage solutions like Amazon S3 Glacier.

---

5. Configuring AWS DataSync for Hybrid Data Transfers

Step 1: Install the DataSync Agent

1. Deploy the DataSync agent on an on-premises server or VM.
2. Configure network settings to enable communication with AWS.

Step 2: Configure Source and Destination

1. Define the source as an on-premises storage system (NFS or SMB).
2. Set the destination as an AWS storage service (Amazon S3, EFS, or FSx).

Step 3: Create a DataSync Task

1. Open the **AWS DataSync Console**.
2. Configure a new task by specifying the source, destination, and desired settings (e.g., transfer schedule, bandwidth limits).

Step 4: Optimize Task Settings

1. Enable data validation to ensure integrity.
2. Configure filters to exclude unnecessary files or directories.
3. Set bandwidth throttling to prevent overloading on-premises network resources.

Step 5: Execute and Monitor Transfers

1. Start the DataSync task and monitor progress via the AWS Management Console or CLI.
2. Use **Amazon CloudWatch** to track metrics such as transfer rate, latency, and errors.

---

6. Best Practices for Using AWS DataSync

1. **Plan Transfer Schedules**:
   - Schedule transfers during non-peak hours to minimize network congestion.
2. **Leverage IAM Roles**:

    ○ Use IAM roles with least privilege permissions for secure access to AWS resources.
3. **Optimize Network Bandwidth**:
    ○ Monitor and adjust bandwidth limits to balance transfer speed with on-premises network capacity.
4. **Enable Incremental Transfers**:
    ○ Use incremental sync to transfer only changed data, reducing time and bandwidth usage.
5. **Monitor and Troubleshoot**:
    ○ Use DataSync logs and metrics for proactive monitoring and troubleshooting.

---

7. Challenges and Considerations

- **Network Bandwidth**:
  - Ensure sufficient network bandwidth to accommodate large data transfers.
- **Compatibility**:
  - Verify compatibility of on-premises storage with DataSync protocols (NFS, SMB).
- **Cost Management**:
  - Monitor costs for data transfers, especially for large datasets.
- **Latency**:
  - Consider transfer latency for time-sensitive workloads.

Conclusion

AWS DataSync is a vital tool for organizations leveraging hybrid cloud architectures. By simplifying and automating data transfers, it enables seamless integration between on-premises systems and AWS storage solutions. With its robust security, scalability, and cost-efficiency, AWS DataSync empowers businesses to optimize their hybrid cloud operations.

Networking Automation and Optimization

Using AWS CLI for Networking Tasks

The AWS Command Line Interface (CLI) is a powerful tool that simplifies and automates the management of AWS services, including networking tasks. By providing direct access to AWS APIs, the CLI enables network engineers and administrators to efficiently manage, configure, and monitor their cloud infrastructure through scripts and commands.

This chapter delves into the essentials of using AWS CLI for networking tasks, from setting up your environment to executing common commands and leveraging automation for optimal efficiency.

1. Introduction to AWS CLI

AWS CLI is a unified tool that provides a consistent interface for managing AWS resources from the command line. It eliminates the need for manual operations in the AWS Management Console, making repetitive tasks faster and less error-prone.

Key Features:

- **Cross-Platform Compatibility**: Works on Windows, macOS, and Linux.
- **Scripting and Automation**: Facilitates the creation of scripts for repetitive networking tasks.
- **Wide Service Coverage**: Supports all AWS networking services, including Amazon VPC, Route 53, and Elastic Load Balancing.

2. Setting Up AWS CLI

Step 1: Install AWS CLI

1. Download the AWS CLI installer from the [AWS CLI official page] (https://aws.amazon.com/cli/).
2. Follow the installation instructions for your operating system.

Step 2: Configure AWS CLI

1. Run the following command to configure AWS CLI:

```
aws configure
```

2. Provide the following details when prompted:
    - **Access Key ID**: Found in the AWS Management Console under IAM.
    - **Secret Access Key**: Corresponds to the Access Key ID.
    - **Default Region**: Specify the AWS Region (e.g., us-east-1).
    - **Default Output Format**: Choose json, table, or text.

3. Common AWS CLI Networking Commands

Managing Virtual Private Cloud (VPC)

- **Create a VPC**:

  ```
  aws ec2 create-vpc --cidr-block 10.0.0.0/16
  ```

  This creates a VPC with a specified CIDR block.

- **Describe VPCs**:

  ```
  aws ec2 describe-vpcs
  ```

  Lists all VPCs in the selected Region.

Configuring Subnets

- **Create a Subnet**:

  ```
  aws ec2 create-subnet --vpc-id vpc-12345678 --cidr-block 10.0.1.0/24
  ```

  Adds a subnet to an existing VPC.

- **Describe Subnets**:

  ```
  aws ec2 describe-subnets
  ```

  Retrieves details of all subnets.

Managing Route Tables

- **Create a Route Table**:

  ```
  aws ec2 create-route-table --vpc-id vpc-12345678
  ```

- **Add a Route to a Route Table**:

  ```
  aws ec2 create-route --route-table-id rtb-12345678 --destination-cidr-block
  0.0.0.0/0 --gateway-id igw-12345678
  ```

Elastic Load Balancing

- **Create an Application Load Balancer**:

  ```
  aws elbv2 create-load-balancer --name my-load-balancer --subnets
  subnet-12345678 subnet-87654321
  ```

- **Describe Load Balancers**:

  ```
  aws elbv2 describe-load-balancers
  ```

Amazon Route 53

- **List Hosted Zones**:

  ```
  aws route53 list-hosted-zones
  ```

- **Create a DNS Record**:

  ```
  aws route53 change-resource-record-sets --hosted-zone-id Z123456789
  --change-batch file://record.json
  ```

Note: The record.json file must include DNS record details.

---

4. Automating Networking Tasks with AWS CLI

Task Automation Using Shell Scripts

Scripts can automate multiple tasks, such as creating a VPC, subnets, and routing rules in one go.

Example Script: Create VPC with Subnets

```bash
#!/bin/bash

# Create a VPC
VPC_ID=$(aws ec2 create-vpc --cidr-block 10.0.0.0/16 --query 'Vpc.VpcId' --output
text)

# Create Subnets
SUBNET_ID=$(aws ec2 create-subnet --vpc-id $VPC_ID --cidr-block 10.0.1.0/24 --query
'Subnet.SubnetId' --output text)

# Attach an Internet Gateway
IGW_ID=$(aws ec2 create-internet-gateway --query
'InternetGateway.InternetGatewayId' --output text)
aws ec2 attach-internet-gateway --vpc-id $VPC_ID --internet-gateway-id $IGW_ID

# Create and Associate a Route Table
RTB_ID=$(aws ec2 create-route-table --vpc-id $VPC_ID --query
'RouteTable.RouteTableId' --output text)
aws ec2 associate-route-table --route-table-id $RTB_ID --subnet-id $SUBNET_ID
aws ec2 create-route --route-table-id $RTB_ID --destination-cidr-block 0.0.0.0/0
--gateway-id $IGW_ID

echo "VPC, Subnet, and Routing successfully created!"
```

Scheduling CLI Tasks with CRON

- Use **CRON jobs** to run scripts at predefined intervals for tasks like monitoring or updating configurations.

Example CRON Job

- Edit CRON jobs:

  ```
  crontab -e
  ```

- Add a scheduled task:

  ```
  0 2 * * * /path/to/script.sh
  ```

---

5. Best Practices for Using AWS CLI in Networking

1. **Secure Credentials**:
   - Use AWS IAM roles and policies instead of hardcoding credentials in scripts.
2. **Enable Logging**:
   - Use --debug mode to troubleshoot issues during execution.
3. **Validate Commands**:

- o Use the `--dry-run` option to validate commands without making actual changes.
4. **Leverage Profiles**:
    - o Configure multiple profiles for different environments (e.g., production, development).
5. **Monitor Costs**:
    - o Use AWS CLI commands to analyze costs and ensure efficient use of resources:

```
aws ce get-cost-and-usage --time-period Start=YYYY-MM-DD,End=YYYY-MM-DD
--granularity MONTHLY
```

Conclusion

AWS CLI is an indispensable tool for managing networking tasks in AWS. It provides flexibility, scalability, and efficiency, enabling administrators to automate repetitive tasks and streamline operations. By mastering AWS CLI commands and leveraging automation, organizations can significantly enhance their networking workflows and reduce operational overhead.

Automation with AWS CloudFormation

AWS CloudFormation is a service that allows users to automate the deployment and management of AWS resources, including networking components, by using infrastructure as code (IaC). This approach simplifies complex networking configurations, ensures consistency, and reduces manual intervention in resource management.

This chapter focuses on leveraging AWS CloudFormation to automate networking tasks, covering its core concepts, advantages, and practical examples.

1. Introduction to AWS CloudFormation

AWS CloudFormation enables users to define their AWS infrastructure, including networking resources, in templates written in JSON or YAML. These templates describe all the resources required for an application or service, such as Virtual Private Clouds (VPCs), subnets, route tables, and security groups.

Key Features of CloudFormation:

- **Infrastructure as Code**: Declaratively manage resources using templates.
- **Repeatability**: Deploy consistent environments across different accounts and regions.
- **Dependency Management**: Automatically handles resource dependencies.
- **Change Management**: Enables updates and rollbacks with minimal risk.

2. Benefits of Using AWS CloudFormation for Networking

- **Efficiency**: Automates repetitive tasks, reducing deployment time.
- **Standardization**: Ensures uniform configurations across environments.
- **Version Control**: Templates can be stored in repositories for tracking changes.
- **Scalability**: Easily replicate complex networking setups in multiple regions.

3. Core Components of CloudFormation

- **Templates**: The blueprint for your infrastructure, written in JSON or YAML.
- **Stacks**: A collection of AWS resources created and managed as a single unit.
- **Change Sets**: Previews of how proposed updates to a stack will affect resources.

4. Writing Networking Templates in CloudFormation

Defining Networking Components

1. **VPC**:

```
Resources:
  MyVPC:
    Type: "AWS::EC2::VPC"
    Properties:
      CidrBlock: "10.0.0.0/16"
      EnableDnsSupport: true
      EnableDnsHostnames: true
```

```
      Tags:
        - Key: "Name"
          Value: "MyVPC"
```

2. **Subnets**:

```
Resources:
  PublicSubnet:
    Type: "AWS::EC2::Subnet"
    Properties:
      VpcId: !Ref MyVPC
      CidrBlock: "10.0.1.0/24"
      MapPublicIpOnLaunch: true
      Tags:
        - Key: "Name"
          Value: "PublicSubnet"
```

3. **Route Table and Internet Gateway**:

```
Resources:
  InternetGateway:
    Type: "AWS::EC2::InternetGateway"
  RouteTable:
    Type: "AWS::EC2::RouteTable"
    Properties:
      VpcId: !Ref MyVPC
  Route:
    Type: "AWS::EC2::Route"
    Properties:
      RouteTableId: !Ref RouteTable
      DestinationCidrBlock: "0.0.0.0/0"
      GatewayId: !Ref InternetGateway
```

---

5. Deploying and Managing Networking Stacks

Creating a Stack

1. Save your template file locally (e.g., `networking-template.yaml`).
2. Use the AWS Management Console, AWS CLI, or AWS SDKs to create a stack.

```
aws cloudformation create-stack --stack-name MyNetworkStack --template-body
file://networking-template.yaml
```

Monitoring Stack Deployment

- Check the status of the stack using:

```
aws cloudformation describe-stacks --stack-name MyNetworkStack
```

Updating a Stack

- Modify the template and update the stack:

```
aws cloudformation update-stack --stack-name MyNetworkStack --template-body
file://updated-template.yaml
```

Deleting a Stack

- Remove all resources in a stack with a single command:

```
aws cloudformation delete-stack --stack-name MyNetworkStack
```

---

6. Advanced Features for Networking Automation

Nested Stacks

- Reuse templates by nesting them within a parent template to manage large infrastructures.

Example:

```
Resources:
  VPCStack:
    Type: "AWS::CloudFormation::Stack"
    Properties:
      TemplateURL: "https://s3.amazonaws.com/mybucket/vpc-template.yaml"
  SubnetStack:
    Type: "AWS::CloudFormation::Stack"
    Properties:
      TemplateURL: "https://s3.amazonaws.com/mybucket/subnet-template.yaml"
      Parameters:
        VPCID: !GetAtt VPCStack.Outputs.VPCID
```

Parameters

- Use parameters to make templates dynamic.

Example:

```
Parameters:
  VPCName:
    Type: String
    Default: "MyVPC"
Resources:
  MyVPC:
    Type: "AWS::EC2::VPC"
    Properties:
      CidrBlock: "10.0.0.0/16"
      Tags:
        - Key: "Name"
          Value: !Ref VPCName
```

Outputs

- Define outputs to share information between stacks or for reference.

Example:

```
Outputs:
  VPCID:
    Value: !Ref MyVPC
    Description: "The ID of the VPC"
```

7. Best Practices for Networking Automation with CloudFormation

1. **Use Modular Templates**: Break large configurations into smaller, reusable templates.
2. **Validate Templates**: Use the AWS CloudFormation Linter (`cfn-lint`) to check for errors.

```
cfn-lint networking-template.yaml
```

3. **Version Control**: Store templates in repositories like GitHub or CodeCommit for tracking changes.
4. **Tagging**: Apply consistent tags to resources for better organization and cost tracking.
5. **Test in Non-Production Environments**: Validate changes in a test environment before applying to production.

8. Example Use Case: Automating Multi-Region VPC Setup

```
Resources:
  VPC:
    Type: "AWS::EC2::VPC"
    Properties:
      CidrBlock: "10.0.0.0/16"
  PublicSubnet:
    Type: "AWS::EC2::Subnet"
    Properties:
      VpcId: !Ref VPC
      CidrBlock: "10.0.1.0/24"
  InternetGateway:
    Type: "AWS::EC2::InternetGateway"
  RouteTable:
    Type: "AWS::EC2::RouteTable"
    Properties:
      VpcId: !Ref VPC
  Route:
    Type: "AWS::EC2::Route"
    Properties:
      RouteTableId: !Ref RouteTable
      DestinationCidrBlock: "0.0.0.0/0"
      GatewayId: !Ref InternetGateway
Outputs:
  VPCID:
    Description: "VPC ID"
    Value: !Ref VPC
```

Conclusion

AWS CloudFormation revolutionizes how networking infrastructure is managed by enabling automation, consistency, and scalability. By using templates, organizations can deploy and maintain complex networking setups with ease, reduce human error, and focus on optimizing network performance.

Networking with AWS CDK (Cloud Development Kit)

The AWS Cloud Development Kit (CDK) is a powerful tool that allows you to define cloud infrastructure using programming languages like Python, TypeScript, Java, C#, and Go. By leveraging the AWS CDK, you can programmatically design and deploy networking resources with the benefits of version control, reusability, and automation. This chapter focuses on how the AWS CDK can be utilized for automating and optimizing AWS networking tasks.

1. Introduction to AWS CDK for Networking

The AWS CDK is an Infrastructure-as-Code (IaC) framework that provides a high-level abstraction for defining AWS resources, including networking components. Unlike traditional CloudFormation templates, the CDK allows you to use familiar programming languages, making it easier to integrate infrastructure management into your application development process.

Key Features of AWS CDK:

- **Programming Language Support**: Use Python, TypeScript, Java, Go, and C# to define resources.
- **Reusable Constructs**: Modular components that simplify complex resource definitions.
- **Synthesis to CloudFormation**: Automatically generates CloudFormation templates.
- **Ecosystem Support**: Access to pre-built constructs in the AWS Construct Library.

2. Benefits of Using AWS CDK for Networking Automation

- **Simplified Development**: Reduces the learning curve for non-YAML/JSON users.
- **Dynamic Resource Management**: Enables conditional logic and loops in infrastructure definitions.
- **Version Control**: Seamlessly integrate with Git or other version control systems.
- **Efficient Reusability**: Share and reuse constructs across projects and teams.
- **Improved Scalability**: Easily replicate and manage networking setups across regions or accounts.

3. Core Concepts of AWS CDK

1. **Stacks**: Represents a single unit of deployment (e.g., a VPC or networking stack).
2. **Constructs**: Reusable components representing AWS resources or logical groupings.
3. **App**: A container for one or more stacks, representing your entire CDK application.
4. **Synthesis**: The process of converting CDK code into a CloudFormation template.

4. Setting Up AWS CDK

To get started with AWS CDK:

1. **Install the AWS CDK CLI**:

```
npm install -g aws-cdk
```

2. **Bootstrap Your Environment**:

```
cdk bootstrap aws://<account-id>/<region>
```

3. **Initialize a New CDK Project**:

```
cdk init app --language typescript
```

4. **Install Required Libraries**:

```
npm install @aws-cdk/aws-ec2 @aws-cdk/core
```

---

5. Building Networking Resources with CDK

Example: Creating a VPC with Subnets

Below is a TypeScript example to create a VPC with public and private subnets:

```typescript
import * as cdk from 'aws-cdk-lib';
import { Vpc, SubnetType } from 'aws-cdk-lib/aws-ec2';

class NetworkingStack extends cdk.Stack {
  constructor(scope: cdk.App, id: string, props?: cdk.StackProps) {
    super(scope, id, props);

    // Create a VPC with public and private subnets
    const vpc = new Vpc(this, 'MyVpc', {
      cidr: '10.0.0.0/16',
      maxAzs: 2,
      subnetConfiguration: [
        {
          cidrMask: 24,
          name: 'PublicSubnet',
          subnetType: SubnetType.PUBLIC,
        },
        {
          cidrMask: 24,
          name: 'PrivateSubnet',
          subnetType: SubnetType.PRIVATE_WITH_NAT,
        },
      ],
    });
  }
}

const app = new cdk.App();
new NetworkingStack(app, 'NetworkingStack');
app.synth();
```

Example: Adding an Internet Gateway

To add an Internet Gateway to the VPC:

```typescript
import { InternetGateway, Vpc, SubnetType } from 'aws-cdk-lib/aws-ec2';

const vpc = new Vpc(this, 'MyVpc', {
```

```
  cidr: '10.0.0.0/16',
  maxAzs: 2,
});


const igw = new InternetGateway(this, 'MyInternetGateway', {
  vpc,
});
```

Example: Setting Up Security Groups

```
import { SecurityGroup, Port, Peer } from 'aws-cdk-lib/aws-ec2';

const securityGroup = new SecurityGroup(this, 'MySecurityGroup', {
  vpc,
  description: 'Allow SSH and HTTP traffic',
  allowAllOutbound: true,
});

securityGroup.addIngressRule(Peer.anyIpv4(), Port.tcp(22), 'Allow SSH');
securityGroup.addIngressRule(Peer.anyIpv4(), Port.tcp(80), 'Allow HTTP');
```

---

6. Deploying CDK Applications

1. **Synthesize CloudFormation Templates**:

   ```
   cdk synth
   ```

2. **Deploy the Stack**:

   ```
   cdk deploy
   ```

3. **View Stack Outputs**: Outputs defined in the CDK application can be retrieved using:

   ```
   cdk outputs
   ```

4. **Destroy the Stack**: Remove all resources created by the stack:

   ```
   cdk destroy
   ```

---

7. Advanced Networking Scenarios with CDK

Multi-VPC Setup with Peering

```
import { Vpc, VpcPeeringConnection } from 'aws-cdk-lib/aws-ec2';

// Create two VPCs
const vpc1 = new Vpc(this, 'Vpc1', { cidr: '10.0.0.0/16' });
const vpc2 = new Vpc(this, 'Vpc2', { cidr: '10.1.0.0/16' });

// Establish VPC peering
const peering = new VpcPeeringConnection(this, 'VpcPeering', {
  vpc: vpc1,
```

```
  peerVpc: vpc2,
});
```

8. Best Practices for Networking Automation with CDK

1. **Use Constructs for Reusability**: Create reusable constructs for common networking configurations.
2. **Adopt Modular Design**: Divide large deployments into multiple stacks for better manageability.
3. **Leverage CDK Toolkit**: Use the CDK CLI for testing and deploying stacks efficiently.
4. **Use Parameterization**: Utilize context variables to make your applications dynamic and reusable:

```
cdk deploy --context region=us-east-1
```

5. **Validate Before Deployment**: Test the CDK application in a development environment before deploying to production.

Conclusion

AWS CDK simplifies the automation and management of networking resources by allowing you to write code in familiar programming languages. With its powerful constructs and integration with the AWS ecosystem, CDK provides an efficient way to define, deploy, and manage AWS networking infrastructure at scale.

Monitoring with Amazon CloudWatch

Amazon CloudWatch is a comprehensive monitoring and observability service designed to provide actionable insights into your AWS resources and applications. For networking tasks, CloudWatch helps track network performance, identify issues, and optimize network usage through real-time metrics, logs, and alarms.

This chapter focuses on leveraging Amazon CloudWatch for monitoring AWS networking components and ensuring high availability, scalability, and reliability in your cloud infrastructure.

1. Introduction to Amazon CloudWatch

Amazon CloudWatch acts as a unified monitoring service that collects and visualizes metrics and logs from AWS resources. By monitoring networking components like VPCs, Load Balancers, and Route 53, CloudWatch helps maintain optimal network performance.

Key Features of CloudWatch:

- **Metrics Monitoring**: Collects data points such as latency, throughput, and packet loss.
- **Alarms**: Automatically triggers actions when thresholds are breached.
- **Logs Insights**: Enables querying of logs for troubleshooting and debugging.
- **Dashboards**: Provides centralized visualization of metrics and logs.

2. Benefits of Monitoring AWS Networking with CloudWatch

- **Real-Time Visibility**: Monitor networking metrics such as data transfer, latency, and error rates.
- **Proactive Alerts**: Receive notifications for threshold breaches to prevent downtime.
- **Enhanced Troubleshooting**: Analyze logs for debugging networking issues.
- **Cost Optimization**: Identify and manage underutilized resources.
- **Integrated Solutions**: Seamlessly integrates with AWS services like CloudTrail, Lambda, and SNS for automated responses.

3. Key Networking Metrics in CloudWatch

CloudWatch collects a wide range of metrics for networking components. Below are some critical metrics to monitor:

VPC Flow Logs

- **BytesTransferred**: Volume of data transferred.
- **Packets**: Number of packets sent and received.
- **RejectCount**: Count of rejected packets.

Elastic Load Balancers

- **HealthyHostCount**: Number of healthy instances.
- **UnHealthyHostCount**: Number of unhealthy instances.
- **RequestCount**: Total requests handled.
- **Latency**: Time taken to serve requests.

Route 53

- **HealthCheckStatus**: Status of Route 53 health checks.
- **DNSQueries**: Number of DNS queries processed.

Direct Connect

- **ConnectionBps**: Bandwidth usage of the connection.
- **ConnectionStatus**: Status of the Direct Connect link.

---

4. Setting Up Monitoring for Networking Components

Step 1: Enabling Metrics Collection

Most AWS networking services automatically publish metrics to CloudWatch. Ensure that:

- VPC Flow Logs are enabled for your VPC.
- Load Balancer metrics are being collected.
- Health checks for Route 53 are configured.

Step 2: Configuring Alarms

Use CloudWatch Alarms to monitor critical metrics and trigger automated actions when thresholds are crossed.

Example: Creating an alarm for high latency on a Load Balancer:

```
aws cloudwatch put-metric-alarm \
  --alarm-name HighLatencyAlarm \
  --metric-name Latency \
  --namespace AWS/ApplicationELB \
  --statistic Average \
  --threshold 0.5 \
  --comparison-operator GreaterThanThreshold \
  --evaluation-periods 2 \
  --dimensions Name=LoadBalancer,Value=my-load-balancer \
  --alarm-actions arn:aws:sns:region:account-id:my-sns-topic
```

Step 3: Creating Dashboards

Visualize metrics using CloudWatch Dashboards for better monitoring.

```
aws cloudwatch put-dashboard \
  --dashboard-name NetworkDashboard \
  --dashboard-body file://dashboard.json
```

Example dashboard.json:

```
{
  "widgets": [
    {
      "type": "metric",
      "properties": {
        "metrics": [
          ["AWS/ApplicationELB", "Latency", "LoadBalancer", "my-load-balancer"],
          ["AWS/NetworkELB", "ActiveFlowCount", "LoadBalancer",
"my-network-load-balancer"]
        ],
        "view": "timeSeries",
        "stacked": false,
```

```
        "region": "us-east-1"
      }
    }
  ]
}
```

5. Log Analysis with CloudWatch Logs

VPC Flow Logs

VPC Flow Logs capture information about network traffic to and from interfaces within your VPC.

Steps to Enable:

1. Go to the VPC console.
2. Select your VPC and click on **Flow Logs**.
3. Choose a CloudWatch Log Group to store the logs.

Example Log Entry:

2 123456789012 eni-abc123 192.168.0.1 10.0.0.1 443 50500 6 10 840 1625678901 1625678902 ACCEPT OK

Analyzing Flow Logs with Logs Insights

Run queries to analyze logs:

```
fields @timestamp, srcAddr, dstAddr, action
| filter action = "REJECT"
| sort @timestamp desc
| limit 20
```

6. Automating Responses with CloudWatch

Integrate CloudWatch Alarms with AWS services to automate responses:

- **Scaling Instances**: Trigger Auto Scaling when load balancer requests increase.
- **Network Configuration Changes**: Use Lambda to reconfigure security groups if a traffic anomaly is detected.
- **Notifications**: Send alerts via SNS to administrators for immediate action.

Example SNS Notification:

```
aws sns publish \
  --topic-arn arn:aws:sns:region:account-id:my-sns-topic \
  --message "High latency detected on Load Balancer"
```

7. Best Practices for Network Monitoring

- **Set Meaningful Thresholds**: Avoid false alarms by defining appropriate thresholds for alarms.
- **Use Aggregated Metrics**: Monitor aggregated metrics for multi-region architectures.
- **Enable Detailed Monitoring**: Opt for detailed monitoring where real-time insights are critical.
- **Centralize Logs**: Use log groups to organize logs for easy access and analysis.

Conclusion

Amazon CloudWatch provides robust tools for monitoring AWS networking components, ensuring that you can maintain high performance and availability. By setting up metrics, alarms, and dashboards, and integrating log analysis, you can proactively address issues and optimize your network's efficiency.

Optimizing Network Costs in AWS

Managing costs effectively is a critical aspect of building and maintaining cloud networks on AWS. While AWS offers robust networking tools and services, their usage can quickly accumulate costs if not optimized properly. This chapter provides a comprehensive guide to understanding AWS networking cost components and strategies to optimize them without compromising performance or scalability.

---

1. Understanding AWS Networking Costs

AWS networking costs are primarily based on data transfer, resource usage, and service configurations. The key factors influencing networking costs include:

1.1. Data Transfer Costs

- **Inbound Data Transfer**: Generally free for most services.
- **Outbound Data Transfer**: Charged based on the volume of data leaving AWS regions, services, or VPCs.
- **Cross-Region Traffic**: Transferring data between regions incurs higher costs.
- **Inter-AZ Data Transfer**: Traffic between Availability Zones within the same region is billed separately.

1.2. Service-Specific Costs

- **Elastic Load Balancing (ELB)**: Costs depend on the volume of requests and processed data.
- **Direct Connect**: Includes port-hour charges and additional data transfer fees.
- **CloudFront**: Pricing depends on the region, volume of requests, and data served.

1.3. DNS and Content Delivery

- **Amazon Route 53**: Costs are incurred for hosted zones, DNS queries, and health checks.
- **AWS CloudFront**: Charged based on data transfer and request volume.

---

2. Strategies for Cost Optimization

Cost optimization involves using the right tools and strategies to reduce unnecessary expenses while maintaining network performance.

2.1. Optimize Data Transfer

- **Use AWS CloudFront**: Cache frequently accessed content at edge locations to minimize data transfer from origin servers.
- **Enable VPC Endpoints**: Use VPC endpoints for private connectivity to AWS services, eliminating public traffic costs.
- **Minimize Cross-Region Traffic**: Where possible, keep traffic within the same region to avoid higher cross-region charges.

2.2. Leverage Pricing Models

- **Savings Plans**: Use Compute Savings Plans for consistent workloads to save up to 72% on EC2 and networking-related services.

- **Spot Instances**: For flexible workloads, use Spot Instances to lower the cost of compute and networking.

2.3. Optimize Load Balancing

- **Use Appropriate Load Balancers**: Choose between Application Load Balancer (ALB), Network Load Balancer (NLB), or Gateway Load Balancer (GLB) based on your application requirements.
- **Enable Sticky Sessions**: Reduce repeated traffic by enabling session stickiness on load balancers.

2.4. Monitor and Adjust Resource Utilization

- **Resize NAT Gateways**: Optimize the number of NAT Gateways to reduce over-provisioning.
- **Analyze Flow Logs**: Use VPC Flow Logs to identify unnecessary traffic patterns and optimize routing.

---

3. Tools for Cost Optimization

AWS provides several tools to analyze and optimize networking costs effectively:

3.1. AWS Cost Explorer

- **Track Networking Costs**: Visualize data transfer costs and identify trends.
- **Set Alerts**: Create alerts for unusual cost spikes.

3.2. AWS Trusted Advisor

- **Optimize Resource Usage**: Provides recommendations to reduce costs, such as removing idle resources or resizing services.
- **Networking Insights**: Highlights underutilized resources and over-provisioned networking components.

3.3. Amazon CloudWatch

- **Monitor Traffic Metrics**: Analyze data transfer volumes and costs associated with specific resources.
- **Set Alarms**: Trigger alarms for high traffic or unexpected costs.

3.4. AWS Budgets

- **Set Budget Limits**: Monitor costs against defined budgets for networking services.
- **Automated Notifications**: Notify stakeholders when costs approach defined limits.

---

4. Best Practices for Cost Optimization

To ensure sustained cost savings, follow these best practices:

- **Plan for Data Transfers**: Optimize your architecture to minimize cross-region and inter-AZ traffic.
- **Use Compression**: Compress data for transfers, especially for bandwidth-intensive applications.
- **Rightsize Resources**: Regularly analyze and adjust the size of networking components to match actual usage.
- **Implement Lifecycle Policies**: Use lifecycle policies to archive less frequently accessed data, reducing transfer costs.
- **Leverage Free Tiers**: Use AWS free-tier offerings for testing and development environments.

5. Real-World Use Case: Cost Optimization for a Multi-Region Architecture

A company operating a multi-region application was experiencing high networking costs due to cross-region traffic. By implementing the following changes, they reduced costs by 30%:

- Deployed Amazon CloudFront to cache content closer to users.
- Consolidated data processing to a single region for applications that did not require multi-region deployment.
- Established Direct Connect links for consistent and cost-effective high-volume transfers.
- Enabled VPC Flow Logs to identify and eliminate unnecessary inter-region traffic.

Conclusion

Optimizing networking costs in AWS requires a thorough understanding of pricing structures, proactive monitoring, and strategic implementation of AWS tools. By leveraging services like CloudFront, VPC endpoints, and Trusted Advisor, you can build cost-efficient networks without sacrificing performance or scalability.

AWS Trusted Advisor for Networking

AWS Trusted Advisor is a comprehensive cloud optimization service designed to assist users in improving the performance, security, fault tolerance, and cost efficiency of their AWS environments. For networking, Trusted Advisor offers actionable insights to optimize network configurations and maintain best practices. This chapter explores how to utilize AWS Trusted Advisor for networking tasks, identify key recommendations, and implement them effectively.

1. Introduction to AWS Trusted Advisor

AWS Trusted Advisor is an advisory tool that checks your AWS environment against a set of predefined best practices across multiple categories, including:

- **Cost Optimization**
- **Performance**
- **Security**
- **Fault Tolerance**
- **Service Limits**

For networking, Trusted Advisor focuses on identifying misconfigurations, cost inefficiencies, and security vulnerabilities in your network infrastructure.

2. Networking-Specific Checks in Trusted Advisor

Trusted Advisor provides several checks that are highly relevant to networking. Some key checks include:

2.1. Security Checks

- **Open Access Security Groups**: Identifies security groups allowing unrestricted access to specific ports (e.g., SSH or RDP) and provides recommendations to tighten access.
- **Network ACL Misconfigurations**: Highlights any overly permissive or conflicting ACL rules.
- **CloudFront HTTPS Usage**: Ensures HTTPS is enforced for secure content delivery via CloudFront.

2.2. Cost Optimization Checks

- **Idle Load Balancers**: Identifies load balancers that are not actively serving traffic, suggesting termination to save costs.
- **Unassociated Elastic IPs**: Detects Elastic IP addresses that are allocated but not associated with running instances.

2.3. Performance and Fault Tolerance Checks

- **Overutilized or Underutilized NAT Gateways**: Highlights inefficient configurations of NAT Gateways to ensure optimal resource usage.
- **VPC Peering Connections**: Ensures peering connections are correctly established and actively used.

2.4. Service Limits

- **Service Limit Monitoring**: Warns when nearing service limits for key networking resources like Elastic IPs, NAT Gateways, and load balancers.

3. Enabling and Accessing Trusted Advisor

To use Trusted Advisor for networking tasks:

1. **Enable Trusted Advisor**: Trusted Advisor is available for all AWS accounts, but certain checks require a Business or Enterprise Support Plan.
2. **Access via Console**:
   - Navigate to the **AWS Management Console**.
   - Select **Trusted Advisor** under the Support section.
3. **Access via API**:
   - Use the AWS Trusted Advisor API to automate report generation and integrate it into workflows.

4. Implementing Networking Recommendations

Trusted Advisor provides actionable recommendations for optimizing network configurations. Here's how to implement these recommendations effectively:

4.1. Enhancing Security

- **Restrict Security Group Rules**: Replace "0.0.0.0/0" with specific IP ranges or VPN endpoints for tighter control.
- **Audit Publicly Accessible Resources**: Identify and secure resources that should not be exposed to the internet.
- **Enforce HTTPS for CloudFront**: Update CloudFront distributions to require HTTPS for secure data delivery.

4.2. Optimizing Costs

- **Terminate Idle Load Balancers**: Use Amazon CloudWatch metrics to confirm inactivity before termination.
- **Release Unused Elastic IPs**: Deallocate unused IP addresses to avoid unnecessary charges.
- **Consolidate NAT Gateways**: Evaluate traffic patterns to reduce the number of NAT Gateways where feasible.

4.3. Improving Fault Tolerance

- **Monitor VPC Peering Connections**: Ensure peering connections are active and routes are correctly configured.
- **Evaluate Subnet Utilization**: Balance traffic distribution across subnets for high availability.

5. Automating Trusted Advisor Recommendations

Automation can simplify the process of monitoring and addressing Trusted Advisor recommendations:

5.1. AWS Lambda

- Use AWS Lambda functions to periodically check Trusted Advisor reports and apply predefined fixes (e.g., deleting idle resources).

5.2. AWS CloudWatch Alarms

- Set up alarms based on Trusted Advisor findings to notify administrators of critical issues, such as open access security groups.

5.3. Integration with AWS CLI

- Use the AWS CLI to script checks and automate tasks like updating security group rules or releasing unused IPs.

---

6. Best Practices for Trusted Advisor in Networking

- **Enable All Checks**: Ensure all relevant networking checks are enabled, especially for security and cost optimization.
- **Review Regularly**: Schedule periodic reviews of Trusted Advisor reports to identify and address potential issues proactively.
- **Combine with AWS Config**: Use AWS Config to track changes in network configurations and align them with Trusted Advisor recommendations.
- **Train Teams**: Educate network administrators on interpreting and applying Trusted Advisor insights effectively.

---

7. Real-World Use Case: Enhancing Security with Trusted Advisor

A financial services company identified multiple open security group rules via Trusted Advisor, exposing sensitive resources to the public internet. By implementing the recommendations:

- They restricted access to internal IP ranges.
- Automated regular audits with AWS Lambda.
- Reduced the attack surface by 40%.

This proactive approach enhanced their security posture while maintaining compliance with industry standards.

Conclusion

AWS Trusted Advisor is an invaluable tool for maintaining best practices in your network configurations. By leveraging its insights, you can ensure cost efficiency, security, and performance across your AWS networking stack. Combine it with automation tools like Lambda and CloudWatch for continuous optimization.

Performance and Monitoring

Network Performance Metrics in AWS

Monitoring network performance is a critical aspect of managing and optimizing your AWS infrastructure. Understanding key performance metrics enables you to assess the health, efficiency, and reliability of your networking resources, ensuring optimal operation and user satisfaction. This chapter explores the essential network performance metrics in AWS, tools to monitor them, and best practices for analysis and optimization.

1. Importance of Network Performance Metrics

Network performance metrics are vital for:

- **Ensuring Reliability**: Identify and resolve issues proactively.
- **Optimizing Costs**: Monitor resource utilization to eliminate waste.
- **Improving User Experience**: Minimize latency and maximize throughput.
- **Compliance**: Meet SLAs (Service Level Agreements) and regulatory requirements.

2. Key Network Performance Metrics in AWS

AWS provides a rich set of metrics through **Amazon CloudWatch** and other monitoring tools. The primary metrics for network performance include:

2.1. Network Throughput

- **Definition**: Measures the rate of data transfer between resources, typically in Mbps or Gbps.
- **Usage**: Identifies bandwidth bottlenecks in VPCs, load balancers, and gateways.

2.2. Latency

- **Definition**: Measures the time taken for data to travel between two endpoints.
- **Usage**: Crucial for applications requiring low-latency connections like gaming or streaming.

2.3. Packet Loss

- **Definition**: Indicates the percentage of packets dropped during transmission.
- **Usage**: High packet loss can affect application performance and user experience.

2.4. Connection Errors

- **Definition**: Tracks failed or incomplete network connections.
- **Usage**: Helps identify issues with configurations, routing, or resource limits.

2.5. Traffic Distribution

- **Definition**: Monitors the distribution of traffic across resources like load balancers or VPC endpoints.
- **Usage**: Ensures balanced resource utilization to prevent overloading.

2.6. Network Packet Rate

- **Definition**: Measures the number of packets sent or received per second.
- **Usage**: Detects potential resource overloading or inefficiencies in data handling.

2.7. Data Transfer Costs

- **Definition**: Tracks the cost associated with inbound and outbound data transfer.
- **Usage**: Helps optimize configurations to minimize unnecessary expenses.

---

3. Monitoring Network Metrics with AWS Tools

AWS offers a suite of tools to collect and analyze network performance data:

3.1. Amazon CloudWatch

- **Capabilities**:
  - Real-time monitoring of metrics like bandwidth usage, latency, and packet loss.
  - Integration with alarms to notify administrators of anomalies.
- **Key Metrics**:
  - NetworkIn and NetworkOut for EC2 instances.
  - HealthyHostCount and UnHealthyHostCount for load balancers.

3.2. AWS X-Ray

- **Capabilities**:
  - Provides end-to-end tracing of application requests.
  - Identifies latency and bottlenecks in networking layers.
- **Use Case**: Debugging distributed applications or APIs.

3.3. AWS CloudTrail

- **Capabilities**:
  - Logs API calls and user activities affecting network configurations.
  - Tracks changes to security groups, VPCs, and other resources.
- **Use Case**: Auditing and troubleshooting.

3.4. VPC Flow Logs

- **Capabilities**:
  - Captures detailed information about traffic entering and exiting your VPC.
  - Analyzes metrics like IP addresses, ports, and packet counts.
- **Use Case**: Diagnosing connectivity issues or optimizing traffic flows.

---

4. Best Practices for Network Performance Monitoring

Implement these best practices to maximize the effectiveness of network performance monitoring:

4.1. Set Baseline Metrics

- Monitor network performance under normal operating conditions to establish benchmarks.
- Use these baselines to identify deviations or anomalies.

4.2. Enable Multi-Level Monitoring

- Collect metrics at multiple layers, including VPCs, instances, and load balancers, for a comprehensive view.
- Leverage tools like CloudWatch for high-level monitoring and Flow Logs for granular analysis.

4.3. Automate Alerts

- Set up CloudWatch Alarms to receive notifications when metrics exceed predefined thresholds (e.g., high latency or packet loss).

4.4. Regularly Analyze Logs

- Use VPC Flow Logs and CloudTrail to identify trends or recurring issues.
- Automate log analysis with AWS Lambda or third-party tools.

4.5. Optimize Resources

- Use metrics like throughput and traffic distribution to adjust instance types, increase bandwidth, or reconfigure load balancers.

---

5. Real-World Example: Monitoring Latency for a Web Application

A retail company observed increased latency in their e-commerce application. Using CloudWatch and X-Ray:

1. They identified increased response times from a specific region.
2. Analysis revealed a misconfigured Route 53 DNS failover policy.
3. They corrected the configuration and optimized traffic routing, reducing latency by 35%.

Conclusion

Monitoring network performance metrics is a cornerstone of maintaining a robust and scalable AWS network. By leveraging tools like CloudWatch, X-Ray, and Flow Logs, administrators can gain deep insights into their network's health, optimize configurations, and ensure superior performance.

Troubleshooting AWS Networking Issues

Managing and maintaining an AWS network involves identifying and resolving issues that can disrupt workflows, compromise security, or degrade performance. This chapter provides a systematic approach to troubleshooting common AWS networking issues, leveraging AWS tools, best practices, and strategies to restore network functionality quickly and effectively.

---

1. The Importance of Effective Troubleshooting

Networking issues can manifest in several ways, such as:

- **Connectivity Problems**: Instances or services failing to communicate.
- **Performance Bottlenecks**: High latency or low throughput impacting applications.
- **Misconfigurations**: Errors in security groups, route tables, or VPC configurations.

Effective troubleshooting ensures:

- Minimal downtime and service disruptions.
- Optimal network performance and security.
- Compliance with SLAs and operational requirements.

---

2. Common AWS Networking Issues and Their Causes

2.1. Connectivity Issues

- **Symptoms**: Instances or services are unable to communicate.
- **Potential Causes**:
  - Misconfigured security groups or NACLs.
  - Incorrect route table entries.
  - Missing or misconfigured internet gateways or NAT gateways.

2.2. Performance Degradation

- **Symptoms**: Increased latency, reduced throughput, or packet loss.
- **Potential Causes**:
  - Insufficient bandwidth allocation.
  - Overloaded instances or load balancers.
  - Inefficient traffic routing.

2.3. Incorrect DNS Resolution

- **Symptoms**: Failure to resolve hostnames or delayed resolution.
- **Potential Causes**:
  - Misconfigured Amazon Route 53 DNS settings.
  - Incorrect private or public hosted zones.

2.4. Security and Access Problems

- **Symptoms**: Denied access or unintended access to resources.
- **Potential Causes**:
  - Incorrect IAM policies or roles.
  - Overly restrictive security group or NACL settings.

○ Misconfigured AWS PrivateLink or Direct Connect.

2.5. Resource Limits

- **Symptoms**: New connections failing or network interruptions.
- **Potential Causes**:
  ○ Exceeding service limits like VPC, NAT gateways, or ENI limits.
  ○ Exhausted IP address ranges in subnets.

---

3. Tools for Troubleshooting AWS Networking

3.1. Amazon CloudWatch

- Monitors network metrics like latency, throughput, and error rates.
- Set alarms for unusual metric behavior.

3.2. VPC Flow Logs

- Captures information about traffic entering and exiting VPCs.
- Helps analyze connectivity issues and unauthorized traffic.

3.3. AWS CloudTrail

- Logs API calls and changes to network configurations.
- Useful for identifying accidental or malicious changes.

3.4. AWS Trusted Advisor

- Provides recommendations on improving security, performance, and cost optimization.
- Identifies misconfigurations in security groups, NACLs, and other resources.

3.5. AWS Reachability Analyzer

- Simulates connectivity between resources to identify potential issues.
- Pinpoints misconfigurations in security or routing.

3.6. Network Manager

- Monitors and visualizes global networks.
- Provides insights into network health across regions.

---

4. Systematic Troubleshooting Approach

Step 1: Define the Problem

- Document the symptoms (e.g., connection timeout, high latency).
- Identify affected resources and applications.

Step 2: Isolate the Issue

- Determine if the problem is local (specific to a resource) or global (across the network).
- Use VPC Flow Logs and CloudWatch to narrow down the scope.

Step 3: Analyze Configurations

- Check security group rules, NACLs, and route tables.
- Verify DNS configurations in Amazon Route 53.

Step 4: Monitor Metrics

- Review metrics like NetworkIn, NetworkOut, and PacketDropCount in CloudWatch.
- Look for deviations from baseline performance.

Step 5: Test Connectivity

- Use Reachability Analyzer to simulate and diagnose connectivity between resources.
- Perform ping and traceroute tests from affected instances.

Step 6: Implement Solutions

- Update configurations, adjust resource limits, or optimize traffic flows.
- Redeploy or restart resources if necessary.

Step 7: Validate and Monitor

- Confirm the issue is resolved by testing applications and services.
- Continue monitoring metrics to ensure long-term stability.

---

5. Real-World Example: Resolving a VPC Connectivity Issue

Scenario: An application hosted in a private subnet is unable to connect to the internet.

Steps Taken:

1. **Problem Identification**:
   - Verified that the application is unreachable from the internet.
2. **Analysis**:
   - Checked security group and NACL rules: No outbound rules were blocking traffic.
   - Inspected route table: Found that the route to the NAT gateway was missing.
3. **Solution**:
   - Updated the route table to include a route to the NAT gateway for internet-bound traffic.
4. **Validation**:
   - Retested the application and confirmed internet connectivity.

---

6. Best Practices for Avoiding Networking Issues

- **Automate Configuration Management**:
  - Use AWS CloudFormation or AWS CDK to define and deploy consistent network configurations.
- **Enable Detailed Monitoring**:
  - Activate VPC Flow Logs, CloudTrail, and CloudWatch for proactive monitoring.
- **Implement Redundancy**:
  - Use multiple Availability Zones for critical resources to minimize the impact of failures.
- **Set Alarms and Alerts**:
  - Configure CloudWatch alarms to notify administrators of unusual activity or performance metrics.
- **Regularly Review Security Policies**:
  - Audit security groups, NACLs, and IAM roles to ensure compliance and minimize risk.

Conclusion

Troubleshooting AWS networking issues requires a systematic approach, a solid understanding of AWS tools, and a proactive monitoring strategy. By leveraging the powerful suite of AWS monitoring and diagnostic tools, administrators can quickly identify and resolve issues, ensuring high availability and performance.

Configuring Flow Logs for Monitoring

Monitoring network traffic within your AWS environment is essential for maintaining security, optimizing performance, and troubleshooting connectivity issues. **VPC Flow Logs** provide a detailed view of traffic entering and exiting network interfaces within a Virtual Private Cloud (VPC), making it a critical tool for AWS administrators. In this chapter, we explore the setup, configuration, and best practices for using Flow Logs to monitor AWS network traffic effectively.

1. Understanding VPC Flow Logs

VPC Flow Logs capture detailed metadata about the IP traffic flowing to and from network interfaces in a VPC. The captured data can include:

- **Accepted and Rejected Traffic**: Understand which connections are permitted or blocked.
- **Source and Destination Information**: Identify traffic origins and destinations.
- **Traffic Flow Statistics**: Monitor packet counts, bytes transferred, and protocols used.

Use Cases:

- **Security Monitoring**: Detect unauthorized access attempts and traffic anomalies.
- **Troubleshooting Connectivity Issues**: Diagnose routing and configuration problems.
- **Performance Optimization**: Analyze traffic patterns to improve resource allocation.

2. Setting Up Flow Logs

Step 1: Define the Scope

Flow Logs can be configured for:

- **VPC Level**: Captures all traffic within a VPC.
- **Subnet Level**: Captures traffic for specific subnets.
- **Network Interface Level**: Targets individual Elastic Network Interfaces (ENIs).

Step 2: Choose the Destination

You can store Flow Log data in:

- **Amazon CloudWatch Logs**: Ideal for real-time monitoring and alerting.
- **Amazon S3**: Suitable for long-term storage and integration with data analysis tools.

Step 3: Create the Flow Log

1. Navigate to the **VPC Console**.
2. Select the VPC, subnet, or network interface for which you want to enable Flow Logs.
3. Click on **Actions → Create Flow Log**.
4. Configure the settings:
   - **Filter**: Choose between ALL, ACCEPT, or REJECT traffic.
   - **Destination**: Specify CloudWatch Logs or S3.
   - **IAM Role**: Ensure a role with the necessary permissions is assigned.

Step 4: Enable and Test

Once the Flow Log is created:

- Confirm that logs are being delivered to the specified destination.
- Test by generating traffic (e.g., ping or HTTP requests) and verify the logs reflect this activity.

---

3. Analyzing Flow Log Data

Log Record Format

Each Flow Log record consists of:

- **Version**: The format version of the Flow Log record.
- **Account ID**: The AWS account ID generating the traffic.
- **Interface ID**: The network interface from which traffic originated or terminated.
- **Traffic Type**: Inbound or outbound.
- **Action**: ACCEPT or REJECT based on security group or NACL rules.

Example Record:

```
2 123456789012 eni-abc12345 10.0.0.1 10.0.0.2 443 80 6 10 1000 1625140800
1625140860 ACCEPT OK
```

Analyzing with CloudWatch

- Use **CloudWatch Logs Insights** to query Flow Log data.
- Example Query: Identify rejected traffic.

```
fields @timestamp, sourceAddress, destinationAddress, protocol, action
| filter action = "REJECT"
```

Analyzing with S3

- Use Amazon Athena or AWS Glue to query logs stored in S3.
- Integrate with third-party analytics tools for advanced visualization.

---

4. Best Practices for Flow Logs

4.1. Scope Configuration

- Start with a VPC-level Flow Log to get a holistic view.
- Narrow the scope to subnets or ENIs for targeted analysis.

4.2. Optimize Storage

- Use lifecycle policies for S3 to archive older logs or delete unnecessary data.
- Aggregate logs to reduce storage costs and improve query performance.

4.3. Enable Monitoring

- Set up CloudWatch alarms based on Flow Log data to detect anomalies in real-time.
- Example: Trigger an alarm for repeated rejected connections from a specific IP.

4.4. Regularly Review Logs

- Periodically analyze Flow Logs to identify unused routes, misconfigured security groups, or malicious traffic patterns.
- Use findings to refine firewall and routing configurations.

5. Real-World Example: Debugging Connectivity Issues

Scenario: A web server instance is unable to connect to an external API.

Steps:

1. **Enable Flow Logs**:
   - Create a Flow Log at the ENI level for the web server instance.
2. **Analyze Traffic**:
   - Query Flow Logs for REJECT actions to identify blocked connections.
   - Locate records showing traffic from the web server's private IP to the API's public IP.
3. **Identify Root Cause**:
   - Found that an outbound rule in the security group was missing.
4. **Solution**:
   - Updated the security group to allow outbound traffic to the API's IP and port.

6. Troubleshooting Tips

- **Logs Not Delivering**: Ensure the IAM role has permissions for CloudWatch Logs or S3.
- **Empty Logs**: Confirm traffic is flowing through the monitored scope and that filters are set correctly.
- **Performance Overhead**: Minimize by narrowing the scope and optimizing log storage.

Conclusion

VPC Flow Logs are an indispensable tool for AWS networking professionals. They provide insights into traffic patterns, help identify configuration issues, and enhance security monitoring. By effectively configuring and analyzing Flow Logs, you can ensure your network is optimized and secure.

Best Practices for AWS Network Performance

Efficient network performance is crucial for maintaining the reliability, scalability, and cost-effectiveness of your AWS environment. AWS offers a variety of tools, services, and strategies that help optimize network performance. This chapter provides a comprehensive guide to best practices for enhancing network performance across your AWS workloads.

1. Understand Your Network Requirements

The first step in optimizing network performance is understanding your workload's specific needs. Consider:

- **Bandwidth Requirements**: Determine the data transfer rates your applications need.
- **Latency Tolerance**: Identify acceptable delays in data transfer.
- **Traffic Patterns**: Analyze whether your traffic is bursty, consistent, or variable.

Actionable Tip: Use tools like **Amazon CloudWatch** and **VPC Flow Logs** to monitor network behavior and identify bottlenecks.

2. Choose the Right Network Architecture

AWS provides multiple options for designing your network. Ensure that your architecture aligns with your performance goals:

- Use **AWS Transit Gateway** for interconnecting multiple VPCs efficiently.
- Leverage **Direct Connect** for low-latency and high-bandwidth connections to on-premise data centers.
- Deploy **Edge Locations** with **Amazon CloudFront** to reduce latency for globally distributed users.

Best Practice: Minimize hops in your architecture by placing compute resources close to data sources.

3. Optimize Data Transfer and Bandwidth

Efficient data transfer ensures optimal utilization of network resources. Consider:

- **Compression**: Use compression algorithms to reduce data size.
- **Amazon S3 Transfer Acceleration**: Enable faster uploads to S3 buckets across geographical locations.
- **AWS Global Accelerator**: Optimize routing paths for high-priority traffic.

Actionable Tip: Use **Elastic Load Balancing** to distribute traffic evenly and avoid network congestion.

4. Leverage Auto Scaling

Auto Scaling dynamically adjusts resources to match demand, ensuring consistent performance:

- Use **Auto Scaling Groups** for EC2 instances to handle variable traffic loads.
- Configure scaling policies based on network metrics such as incoming traffic volume or connection count.

Best Practice: Set up proactive scaling policies for predictable traffic spikes.

---

5. Monitor and Analyze Network Metrics

Continuous monitoring is critical to maintaining network health. AWS provides tools to track key metrics:

- **CloudWatch Metrics**: Monitor latency, packet loss, and throughput.
- **VPC Flow Logs**: Analyze traffic patterns to identify anomalies.
- **AWS Network Manager**: Gain a centralized view of your network performance.

Actionable Tip: Set up CloudWatch alarms to receive alerts for critical performance thresholds.

---

6. Utilize Advanced AWS Networking Tools

AWS offers specialized tools to enhance network performance:

- **Elastic Fabric Adapter (EFA)**: Optimize high-performance computing (HPC) workloads.
- **AWS Direct Connect**: Reduce latency for hybrid cloud scenarios.
- **AWS Outposts**: Extend AWS infrastructure to on-premise locations for low-latency requirements.

Best Practice: Evaluate these tools based on your specific workload needs.

---

7. Implement Security Best Practices

Security misconfigurations can lead to network performance issues. Ensure:

- **Proper Firewall Rules**: Optimize Security Groups and Network ACLs to avoid unnecessary traffic filtering.
- **Encryption Optimization**: Use hardware-accelerated encryption options for data in transit.

Actionable Tip: Use **AWS Shield Advanced** for DDoS protection, ensuring uninterrupted performance during attacks.

---

8. Optimize DNS Resolution

Efficient DNS resolution reduces latency:

- Use **Amazon Route 53** for scalable and reliable DNS management.
- Leverage **Health Checks** in Route 53 to route traffic to healthy endpoints.

Best Practice: Configure multi-region DNS failover to ensure global availability.

---

9. Test and Validate Performance

Regular testing ensures that your network is optimized for current and future workloads:

- Use **AWS Trusted Advisor** to review your environment for performance optimization recommendations.
- Perform load testing using tools like **AWS CloudFormation** or third-party solutions.

Actionable Tip: Validate throughput and latency by simulating peak traffic conditions.

---

10. Follow Cost Optimization Strategies

High performance often correlates with higher costs. Implement strategies to balance performance and cost:

- Use **Savings Plans** or **Reserved Instances** for predictable workloads.
- Review and optimize **Data Transfer Costs** using the AWS Cost Explorer.
- Enable **S3 Lifecycle Policies** to move less-frequently accessed data to lower-cost storage tiers.

Best Practice: Regularly review your AWS billing reports to identify and mitigate cost spikes.

---

11. Real-World Example: Optimizing a High-Traffic E-Commerce Site

Scenario: An e-commerce site experiences periodic spikes in traffic during sales events.

Steps:

1. **Use Elastic Load Balancing**: Distribute incoming traffic across multiple instances to prevent bottlenecks.
2. **Enable Auto Scaling**: Automatically add instances to handle increased demand.
3. **Leverage CloudFront**: Cache static content at edge locations to reduce latency for global users.
4. **Monitor Performance**: Use CloudWatch alarms to track and address anomalies in real-time.

Outcome: The site maintained high performance and availability during traffic spikes, ensuring a positive customer experience.

Conclusion

Optimizing network performance in AWS requires a combination of architectural best practices, effective use of AWS tools, and continuous monitoring. By implementing the strategies outlined in this chapter, you can ensure that your AWS environment operates efficiently, meets performance demands, and remains cost-effective.

AWS Network Manager for Centralized Monitoring

Efficient monitoring and management are critical for ensuring that complex networks function optimally. AWS Network Manager is a powerful tool designed to simplify the monitoring and management of global networks in AWS, providing a centralized view of your networking resources. This chapter explores its features, use cases, and best practices for leveraging AWS Network Manager for centralized monitoring.

1. What is AWS Network Manager?

AWS Network Manager is a service that provides a unified operational view of your network resources. It allows you to:

- Visualize your global network topology.
- Monitor performance metrics across your network.
- Manage AWS Transit Gateway and VPN connections.
- Troubleshoot network issues with real-time insights.

Key Features:

- Centralized monitoring of multiple regions.
- Integration with other AWS services like CloudWatch.
- Network topology visualizations.
- Alerts and notifications for network events.

2. Key Components of AWS Network Manager

AWS Network Manager relies on several integrated components to deliver its functionality:

- **Global Network**: The logical representation of your interconnected network resources.
- **AWS Transit Gateway**: Used for connecting VPCs and on-premises networks.
- **VPN Connections**: Allows monitoring of Site-to-Site VPN links.
- **Third-Party Connectivity**: Extends monitoring to non-AWS resources.

Actionable Tip: Define your global network in AWS Network Manager to monitor all associated resources effectively.

3. Setting Up AWS Network Manager

Step 1: Define Your Global Network

- Access the **AWS Management Console** and navigate to Network Manager.
- Create a **global network**, which will serve as the central hub for monitoring.

Step 2: Register AWS Resources

- Attach AWS Transit Gateways, VPN connections, and Direct Connect resources.
- Register on-premises networks using **Network Manager APIs** or the **console**.

Step 3: Configure Real-Time Monitoring

- Enable CloudWatch integration for metrics collection.

- Configure **Flow Logs** for detailed traffic analysis.

Step 4: Visualize the Network

- Use the topology map to understand connectivity and resource relationships.

---

4. Use Cases for AWS Network Manager

1. **Centralized Network Visibility**
   - Manage multiple AWS regions and on-premises networks from a single console.
2. **Performance Monitoring**
   - Monitor latency, packet loss, and throughput across all connections.
3. **Cost Management**
   - Identify underutilized resources and optimize cost through detailed usage insights.
4. **Issue Resolution**
   - Detect and troubleshoot issues using network events and performance metrics.

Example: A retail company uses Network Manager to monitor their multi-region AWS network, ensuring seamless customer experience during high-traffic events like Black Friday.

---

5. Monitoring and Alerts with AWS Network Manager

Metrics to Monitor:

- **VPN Connection Status**: Ensure connectivity is up and stable.
- **Transit Gateway Metrics**: Analyze packet drops and throughput.
- **Link Health**: Monitor site-to-site connectivity.

Configuring Alerts:

- Set up CloudWatch alarms for critical metrics.
- Use AWS EventBridge to trigger automated actions based on network events.

---

6. Integrating with Other AWS Services

AWS Network Manager works seamlessly with other AWS tools for enhanced functionality:

- **CloudWatch**: For monitoring and alerts.
- **AWS Trusted Advisor**: For cost and performance optimization recommendations.
- **AWS Systems Manager**: For automating troubleshooting workflows.

Best Practice: Use CloudWatch dashboards to visualize key metrics collected by AWS Network Manager.

---

7. Best Practices for Using AWS Network Manager

1. **Regularly Review Topology Maps**
   - Ensure the network topology aligns with your architectural design.
2. **Automate Monitoring Tasks**
   - Use CloudFormation templates to automate resource registration and monitoring configurations.

3. **Enable Logging**
   ○ Activate **Flow Logs** for deeper insights into network traffic.
4. **Optimize for Scale**
   ○ Leverage Network Manager's scalability to handle thousands of resources across multiple regions.

---

8. Limitations and Considerations

While AWS Network Manager is powerful, it has some limitations:

- It is primarily focused on AWS and associated resources.
- Non-AWS integrations may require additional setup using APIs.

Workaround: Use third-party tools like Cisco or Palo Alto for advanced non-AWS network integrations.

---

9. Real-World Scenario: Optimizing a Global Retail Network

Scenario: A global retailer operates multiple VPCs across regions with Direct Connect links to their on-premises data centers.

Steps Taken:

1. Set up AWS Network Manager to define their global network.
2. Integrated Transit Gateways and VPN connections into the topology.
3. Monitored real-time performance metrics to ensure low latency for transactions.

Outcome: The retailer improved network performance and reduced downtime by proactively identifying and resolving connectivity issues.

Conclusion

AWS Network Manager simplifies the complex task of managing and monitoring global networks. By centralizing the visibility of AWS and hybrid networking resources, it ensures better performance, scalability, and reliability. Implementing the practices outlined in this chapter will enhance your ability to maintain a robust AWS network infrastructure.

Security Best Practices

Advanced Firewall Configurations in AWS

Firewalls play a critical role in securing network traffic and ensuring only authorized connections are permitted to your resources. AWS provides a range of configurable firewall options that offer both fine-grained control and scalability to meet the diverse needs of modern enterprises. In this chapter, we will explore advanced firewall configurations in AWS, focusing on best practices, advanced features, and tools available for robust security.

1. Overview of Firewall Options in AWS

AWS offers several types of firewalls designed to cater to different layers of the network stack:

1. **Security Groups**: Operate at the instance level to control inbound and outbound traffic.
2. **Network Access Control Lists (NACLs)**: Function at the subnet level to provide stateless filtering of traffic.
3. **AWS Network Firewall**: A fully managed service providing deep packet inspection and intrusion detection/prevention.
4. **WAF (Web Application Firewall)**: Protects web applications from common exploits like SQL injection or cross-site scripting.
5. **Firewall Manager**: Centralized management for firewall rules across accounts and resources.

Each option serves a specific purpose and can be combined for a layered security approach.

2. Configuring Security Groups for Granular Access Control

Security Groups are stateful firewalls that automatically allow return traffic. Advanced configurations include:

- **IP-Based Rules**: Restrict traffic to specific IP ranges or addresses.
- **Port-Based Rules**: Permit only necessary ports (e.g., 80 for HTTP, 443 for HTTPS).
- **Protocol-Specific Rules**: Configure rules based on protocols like TCP, UDP, or ICMP.

Example: To secure an application server, configure rules such as:

- Allow inbound HTTP and HTTPS traffic from the public internet.
- Restrict SSH access to specific IP addresses (e.g., corporate office IP).

Best Practice: Regularly review and tighten security group rules to follow the principle of least privilege.

3. Advanced Use of Network Access Control Lists (NACLs)

Unlike security groups, **NACLs** are stateless, meaning inbound and outbound rules need to be explicitly configured.

- **Use Case**: Denying specific IP ranges or traffic types at the subnet level.

- **Rule Evaluation**: Rules are evaluated in numerical order, so prioritize critical rules with lower rule numbers.

Advanced Configuration:

- Create explicit **deny rules** to block malicious IP ranges.
- Use NACLs as an additional layer of security for public-facing subnets.

Caution: Be mindful of overlapping rules that can unintentionally block legitimate traffic.

---

4. AWS Network Firewall: Advanced Packet Filtering

The **AWS Network Firewall** provides deep packet inspection and advanced traffic filtering for VPCs. Key features include:

- **Stateful and Stateless Rule Engines**: Configure rules for monitoring and blocking traffic based on patterns.
- **Threat Intelligence Feeds**: Block traffic from known malicious IP addresses.
- **Intrusion Prevention System (IPS)**: Detect and mitigate sophisticated attacks.

Example Use Case:

- Protect sensitive workloads by inspecting inbound traffic for known attack signatures.
- Enforce compliance with regulations like PCI DSS by monitoring and logging traffic.

Best Practice: Integrate AWS Network Firewall with CloudWatch for real-time monitoring of security events.

---

5. Web Application Firewall (WAF): Application-Level Protection

AWS WAF is a specialized firewall for protecting web applications. Advanced configurations include:

- **Custom Rule Groups**: Block specific traffic patterns unique to your application.
- **Rate-Based Rules**: Limit the number of requests per IP address to prevent DDoS attacks.
- **Managed Rule Groups**: Use preconfigured rules for common vulnerabilities.

Advanced Features:

- Automate rule updates using AWS WAF APIs.
- Combine WAF with **AWS Shield Advanced** for enhanced DDoS protection.

Use Case: Block SQL injection attempts on a public-facing e-commerce website using AWS WAF.

---

6. Centralized Management with AWS Firewall Manager

AWS Firewall Manager simplifies the management of firewall rules across multiple accounts and regions. It is especially useful for organizations operating under AWS Organizations.

Capabilities:

- Enforce consistent security policies across all resources.
- Automatically apply rules to newly created resources.
- Integrate with AWS Config to ensure compliance.

Example:

- Create a Firewall Manager policy to automatically apply WAF rules to all CloudFront distributions.

---

7. Integrating Logging and Monitoring

Advanced firewall configurations are incomplete without proper logging and monitoring. Enable and analyze logs to detect anomalies and potential breaches.

- **VPC Flow Logs**: Capture information about allowed and denied traffic.
- **CloudWatch Logs**: Monitor and create alerts for unusual traffic patterns.
- **AWS Security Hub**: Aggregate findings from firewalls and other security services.

Best Practice: Regularly review logs and automate anomaly detection using Amazon GuardDuty.

---

8. Automation for Firewall Rule Management

Automation ensures that firewall configurations remain consistent and reduce manual errors.

- Use **AWS CloudFormation** templates to deploy security group and NACL configurations.
- Automate rule updates using **AWS Lambda** functions.
- Leverage **AWS Systems Manager** to enforce compliance policies across accounts.

Example: Create a Lambda function to automatically block IP addresses identified by GuardDuty as malicious.

---

9. Common Pitfalls and How to Avoid Them

- **Overly Permissive Rules**: Avoid rules that allow wide-open access, such as 0.0.0.0/0 for inbound traffic.
- **Rule Conflicts**: Regularly audit rules to identify and resolve conflicts between security groups and NACLs.
- **Neglecting Logging**: Always enable logging to track and troubleshoot issues effectively.

Conclusion

Advanced firewall configurations in AWS provide robust security for your network infrastructure. By combining services like Security Groups, NACLs, AWS Network Firewall, and WAF, you can build a multi-layered security strategy tailored to your specific needs. Regular monitoring, automation, and adherence to best practices ensure that your network remains secure and compliant with industry standards.

Network Security Automation with AWS Tools

As modern network architectures grow in complexity, manual management of security configurations becomes increasingly challenging and error-prone. AWS offers a suite of tools and services that enable automation of network security tasks, ensuring consistent application of policies, quicker response times to threats, and overall improved efficiency in securing your cloud environment.

1. Introduction to Network Security Automation

Network security automation involves the use of tools and services to automatically enforce security policies, monitor network activity, and respond to potential threats. AWS provides built-in services and integrations that allow you to automate key aspects of your network security.

Benefits of Automation:

- Reduces human error in configuring and managing security.
- Ensures compliance with organizational and regulatory standards.
- Speeds up detection and mitigation of security risks.
- Improves scalability by applying security configurations across large infrastructures.

2. AWS Tools for Network Security Automation

AWS offers several services to automate and enhance network security:

1. **AWS Firewall Manager**:
   - Enables centralized management of firewall rules across multiple accounts.
   - Automates rule application to new resources as they are created.
   - Integrates with AWS WAF, AWS Network Firewall, and Shield Advanced.
2. **AWS Config**:
   - Continuously monitors and records resource configurations.
   - Automates compliance by enforcing predefined security rules.
   - Triggers remediation workflows when non-compliant configurations are detected.
3. **AWS Security Hub**:
   - Aggregates security findings from multiple AWS services.
   - Automates security checks based on industry standards like CIS benchmarks.
   - Provides insights for improving security posture.
4. **AWS Lambda**:
   - Enables custom automation workflows for responding to security events.
   - Useful for tasks like blocking malicious IPs or updating security groups dynamically.
5. **Amazon GuardDuty**:
   - Uses machine learning to detect unusual or unauthorized activity.
   - Integrates with other services to automate responses to threats.
6. **AWS Systems Manager**:
   - Automates patching and compliance across instances.
   - Executes runbooks for security-related tasks.

3. Automating Security Group Management

Automation can simplify the management and ensure consistency.

Use Cases:

- Automatically remove overly permissive rules, such as 0.0.0.0/0.
- Update security group rules based on real-time threat intelligence.
- Apply standardized security group configurations to new instances.

Example: Use AWS Lambda and Amazon GuardDuty integration to dynamically block IPs flagged as malicious by GuardDuty.

Automation Workflow:

1. GuardDuty identifies a malicious IP address.
2. A Lambda function is triggered to add the IP to a deny rule in the relevant security group.
3. Logs are updated in CloudWatch for auditing purposes.

---

4. Using AWS Config for Compliance Automation

AWS Config continuously evaluates your resources against compliance rules you define.

Key Features:

- Predefined security rules, such as ensuring all internet-facing instances use secure protocols.
- Automatic remediation via AWS Config Rules.
- Integration with AWS Systems Manager for advanced automation.

Example: Ensure all subnets have NACLs configured with explicit deny rules for known malicious IPs.

Automation Steps:

1. Define a Config rule for NACL compliance.
2. Use a remediation action to automatically apply missing rules to non-compliant NACLs.
3. Notify administrators via Amazon SNS when a remediation action is taken.

---

5. Streamlining WAF and AWS Network Firewall Management

Automation simplifies the management of complex firewall configurations:

- **AWS WAF Automation**:
  - Automatically apply rate-based rules for DDoS mitigation.
  - Use AWS Firewall Manager to deploy WAF rules across accounts and regions.
  - Dynamically update WAF rules using threat intelligence feeds.
- **AWS Network Firewall**:
  - Automate the deployment of stateful and stateless rule sets across multiple VPCs.
  - Use AWS Firewall Manager to maintain consistent rule sets across environments.

Best Practice: Regularly update firewall rules using automated scripts to account for evolving threat landscapes.

---

6. Incident Response Automation

AWS tools enable swift and automated responses to security incidents:

1. **Using GuardDuty and Lambda**:
   - Detect anomalous activities such as port scanning or data exfiltration.
   - Trigger a Lambda function to isolate compromised instances by modifying security group rules.
2. **Integrating with AWS Security Hub**:
   - Aggregate findings from services like GuardDuty, Inspector, and Firewall Manager.
   - Automatically generate tickets in third-party incident management systems like ServiceNow.
3. **Automated Forensics with Systems Manager**:
   - Use Systems Manager to capture logs, memory dumps, and other forensic data from instances under investigation.

---

7. Centralized Management with AWS Firewall Manager

AWS Firewall Manager provides a centralized platform for managing firewall rules across your organization.

Capabilities:

- Automatically apply rules to new accounts and resources.
- Enforce compliance with organization-wide policies.
- Integrate with AWS Organizations for hierarchical rule management.

Example: Use Firewall Manager to enforce consistent WAF rules on all CloudFront distributions and ALBs in your environment.

---

8. Monitoring and Logging for Security Automation

Effective automation requires comprehensive logging and monitoring:

- Enable **VPC Flow Logs** to capture network traffic information.
- Use **CloudWatch Logs** and metrics for real-time monitoring of firewall activity.
- Integrate **AWS CloudTrail** to track changes to security configurations.

Best Practice: Use Amazon Kinesis to analyze flow log data in real-time for suspicious patterns.

---

9. Best Practices for Security Automation

- **Use the Principle of Least Privilege**: Ensure all automation scripts and services operate with the minimum permissions required.
- **Leverage AWS Tags**: Tag resources to apply targeted security policies programmatically.
- **Regular Audits**: Periodically review automation workflows to ensure they align with evolving security requirements.

Conclusion

Automating network security with AWS tools not only enhances your security posture but also reduces operational overhead. By leveraging services like AWS Firewall Manager, Config, and GuardDuty, you can enforce consistent policies, quickly respond to threats, and ensure compliance across your cloud infrastructure.

Securing Public-Facing Applications

Public-facing applications, such as web portals and APIs, are critical entry points for users and systems but also serve as potential attack vectors for malicious actors. Securing these applications in AWS is essential to ensure data integrity, availability, and user trust. This chapter focuses on AWS tools and strategies to protect public-facing applications while maintaining their performance and accessibility.

---

1. Understanding the Challenges of Public-Facing Applications

Public-facing applications are inherently exposed to external users and threats, making them vulnerable to attacks like:

- **Distributed Denial of Service (DDoS)**: Overwhelming the application with traffic to disrupt service.
- **SQL Injection and Cross-Site Scripting (XSS)**: Exploiting application vulnerabilities to manipulate data or execute malicious scripts.
- **Credential Stuffing**: Automated attempts to gain unauthorized access using stolen credentials.
- **Man-in-the-Middle Attacks**: Intercepting communication between the client and server.

To address these challenges, AWS provides a robust set of security tools and best practices.

---

2. AWS Tools for Securing Public-Facing Applications

AWS offers multiple services to enhance the security of public-facing applications:

1. **AWS Web Application Firewall (WAF)**:
   - Filters and monitors HTTP/S traffic to and from your application.
   - Protects against common threats like SQL injection and XSS.
   - Supports custom rules to enforce application-specific security requirements.
2. **AWS Shield**:
   - Provides managed DDoS protection.
   - AWS Shield Standard is included with AWS services and offers basic protection.
   - AWS Shield Advanced provides enhanced DDoS mitigation, cost protection, and 24/7 access to the AWS DDoS Response Team (DRT).
3. **Amazon CloudFront**:
   - Distributes application content securely via edge locations.
   - Offers integration with AWS WAF for additional security at the edge.
   - Reduces exposure by caching responses and minimizing requests to the origin server.
4. **AWS Certificate Manager (ACM)**:
   - Simplifies SSL/TLS certificate management.
   - Ensures secure communication with HTTPS for public-facing applications.
5. **AWS Identity and Access Management (IAM)**:
   - Manages user authentication and authorization.
   - Enables fine-grained access control to application resources.
6. **Amazon Cognito**:
   - Provides user authentication, authorization, and user data management.
   - Protects against credential-based attacks.

---

3. Designing a Secure Public-Facing Architecture

Securing public-facing applications starts with designing a robust architecture:

1. **Use Load Balancers**:
   - Employ **Application Load Balancers (ALBs)** to handle incoming HTTP/S traffic securely.
   - Enforce HTTPS connections using SSL/TLS certificates managed by ACM.
2. **Implement Network Segmentation**:
   - Host public-facing resources in a **demilitarized zone (DMZ)** using public subnets.
   - Place backend resources like databases in private subnets accessible only through specific channels.
3. **Leverage Content Delivery Networks (CDNs)**:
   - Use Amazon CloudFront to cache application content and reduce direct exposure to origin servers.
4. **Restrict Access with Security Groups**:
   - Allow traffic only on specific ports (e.g., 443 for HTTPS).
   - Deny all other inbound traffic by default.
5. **Enable Encryption Everywhere**:
   - Use HTTPS for all communication between users and the application.
   - Encrypt data at rest and in transit using AWS-managed or customer-managed keys.

---

4. Implementing Security with AWS WAF

AWS WAF provides customizable protection against common threats:

- **Predefined Rule Groups**:
  - AWS offers managed rule groups to block common attack patterns.
  - Examples include protection against SQL injection, XSS, and bad bots.
- **Custom Rules**:
  - Define IP-based blocking, rate-based rules, or geographical restrictions.
  - Use regular expressions to detect and block malicious payloads.
- **Integration with ALB and CloudFront**:
  - Deploy WAF rules at the edge using CloudFront or at the application layer using ALB.

Example: Block traffic from specific IP ranges associated with malicious activity:

```
{
  "Name": "BlockMaliciousIPs",
  "IPSetDescriptors": [
    {
      "Type": "IPV4",
      "Value": "192.0.2.0/24"
    }
  ]
}
```

---

5. Enhancing Resilience with AWS Shield

AWS Shield protects public-facing applications against DDoS attacks:

1. **Standard Protection**:
   - Automatic and included at no additional cost with AWS services.
   - Monitors traffic patterns and mitigates common DDoS attacks.
2. **Advanced Protection**:
   - Enhanced protection for sensitive applications.

- ○ Cost protection for scaling during DDoS events.
- ○ Direct access to the DDoS Response Team (DRT).

Best Practice: Use AWS Shield Advanced for critical applications requiring guaranteed availability.

---

6. Securing Application Access with IAM and Amazon Cognito

1. **IAM Policies**:
   - ○ Define permissions for resources, ensuring least privilege.
   - ○ Use conditions in policies to restrict access based on factors like IP address or time of day.
2. **Amazon Cognito**:
   - ○ Manage user sign-up, sign-in, and access controls.
   - ○ Enable multifactor authentication (MFA) for added security.
   - ○ Integrate with social identity providers like Google and Facebook.

Example: Configure MFA for sensitive application actions like viewing user data.

---

7. Monitoring and Logging for Public-Facing Applications

1. **Enable CloudTrail Logging**:
   - ○ Track all API calls to public-facing resources for auditing purposes.
2. **Use VPC Flow Logs**:
   - ○ Monitor network traffic patterns to detect anomalies.
3. **Set Up CloudWatch Alarms**:
   - ○ Trigger alerts for unusual spikes in traffic or failed login attempts.
4. **Integrate with Security Hub**:
   - ○ Centralize security findings and automate responses to potential threats.

---

8. Best Practices for Securing Public-Facing Applications

- **Keep Software Up-to-Date**: Regularly patch application code and dependencies.
- **Use Security Headers**: Enforce headers like Content-Security-Policy (CSP) and X-Frame-Options.
- **Regularly Test Applications**: Perform penetration testing and vulnerability scans to identify weaknesses.
- **Follow the Principle of Least Privilege**: Restrict access to only what is necessary for users and systems.

Conclusion

Securing public-facing applications is an ongoing process that requires the right combination of AWS tools, best practices, and proactive monitoring. By leveraging services like AWS WAF, Shield, and IAM, you can build a robust security posture that protects your applications from a wide range of threats.

DDoS Mitigation with AWS Shield

Distributed Denial of Service (DDoS) attacks are among the most disruptive threats to public-facing applications. These attacks attempt to overwhelm network resources, rendering them inaccessible to legitimate users. AWS Shield is a managed Distributed Denial of Service protection service designed to safeguard applications hosted on AWS against such attacks. This chapter explores the key features, capabilities, and implementation strategies for leveraging AWS Shield to mitigate DDoS risks effectively.

1. Understanding DDoS Attacks

DDoS attacks aim to exhaust application or network resources through various techniques:

- **Volumetric Attacks**: Saturating bandwidth with excessive traffic.
- **Protocol Attacks**: Exploiting network protocol vulnerabilities (e.g., SYN floods).
- **Application-Layer Attacks**: Targeting specific application endpoints, such as login pages, with resource-intensive requests.

The consequences of a successful DDoS attack include:

- Application downtime.
- Revenue loss.
- Damage to reputation and user trust.

2. AWS Shield Overview

AWS Shield provides automatic, always-on DDoS protection for applications running on AWS. It offers two tiers:

1. **AWS Shield Standard**:
   - Included at no additional cost for all AWS customers.
   - Protects against most common and basic DDoS attacks.
   - Integrated with AWS services like Amazon CloudFront and Elastic Load Balancing (ELB).
2. **AWS Shield Advanced**:
   - Offers enhanced protection for critical applications.
   - Includes advanced attack mitigation capabilities, cost protection, and access to the AWS DDoS Response Team (DRT).
   - Protects against more sophisticated and large-scale attacks.

3. Key Features of AWS Shield

1. **Real-Time Detection and Mitigation**:
   - Monitors traffic patterns using AWS global threat intelligence.
   - Automatically mitigates detected DDoS attacks with minimal latency.
2. **Integration with AWS Services**:
   - Natively integrated with CloudFront, Route 53, and ELB for edge-to-origin protection.
   - Optimized to scale dynamically in response to attack traffic.
3. **Cost Protection (Shield Advanced)**:
   - Prevents unexpected costs due to DDoS-related scaling or usage spikes.
4. **Advanced Reporting and Analytics**:
   - Provides detailed attack diagnostics via AWS WAF logs and Amazon CloudWatch metrics.

5. **AWS DDoS Response Team (DRT)** (Shield Advanced only):
   - Offers 24/7 support for identifying and mitigating complex DDoS attacks.
   - Includes tailored recommendations and incident response.

---

4. Using AWS Shield to Protect Your Application

1. **Enable AWS Shield Standard**:
   - Automatically enabled for all AWS services, requiring no additional configuration.
   - Provides baseline protection for most AWS-hosted applications.
2. **Upgrade to AWS Shield Advanced for Critical Applications**:
   - Recommended for applications requiring guaranteed availability, such as e-commerce platforms or financial services.
   - Activate Shield Advanced in the **AWS Management Console** under the **AWS Shield** service.
3. **Leverage Shield in Conjunction with Other AWS Services**:
   - Use **Amazon CloudFront** to distribute traffic across AWS edge locations, reducing direct exposure to backend servers.
   - Integrate with **AWS WAF** to filter malicious traffic based on custom rules.
4. **Monitor and Respond**:
   - Use **AWS Firewall Manager** to enforce Shield Advanced protections across your organization.
   - Configure alerts in **Amazon CloudWatch** to detect unusual traffic patterns or spikes.

---

5. Best Practices for DDoS Mitigation with AWS Shield

1. **Architect for Resiliency**:
   - Distribute workloads across multiple Availability Zones and regions.
   - Use Elastic Load Balancing to manage incoming traffic dynamically.
2. **Implement Layered Security**:
   - Combine AWS Shield with **AWS WAF** for application-layer defense.
   - Use **IAM policies** and **security groups** to restrict access to application resources.
3. **Optimize Edge-to-Origin Protection**:
   - Configure CloudFront to cache static content and reduce load on the origin server.
   - Enable AWS Shield Advanced for CloudFront distributions to protect against edge-based attacks.
4. **Monitor and Test Regularly**:
   - Regularly review traffic patterns and attack reports in the **AWS Shield Management Console**.
   - Conduct simulated DDoS attack tests to identify vulnerabilities and validate your defenses.
5. **Use Rate-Based Rules**:
   - Set rate-based rules in AWS WAF to limit the number of requests from individual IP addresses.
   - Protect against HTTP floods and other application-layer attacks.

---

6. Example Configuration: Protecting a Web Application

To illustrate the implementation of AWS Shield, consider the following scenario:

Objective: Protect a public-facing e-commerce website against DDoS attacks.

1. **Enable CloudFront**:
   - Deploy the website using an Amazon CloudFront distribution.
   - Use edge caching to reduce origin server exposure.
2. **Activate AWS Shield Advanced**:
   - Register the CloudFront distribution under Shield Advanced in the AWS Management Console.
   - Configure cost protection for unexpected scaling due to attack traffic.
3. **Configure AWS WAF**:
   - Apply a managed rule group to block SQL injection and XSS attempts.
   - Add a rate-based rule to limit requests from specific IPs.
4. **Monitor and Alert**:
   - Set up CloudWatch alarms to notify the security team of unusual traffic patterns.
   - Review attack diagnostics in the AWS Shield console for insights into attack vectors.

Conclusion

AWS Shield provides robust, scalable, and automated protection against DDoS attacks, ensuring the availability and security of public-facing applications. By combining Shield with other AWS services like CloudFront and AWS WAF, you can build a multi-layered defense strategy tailored to your application's needs.

Threat Detection Using Amazon GuardDuty

In today's evolving digital landscape, maintaining the security of cloud-based networks is a critical priority for organizations. Amazon GuardDuty offers an intelligent, managed threat detection service that leverages machine learning, anomaly detection, and integrated threat intelligence to identify potential security risks across AWS environments. This chapter explores how to use Amazon GuardDuty to proactively detect, investigate, and respond to security threats in your AWS network.

1. Overview of Amazon GuardDuty

Amazon GuardDuty is a managed threat detection service designed to monitor malicious or unauthorized behavior across AWS accounts and workloads. It provides real-time alerts for issues such as compromised instances, unauthorized access attempts, or malicious IP traffic.

Key Features:

- **Anomaly Detection**: Uses machine learning to identify unusual patterns in network activity.
- **Integrated Threat Intelligence**: Incorporates AWS security research data and external threat feeds for robust detection.
- **Multi-Account Monitoring**: Supports centralized monitoring across multiple AWS accounts via AWS Organizations.
- **Serverless Architecture**: Operates without requiring additional hardware or software installation.

2. How GuardDuty Works

1. **Data Sources**: GuardDuty analyzes data from AWS CloudTrail, Amazon VPC Flow Logs, and DNS logs to detect suspicious activity.
2. **Threat Intelligence**: Cross-references network activity with known threat databases to identify risks like malicious IPs or domains.
3. **Behavioral Insights**: Employs machine learning to detect anomalies in user behavior, such as unauthorized API calls or unusual geographic access.
4. **Findings and Alerts**: Automatically generates findings with detailed information, including the nature of the threat and recommended actions.

3. Key Use Cases

1. **Unauthorized Access Detection**:
   - Identifies brute-force login attempts or unauthorized access to AWS resources.
2. **Malicious Network Activity**:
   - Detects outbound traffic from compromised instances to known malicious IP addresses.
3. **Compromised EC2 Instances**:
   - Alerts when EC2 instances exhibit unusual behavior, such as communicating with command-and-control servers.
4. **Data Exfiltration**:
   - Monitors for potential data theft attempts by analyzing DNS queries and network traffic.

4. Setting Up Amazon GuardDuty

Step 1: Enabling GuardDuty

- Navigate to the **Amazon GuardDuty** console.
- Click **Enable GuardDuty**. If using AWS Organizations, you can enable it across multiple accounts from the **Management Account**.

Step 2: Configuring Data Sources

- Ensure that **CloudTrail**, **VPC Flow Logs**, and **DNS logs** are enabled for your AWS environment.
- GuardDuty automatically ingests data from these sources.

Step 3: Reviewing Findings

- Access findings in the **GuardDuty Console** or via the **AWS CLI**.
- Findings are categorized as low, medium, or high severity, helping prioritize responses.

Step 4: Setting Up Notifications

- Configure Amazon SNS to receive alerts about high-severity findings.
- Integrate with AWS Security Hub for a centralized view of security alerts.

---

5. Interpreting GuardDuty Findings

GuardDuty findings include detailed information about the threat, its source, and recommended actions.

Example Finding: Unauthorized API Call

- **Severity**: High
- **Description**: API calls from an IP address associated with malicious activity.
- **Recommended Action**: Use IAM policies to revoke the compromised user's permissions and investigate the activity with AWS CloudTrail.

Example Finding: Cryptocurrency Mining

- **Severity**: Medium
- **Description**: EC2 instance communicating with a known cryptocurrency mining pool.
- **Recommended Action**: Isolate the instance and review security group configurations.

---

6. Integrating GuardDuty with Other AWS Services

1. **AWS Security Hub**:
   - Aggregate GuardDuty findings alongside security alerts from other AWS services.
   - Automate incident responses with AWS Security Hub's custom workflows.
2. **Amazon CloudWatch**:
   - Create CloudWatch alarms for GuardDuty findings.
   - Trigger automated remediation workflows using AWS Lambda.
3. **AWS Lambda**:
   - Use Lambda functions to automatically remediate threats, such as terminating compromised instances.
4. **AWS Config**:
   - Continuously monitor compliance with security best practices by integrating GuardDuty with AWS Config rules.

---

7. Best Practices for Using GuardDuty

1. **Enable Multi-Region Monitoring**:
   - Activate GuardDuty in all regions to detect region-specific threats.
2. **Implement Centralized Management**:
   - Use AWS Organizations to manage GuardDuty findings across multiple accounts.
3. **Respond to High-Severity Findings Immediately**:
   - Focus on findings classified as high severity and automate responses where possible.
4. **Regularly Review Findings**:
   - Perform routine reviews of GuardDuty findings to detect trends and refine security policies.
5. **Combine with AWS WAF**:
   - Use AWS WAF to block malicious IPs identified by GuardDuty.

---

8. Case Study: Mitigating a Security Threat

Scenario:

A GuardDuty finding indicates that an EC2 instance is communicating with a malicious IP.

Steps Taken:

1. **Investigation**:
   - Access findings in the GuardDuty console and cross-reference with VPC Flow Logs.
   - Confirm the instance's communication with a malicious IP.
2. **Mitigation**:
   - Isolate the instance by modifying its security group to deny outbound traffic.
   - Terminate the instance if necessary and revoke IAM credentials associated with the instance.
3. **Prevention**:
   - Update IAM roles and security group policies.
   - Enable MFA for all users.

Conclusion

Amazon GuardDuty is a powerful tool for proactive threat detection and response in AWS environments. By leveraging its machine learning capabilities and seamless integration with other AWS services, organizations can enhance their cloud security posture and reduce the risk of security incidents.

Use Cases and Practical Applications

Building a Multi-Region Network Architecture

As businesses increasingly operate on a global scale, ensuring high availability, low latency, and disaster recovery capabilities becomes essential. A multi-region network architecture in AWS offers an effective solution for these requirements by distributing resources across multiple AWS regions. This chapter focuses on the design, implementation, and best practices for building robust and efficient multi-region network architectures using AWS networking services.

1. Introduction to Multi-Region Networking

A multi-region network architecture involves deploying AWS resources and services across multiple AWS regions to meet business objectives such as:

- **High Availability**: Minimizing downtime by distributing workloads across regions.
- **Disaster Recovery**: Ensuring business continuity in the event of a region-specific failure.
- **Global Coverage**: Providing low-latency access for geographically dispersed users.
- **Regulatory Compliance**: Adhering to data residency requirements by keeping data in specific regions.

2. Core Components of a Multi-Region Network

Building a multi-region architecture involves leveraging the following AWS components:

1. **Amazon VPC**:
   - Deploy Virtual Private Clouds (VPCs) in each region to isolate and secure your resources.
2. **AWS Transit Gateway**:
   - Establish a hub-and-spoke model to connect VPCs across multiple regions.
3. **AWS Direct Connect**:
   - Use private connections to extend on-premises data centers to multiple AWS regions.
4. **Amazon Route 53**:
   - Implement global DNS routing policies for efficient traffic management.
5. **AWS Global Accelerator**:
   - Optimize latency and improve performance for global applications.
6. **Amazon CloudFront**:
   - Distribute content through an edge network to enhance user experience.

3. Designing a Multi-Region Network Architecture

Step 1: Define Business Requirements

- Identify critical objectives such as availability, latency, compliance, and cost efficiency.
- Determine the regions required to meet user demands and regulatory needs.

Step 2: Plan Network Connectivity

- Design VPCs in each region with non-overlapping IP address ranges.
- Use Transit Gateway to interconnect VPCs within and across regions.

Step 3: Implement Traffic Distribution

- Configure Route 53 DNS routing policies such as geolocation or latency-based routing.
- Deploy Global Accelerator to direct traffic to the optimal region dynamically.

Step 4: Ensure Data Replication

- Use services like Amazon S3 cross-region replication and DynamoDB Global Tables to synchronize data across regions.

Step 5: Establish Disaster Recovery

- Leverage AWS services like Elastic Load Balancing (ELB) and Auto Scaling Groups for failover capabilities.
- Test disaster recovery plans regularly to validate readiness.

---

4. Traffic Management in Multi-Region Architectures

AWS provides several tools for managing traffic in multi-region setups:

1. **Amazon Route 53**:
   - Use latency-based routing to direct users to the nearest region.
   - Configure failover routing for disaster recovery scenarios.
2. **AWS Global Accelerator**:
   - Provides static IP addresses for applications.
   - Automatically redirects traffic to the region with optimal health and performance.
3. **Content Delivery with Amazon CloudFront**:
   - Use edge locations to cache and serve content, reducing latency for end users.

---

5. Data Synchronization and Consistency

Maintaining data consistency across multiple regions is critical for seamless user experiences. AWS offers various services for this purpose:

1. **Amazon S3 Cross-Region Replication**:
   - Automatically replicates objects in S3 buckets across regions.
2. **DynamoDB Global Tables**:
   - Provide multi-master, multi-region replication for low-latency database access.
3. **Amazon RDS Read Replicas**:
   - Set up read replicas in different regions for distributed read workloads.
4. **AWS DataSync**:
   - Simplifies large-scale data transfers between regions.

---

6. Security Considerations

Ensuring security in a multi-region architecture involves:

- **Encryption**:
  - Enable encryption at rest and in transit for all data.

- Use AWS Key Management Service (KMS) for key management across regions.
- **IAM Policies**:
  - Define region-specific IAM roles and permissions to restrict access.
- **Firewall Rules**:
  - Configure Security Groups and Network Access Control Lists (NACLs) for each region.
- **Traffic Inspection**:
  - Use AWS Network Firewall to inspect traffic between regions.

---

7. Monitoring and Optimization

To maintain optimal performance, monitor your multi-region network using:

1. **Amazon CloudWatch**:
   - Set up metrics and alarms for cross-region traffic and resource health.
2. **AWS CloudTrail**:
   - Monitor API activity across regions for auditing and compliance.
3. **AWS Trusted Advisor**:
   - Receive recommendations for optimizing multi-region resource usage.
4. **Cost Optimization**:
   - Use Cost Explorer to identify and manage cross-region data transfer costs.

---

8. Best Practices for Multi-Region Architectures

1. **Plan for Failure**:
   - Design for fault tolerance by distributing resources across regions.
   - Regularly test failover mechanisms.
2. **Use Standardized Configurations**:
   - Automate deployment using AWS CloudFormation templates for consistency.
3. **Minimize Data Transfer Costs**:
   - Leverage caching and local processing to reduce inter-region traffic.
4. **Optimize Latency**:
   - Use Route 53 latency-based routing and Global Accelerator for performance improvements.
5. **Regular Updates**:
   - Keep your architecture updated with the latest AWS features and best practices.

---

9. Case Study: A Global E-Commerce Platform

Scenario: A global e-commerce company requires a network that ensures low-latency access for users in North America, Europe, and Asia-Pacific, with built-in disaster recovery.

Solution:

1. Deploy VPCs in AWS regions near major customer bases (e.g., N. Virginia, Frankfurt, Singapore).
2. Use AWS Transit Gateway to connect VPCs across regions.
3. Implement Route 53 for latency-based routing and failover.
4. Use DynamoDB Global Tables for inventory synchronization.
5. Leverage S3 cross-region replication for image and video assets.

Outcome: The company achieved high availability and seamless user experiences across regions while maintaining cost efficiency.

Conclusion

Building a multi-region network architecture on AWS enables organizations to meet the demands of modern, global business operations. With a combination of AWS networking tools, best practices, and a focus on scalability, security, and reliability, you can ensure that your network architecture supports your enterprise's growth and resilience.

Setting Up a Secure Web Application on AWS

Deploying a secure web application on AWS involves leveraging the platform's robust services and tools to create an infrastructure that ensures scalability, high availability, and security. This chapter provides a detailed guide on building a secure web application environment using AWS resources and implementing best practices for security and performance optimization.

1. Overview of Secure Web Applications

A secure web application protects user data, mitigates threats, and ensures compliance with industry standards. Key objectives for secure web application deployment include:

- **Data Protection**: Safeguarding sensitive data in transit and at rest.
- **Threat Mitigation**: Preventing unauthorized access and attacks, such as DDoS.
- **High Availability**: Ensuring minimal downtime through scalable architectures.
- **Regulatory Compliance**: Adhering to legal and industry requirements for data security.

2. Core Components of a Secure Web Application on AWS

Building a secure web application architecture on AWS typically involves the following components:

1. **Amazon VPC**:
   - Isolate resources within a Virtual Private Cloud (VPC) for enhanced security.
   - Use subnets to segregate public-facing and private resources.
2. **Elastic Load Balancer (ELB)**:
   - Distribute traffic efficiently across application instances.
   - Support secure connections with SSL/TLS certificates.
3. **Amazon EC2 or AWS Fargate**:
   - Host the application using scalable compute services.
   - Apply security group rules to control inbound and outbound traffic.
4. **Amazon RDS or DynamoDB**:
   - Store application data securely in managed database services.
   - Implement encryption at rest and in transit.
5. **Amazon Route 53**:
   - Configure DNS settings for seamless user access.
   - Use health checks to route traffic to healthy endpoints.
6. **Amazon CloudFront**:
   - Enhance performance and security with Content Delivery Network (CDN).
   - Enable HTTPS and block malicious traffic at edge locations.
7. **AWS WAF and Shield**:
   - Protect against common web exploits and DDoS attacks.

3. Steps to Set Up a Secure Web Application

Step 1: Design the VPC

- Create a VPC with subnets for public and private resources.
- Deploy public-facing components (e.g., ELB) in public subnets.
- Place application servers and databases in private subnets for security.

Step 2: Launch and Configure Compute Resources

- Use Amazon EC2 or AWS Fargate to deploy the web application.
- Assign security groups to define allowed IP ranges and ports.
- Enable Auto Scaling to ensure high availability and handle traffic spikes.

Step 3: Set Up Load Balancing

- Use an Application Load Balancer (ALB) to distribute HTTP/HTTPS traffic.
- Install SSL/TLS certificates using AWS Certificate Manager (ACM).

Step 4: Implement Data Layer Security

- Use Amazon RDS or DynamoDB with encryption enabled.
- Set up IAM roles to restrict database access to authorized services.
- Enable Multi-AZ deployments for high availability.

Step 5: Optimize Performance with CloudFront

- Distribute static and dynamic content globally through CloudFront.
- Configure HTTPS for secure communication between users and edge locations.

Step 6: Protect with AWS WAF and Shield

- Define AWS WAF rules to block SQL injection, XSS, and other exploits.
- Enable AWS Shield Standard (included) for DDoS protection or AWS Shield Advanced for enhanced security.

Step 7: Enable Logging and Monitoring

- Use Amazon CloudWatch to monitor application performance and detect anomalies.
- Enable VPC Flow Logs and CloudTrail for auditing network and API activities.

---

4. Security Best Practices

1. **Secure Communication**:
   - Always use HTTPS for secure communication between users and the application.
   - Use ACM to manage SSL/TLS certificates.
2. **Data Encryption**:
   - Encrypt sensitive data at rest using AWS KMS.
   - Enable encryption for S3 buckets, RDS databases, and DynamoDB tables.
3. **Identity and Access Management (IAM)**:
   - Use IAM roles for resource-level access control.
   - Apply the principle of least privilege when assigning permissions.
4. **Web Application Firewall (WAF)**:
   - Create rules to filter out common web vulnerabilities.
   - Regularly update rules to address new threats.
5. **DDoS Mitigation**:
   - Enable AWS Shield to protect against volumetric attacks.
   - Configure Route 53 health checks and failover routing for resilience.

---

5. Performance Optimization

1. **Auto Scaling**:

- Set up Auto Scaling Groups to adjust compute resources dynamically.
- Define scaling policies based on metrics like CPU utilization.

2. **Caching**:
   - Use Amazon ElastiCache for Redis or Memcached to reduce database load.
   - Enable CloudFront caching for frequently accessed content.

3. **Latency Reduction**:
   - Deploy resources closer to users by selecting appropriate AWS regions.
   - Use Route 53 latency-based routing.

4. **Monitoring and Alerts**:
   - Set up CloudWatch alarms for critical metrics like response time and error rates.
   - Use AWS Trusted Advisor to identify performance improvement opportunities.

---

6. Use Case: An E-Commerce Platform

Scenario:
An e-commerce company needs to deploy a secure, scalable web application with high availability and low latency for users in North America and Europe.

Solution:

1. Deploy the application using EC2 instances in multiple Availability Zones.
2. Use ALB with SSL/TLS termination for secure communication.
3. Configure Route 53 with geolocation-based routing to direct users to the nearest region.
4. Enable CloudFront for caching and fast content delivery.
5. Protect the application with AWS WAF and Shield.

Outcome:
The company achieved a secure, scalable, and high-performing web application with global coverage and robust threat protection.

Conclusion

Setting up a secure web application on AWS requires careful planning, the use of AWS's security and networking tools, and adherence to best practices. By implementing a combination of VPCs, load balancers, security groups, and advanced AWS services like WAF and Shield, you can ensure your web application remains secure, scalable, and highly available.

Enabling Real-Time Streaming with AWS Networking

Real-time streaming applications require low latency, high throughput, and robust network architectures to handle dynamic data flows. AWS provides a suite of services that enable seamless real-time streaming for various use cases, such as video streaming, IoT data processing, and live analytics. This chapter focuses on how to set up real-time streaming architectures using AWS networking tools and services.

1. Overview of Real-Time Streaming on AWS

Real-time streaming involves the continuous flow of data between producers and consumers, ensuring minimal delay. Key use cases include:

- **Video Streaming**: Platforms like live sports or webinars.
- **IoT Applications**: Real-time device telemetry and monitoring.
- **Data Analytics**: Processing logs or user behavior data for insights.
- **Gaming**: Low-latency connections for multiplayer games.

AWS supports these use cases through services such as **Amazon Kinesis**, **AWS Elemental Media Services**, and **Amazon CloudFront**, alongside foundational networking components.

2. Core AWS Services for Real-Time Streaming

Amazon Kinesis

- **Kinesis Data Streams**: Enables real-time ingestion of high-throughput data for analytics.
- **Kinesis Video Streams**: Streams video data from connected devices.
- **Kinesis Data Firehose**: Delivers data to destinations like Amazon S3 or Redshift for further processing.

AWS Elemental Media Services

- **MediaLive**: Encodes live video for real-time delivery.
- **MediaPackage**: Prepares and protects video streams for distribution.
- **MediaStore**: Optimized storage for streaming media content.

Amazon CloudFront

- Distributes content globally with low latency.
- Supports live and on-demand video streaming with high availability.

Amazon Route 53

- Configures DNS routing for streaming endpoints, ensuring optimal resource access.

AWS Direct Connect

- Provides high-bandwidth, low-latency dedicated connections for real-time streaming needs.

3. Setting Up a Real-Time Streaming Architecture

Step 1: Define Streaming Requirements

- **Latency**: Specify acceptable delays for data or video delivery.
- **Throughput**: Estimate data volume to select the appropriate AWS services.
- **End Users**: Understand where your audience is located to optimize the network setup.

Step 2: Ingest Data or Video Streams

- Use **Kinesis Data Streams** for high-throughput data ingestion.
- For live video, configure **AWS Elemental MediaLive** to encode and send streams for processing.

Step 3: Process Streaming Data

- Implement real-time analytics pipelines with **Kinesis Analytics**.
- Use **AWS Lambda** functions to trigger actions based on data flows.

Step 4: Distribute Streams to Users

- Deliver content through **Amazon CloudFront** for low latency and global reach.
- Use **AWS Elemental MediaPackage** to format and protect live video streams.

Step 5: Enable High Availability and Fault Tolerance

- Distribute resources across multiple AWS regions and Availability Zones.
- Use **Amazon S3** as a fallback for content storage in case of streaming disruptions.

Step 6: Optimize Network Performance

- Enable **latency-based routing** with **Amazon Route 53**.
- Use **Direct Connect** for reliable connections when high bandwidth is needed.

---

4. Security Considerations for Streaming Applications

1. **Encryption**:
   - Use **SSL/TLS** for secure communication between streaming services and end users.
   - Encrypt data streams with AWS KMS.
2. **Access Control**:
   - Implement IAM policies to control access to streaming resources.
   - Use **Amazon Cognito** for end-user authentication.
3. **DDoS Protection**:
   - Enable **AWS Shield** to protect against DDoS attacks.
   - Configure **AWS WAF** to block malicious traffic targeting streaming endpoints.
4. **Monitoring and Alerts**:
   - Monitor data streams using **Amazon CloudWatch**.
   - Set up alarms for throughput, latency, and error metrics.

---

5. Example Use Case: Live Video Streaming Platform

Scenario:
A media company wants to deliver live sports events globally with minimal delay and high reliability.

Solution:

1. Use **AWS Elemental MediaLive** to encode live video feeds.

2. Store video fragments temporarily in **MediaStore**.
3. Package the video for adaptive bitrate streaming with **MediaPackage**.
4. Deliver streams globally using **Amazon CloudFront**.
5. Optimize routing with **Amazon Route 53** for latency-based distribution.

Outcome:
The company achieves a seamless streaming experience with reduced latency and high scalability, supporting millions of concurrent viewers.

---

6. Best Practices for Real-Time Streaming

- **Optimize Bandwidth Usage**:
  - Use adaptive bitrate streaming to adjust quality based on user bandwidth.
  - Compress video and data streams efficiently.
- **Monitor Streaming Metrics**:
  - Track performance metrics such as throughput, latency, and error rates with **CloudWatch**.
  - Use real-time dashboards to identify and resolve issues proactively.
- **Leverage Edge Locations**:
  - Deliver content closer to users by using **CloudFront edge locations**.
  - Enable caching for static components of streaming applications.
- **Ensure Scalability**:
  - Use **Auto Scaling** for compute resources handling stream processing.
  - Adjust Kinesis shard capacity dynamically based on data volume.

Conclusion

AWS provides a robust ecosystem for enabling real-time streaming applications, catering to a wide range of use cases. By combining services like Amazon Kinesis, AWS Elemental Media Services, and CloudFront with best practices for performance and security, you can deliver reliable, scalable, and secure real-time streaming experiences to your users.

Networking for IoT Applications on AWS

The Internet of Things (IoT) ecosystem has rapidly expanded across industries, connecting devices to collect, process, and analyze real-time data. Networking is a critical component of IoT applications, enabling devices to communicate securely and efficiently. AWS offers a range of tools and services to build scalable and reliable IoT solutions, supported by robust networking architectures.

1. Overview of IoT Applications on AWS

IoT applications span various domains, such as:

- **Smart Cities**: Traffic monitoring, energy management, and public safety.
- **Industrial IoT (IIoT)**: Predictive maintenance, robotics, and process optimization.
- **Healthcare**: Wearable devices for patient monitoring.
- **Consumer IoT**: Smart home devices, connected appliances.

Key networking requirements for IoT include:

- **Low Latency**: Real-time data transmission.
- **High Scalability**: Supporting millions of connected devices.
- **Security**: Protecting sensitive device and user data.
- **Reliability**: Ensuring continuous communication between devices and cloud services.

2. AWS Services for IoT Networking

AWS provides a comprehensive suite of services to facilitate IoT networking:

AWS IoT Core

- Manages device connections and message routing.
- Supports MQTT, HTTP, and WebSocket protocols for communication.
- Provides secure device authentication and authorization.

AWS IoT Greengrass

- Extends cloud capabilities to edge devices.
- Enables devices to run AWS Lambda functions locally.
- Facilitates offline operation with periodic cloud synchronization.

AWS IoT SiteWise

- Collects and processes data from industrial equipment.
- Provides real-time insights into industrial operations.

AWS IoT Analytics

- Processes, stores, and analyzes IoT data streams.
- Integrates with Amazon S3, Amazon Redshift, and Amazon QuickSight.

Amazon Kinesis

- Streams real-time data from IoT devices for analytics and storage.

AWS CloudFront

- Accelerates IoT data delivery globally with low latency.
- Provides content caching for IoT applications with high read demands.

Amazon Route 53

- Directs device traffic to optimal endpoints using latency-based routing.

---

3. Designing a Network for IoT Applications

Step 1: Establish Device Connectivity

- Use **AWS IoT Core** to securely connect devices using lightweight protocols like MQTT.
- Configure unique device endpoints for authentication and secure data exchange.

Step 2: Enable Edge Processing

- Deploy **AWS IoT Greengrass** to enable edge devices to process data locally.
- Reduce latency by minimizing the need for frequent cloud interactions.

Step 3: Build a Reliable Data Stream

- Stream data to AWS services using **Amazon Kinesis** or **AWS IoT Core Rules**.
- Define rules for routing IoT data to AWS services like Lambda, S3, or DynamoDB.

Step 4: Secure Data Transmission

- Encrypt data in transit using TLS.
- Implement device authentication through X.509 certificates.

Step 5: Scale IoT Networks

- Use **Auto Scaling** for backend services handling IoT data.
- Leverage **AWS Direct Connect** for high-bandwidth, low-latency connections.

---

4. Security Considerations for IoT Networks

Security is paramount in IoT applications due to the vast number of devices and data exchanged. AWS IoT provides the following security measures:

1. **Device Authentication**:
   - Use X.509 certificates or Amazon Cognito for secure device authentication.
   - Integrate AWS IoT Core with IAM for fine-grained access control.
2. **Data Encryption**:
   - Encrypt messages with TLS during transmission.
   - Use AWS Key Management Service (KMS) for secure key management.
3. **DDoS Protection**:
   - Deploy **AWS Shield** to protect IoT endpoints from attacks.
   - Implement **AWS WAF** to filter malicious traffic.
4. **Monitoring and Auditing**:
   - Use **AWS IoT Device Defender** for continuous monitoring of IoT devices.
   - Configure CloudWatch alarms for unusual traffic patterns.

5. Example Use Case: Smart Home IoT Network

Scenario:
A company wants to build a smart home IoT system connecting appliances, sensors, and devices to provide real-time control and monitoring for users globally.

Solution:

1. Use **AWS IoT Core** for device registration and secure communication.
2. Deploy **AWS IoT Greengrass** for local processing of sensor data.
3. Stream data to **Amazon Kinesis** for real-time analytics and storage in DynamoDB.
4. Accelerate global delivery of device commands using **AWS CloudFront**.
5. Secure the network with TLS encryption and X.509 certificates.

Outcome:
The smart home system enables seamless device interactions, low-latency command execution, and robust security for end users.

---

6. Best Practices for IoT Networking on AWS

- **Optimize Protocol Usage**:
  - Use MQTT for lightweight, low-bandwidth communication.
  - Leverage WebSocket for real-time interactions with web applications.
- **Ensure High Availability**:
  - Deploy devices across multiple Availability Zones.
  - Use failover configurations with **Amazon Route 53**.
- **Monitor Network Health**:
  - Use **CloudWatch Metrics** to track device connectivity and data throughput.
  - Enable **AWS IoT Device Defender** to detect anomalies in device behavior.
- **Plan for Scalability**:
  - Use shard scaling in **Amazon Kinesis** for data-intensive IoT applications.
  - Employ AWS Global Accelerator for optimal data routing.

Conclusion

IoT networking on AWS empowers organizations to create highly scalable, secure, and reliable IoT solutions. By combining services like AWS IoT Core, Greengrass, and Kinesis with robust networking practices, you can unlock the full potential of IoT applications.

Running Big Data Workloads Over AWS Networks

Big data workloads are critical for modern enterprises aiming to derive insights from massive datasets. These workloads require robust networking to ensure high throughput, low latency, and reliable data transfer. AWS provides a comprehensive ecosystem of services and tools to optimize big data operations, enabling efficient data processing, storage, and analysis.

---

1. Overview of Big Data Workloads on AWS

Big data workloads typically involve:

- **Data Collection**: Aggregating structured and unstructured data from various sources.
- **Data Processing**: Transforming raw data into usable formats through batch or real-time processing.
- **Data Storage**: Persisting data in scalable and accessible repositories.
- **Data Analysis**: Applying machine learning or analytics to extract actionable insights.

Networking plays a vital role in ensuring seamless communication between data sources, processing engines, and storage systems.

---

2. AWS Networking Tools for Big Data

AWS offers specialized services that align with the networking needs of big data workloads:

Amazon S3

- Provides scalable storage for raw and processed data.
- Supports high-speed data transfer through **Amazon S3 Transfer Acceleration**.

AWS Direct Connect

- Establishes dedicated connections between on-premises data centers and AWS for large-scale data transfers.
- Reduces latency and ensures consistent bandwidth.

Amazon Kinesis

- Streams real-time data for analytics and processing.
- Facilitates low-latency communication between data producers and consumers.

AWS DataSync

- Automates data transfers between on-premises systems and AWS storage.
- Ensures secure and efficient data movement.

AWS Snow Family

- Supports offline data transfer for large datasets using **Snowball**, **Snowmobile**, and **Snowcone** devices.
- Ideal for scenarios with limited network connectivity.

Amazon EMR

- Runs big data frameworks like Apache Hadoop and Spark in AWS.
- Uses **Elastic Network Interfaces (ENIs)** for high-bandwidth connections between cluster nodes.

AWS Global Accelerator

- Optimizes global data transfers by routing traffic through AWS's global network backbone.

---

3. Designing a Network for Big Data Workloads

Step 1: Optimize Data Ingestion

- Use **Amazon Kinesis** to stream data from IoT devices, logs, or applications.
- Leverage **AWS Direct Connect** or **DataSync** for bulk data transfers.

Step 2: Build a Reliable Processing Pipeline

- Deploy **Amazon EMR** for distributed data processing.
- Ensure nodes within EMR clusters communicate over private subnets for security and performance.

Step 3: Enhance Data Storage Efficiency

- Store data in **Amazon S3** for scalability and durability.
- Use **S3 Transfer Acceleration** to expedite uploads from distributed data sources.

Step 4: Accelerate Data Analysis

- Integrate **Amazon Redshift** or **Amazon Athena** with S3 for query-based analytics.
- Route queries through **AWS Global Accelerator** to minimize latency.

Step 5: Monitor and Optimize Network Traffic

- Use **Amazon CloudWatch** to monitor data transfer metrics.
- Configure **AWS Trusted Advisor** to optimize network usage and cost.

---

4. Security Considerations for Big Data Networks

Big data workloads often involve sensitive information. AWS networking provides several security measures to protect data in transit and at rest:

1. **Encrypt Data Transfers**:
   - Use **TLS** to encrypt communication between data producers, consumers, and storage services.
   - Enable **AWS Key Management Service (KMS)** for key management.
2. **Implement Network Isolation**:
   - Deploy workloads in private subnets using **VPC**.
   - Restrict access using **Security Groups** and **Network ACLs**.
3. **Monitor for Anomalies**:
   - Use **Amazon GuardDuty** to detect suspicious activity.
   - Enable **VPC Flow Logs** to track network traffic.
4. **Apply IAM Policies**:
   - Use granular policies to control access to data processing and storage resources.
   - Audit roles and permissions regularly.

---

5. Example Use Case: Processing Log Data for Real-Time Insights

Scenario:
A company collects server logs from global data centers and processes them in real time to detect anomalies and optimize server performance.

Solution:

1. Use **Amazon Kinesis Data Streams** to ingest log data from servers.
2. Deploy an **Amazon EMR** cluster to process and analyze logs.
3. Store processed logs in **Amazon S3** with lifecycle policies for archiving.
4. Use **Amazon QuickSight** to visualize insights derived from log data.

Outcome:
The company achieves real-time visibility into server performance, enabling proactive issue resolution and performance optimization.

---

6. Best Practices for Running Big Data Workloads Over AWS Networks

- **Minimize Data Transfer Costs**:
  - Use **VPC endpoints** to avoid public internet traffic.
  - Schedule bulk data transfers during off-peak hours.
- **Leverage Data Partitioning**:
  - Optimize data storage and query performance by partitioning datasets in **Amazon S3** or **Redshift**.
- **Ensure High Availability**:
  - Deploy processing clusters across multiple Availability Zones.
  - Configure **Route 53** for failover routing.
- **Monitor Network Performance**:
  - Use **CloudWatch Logs Insights** to analyze network bottlenecks.
  - Implement alarms for unusual traffic patterns.

Conclusion

Networking is a cornerstone of big data workloads on AWS. By leveraging services like Amazon Kinesis, EMR, and S3, combined with robust networking practices, organizations can handle large-scale data processing with ease.

Emerging Trends and Future of AWS Networking

Edge Networking and 5G Integration in AWS

The growing adoption of edge computing and 5G networks has ushered in a new era of connectivity, transforming the way organizations handle latency-sensitive and real-time workloads. AWS provides comprehensive tools and services to seamlessly integrate edge networking with 5G technology, enabling businesses to enhance application performance, reduce latency, and deliver superior user experiences.

1. Understanding Edge Networking

Edge networking involves placing compute and data resources closer to the end-users or devices that generate and consume data. This proximity reduces latency, enhances real-time processing, and minimizes the bandwidth required for data transfer to centralized cloud regions.

Key benefits of edge networking include:

- **Reduced Latency**: Process data near the source for real-time responsiveness.
- **Optimized Bandwidth Usage**: Reduce the volume of data sent to central cloud regions.
- **Enhanced Privacy and Security**: Process sensitive data locally before transmitting it over the network.

2. Role of 5G in AWS Networking

5G, the fifth generation of cellular network technology, complements edge networking by providing:

- **Ultra-Low Latency**: Enables high-speed data transmission, crucial for real-time workloads.
- **Massive Connectivity**: Supports a high density of IoT devices and sensors.
- **Increased Bandwidth**: Facilitates the transfer of large datasets quickly and efficiently.

AWS leverages 5G technology to power next-generation applications, such as autonomous vehicles, industrial automation, and smart cities.

3. AWS Edge Networking Services

AWS offers several edge networking services to integrate with 5G technologies:

AWS Wavelength

- Extends AWS infrastructure to 5G networks, enabling ultra-low latency applications.
- Deploy compute and storage resources directly in 5G edge locations managed by telecom providers.
- Ideal for applications like AR/VR, autonomous driving, and IoT.

AWS Outposts

- Provides a fully managed infrastructure to run AWS services on-premises.
- Enables edge computing for latency-sensitive workloads and seamless integration with AWS regions.

AWS IoT Greengrass

- Brings AWS compute and machine learning capabilities to edge devices.
- Processes and analyzes IoT data locally, reducing latency and bandwidth consumption.

Amazon CloudFront

- A global content delivery network (CDN) for securely delivering data, videos, applications, and APIs.
- Supports edge locations for caching and accelerating content delivery.

AWS Local Zones

- Places AWS compute, storage, and database services closer to end-users in select locations.
- Enhances latency-sensitive use cases like gaming, live streaming, and machine learning inference.

---

4. Use Cases for AWS Edge Networking and 5G

1. **Autonomous Vehicles**:
   - Process high-frequency sensor data locally using **AWS Wavelength** to make real-time driving decisions.
   - Use 5G connectivity to exchange data with cloud regions for advanced analytics.
2. **Industrial Automation**:
   - Deploy **AWS IoT Greengrass** on manufacturing equipment to enable real-time monitoring and control.
   - Use **AWS Outposts** to manage workloads that require low-latency processing on-site.
3. **Healthcare Applications**:
   - Support telemedicine and remote patient monitoring with **AWS Local Zones** for low-latency video streaming.
   - Use 5G to securely transfer medical imaging data to central AWS regions for analysis.
4. **Smart Cities**:
   - Enable real-time data analysis for traffic management using **AWS Wavelength** at 5G edge locations.
   - Process IoT sensor data locally to optimize resource usage and improve city services.

---

5. Designing an Edge and 5G Network with AWS

Step 1: Identify Latency-Sensitive Components

- Determine which parts of your application require low latency, such as video processing or IoT device communication.

Step 2: Choose Appropriate AWS Services

- Use **AWS Wavelength** for applications that need ultra-low latency.
- Deploy **AWS IoT Greengrass** for localized data processing on edge devices.

Step 3: Leverage 5G Connectivity

- Partner with telecom providers that support **AWS Wavelength** for seamless integration with 5G networks.
- Optimize network configurations to balance local and cloud-based processing.

Step 4: Monitor and Optimize Performance

- Use **Amazon CloudWatch** to monitor the performance of edge applications.
- Optimize content delivery with **Amazon CloudFront** edge locations.

---

6. Security Considerations for Edge and 5G Integration

- **Data Encryption**: Ensure end-to-end encryption for data in transit using AWS Key Management Service (KMS).
- **Access Control**: Implement strict IAM policies for edge resources to prevent unauthorized access.
- **Local Threat Detection**: Use **Amazon GuardDuty** and **AWS IoT Device Defender** for monitoring edge networks.
- **Regular Updates**: Keep edge devices and infrastructure updated to mitigate vulnerabilities.

---

7. Best Practices for Edge Networking with 5G

1. **Minimize Data Transfers**:
   - Use edge computing for pre-processing and send only essential data to AWS regions.
2. **Design for Scalability**:
   - Leverage **AWS Wavelength** and **Local Zones** to scale applications across multiple 5G edge locations.
3. **Optimize Costs**:
   - Use **AWS Cost Explorer** to analyze the cost impact of deploying workloads on the edge.
4. **Implement Redundancy**:
   - Deploy resources across multiple edge locations to ensure high availability.

---

8. Future Trends in Edge and 5G Networking

The convergence of edge computing and 5G is expected to drive innovations in:

- **Augmented and Virtual Reality**: Enhanced user experiences for gaming, education, and training.
- **Smart Manufacturing**: Fully automated production lines with real-time feedback loops.
- **Remote Work and Collaboration**: Seamless virtual meetings and real-time file sharing.

Conclusion

AWS's edge networking services, combined with the power of 5G, are transforming the way businesses handle latency-sensitive workloads. By strategically leveraging tools like **AWS Wavelength**, **AWS IoT Greengrass**, and **CloudFront**, organizations can deliver exceptional performance and scalability.

Exploring AWS's Role in the Metaverse

The metaverse, a digital ecosystem that integrates augmented reality (AR), virtual reality (VR), and blockchain technologies, is poised to redefine how individuals and organizations interact online. AWS, with its robust networking and compute capabilities, plays a critical role in powering this interconnected digital universe. This chapter explores how AWS technologies enable the development, deployment, and scaling of applications for the metaverse.

1. Understanding the Metaverse

The metaverse combines virtual and physical realities, offering users immersive experiences for:

- **Social Interaction**: Virtual environments for communication and collaboration.
- **Commerce**: Digital marketplaces for goods and services.
- **Entertainment**: Gaming, concerts, and events hosted in shared digital spaces.
- **Education and Training**: Virtual classrooms and simulations for skills development.

Creating such experiences requires high-performance networking, real-time data processing, and scalable infrastructure, all of which AWS excels in providing.

2. Key Networking Challenges in the Metaverse

Developing and maintaining the metaverse involves overcoming several networking challenges:

- **Low Latency**: To ensure real-time interactivity in AR/VR applications.
- **High Bandwidth**: To support rich media content like 3D graphics and live streaming.
- **Global Scalability**: To cater to millions of simultaneous users worldwide.
- **Data Security**: To protect sensitive user data and digital assets.

AWS addresses these challenges through its suite of advanced networking services and global infrastructure.

3. AWS Services Supporting the Metaverse

Amazon CloudFront

- Delivers 3D assets, videos, and dynamic content to users with low latency.
- Supports edge caching to reduce the load on origin servers.

AWS Wavelength

- Extends AWS compute and storage capabilities to the edge of 5G networks.
- Enables ultra-low latency applications, essential for AR/VR experiences.

AWS Local Zones

- Brings compute, storage, and networking closer to end-users in metropolitan areas.
- Reduces latency for immersive gaming and real-time simulations.

AWS Outposts

- Provides consistent infrastructure on-premises for edge applications.
- Ideal for hybrid deployments of metaverse components.

AWS AppStream 2.0

- Streams virtual applications to end-users without requiring high-end hardware.
- Enables device-agnostic access to metaverse environments.

AWS GameLift

- Optimizes game server hosting for multiplayer metaverse experiences.
- Balances workloads dynamically for enhanced user experiences.

---

4. Building the Infrastructure for the Metaverse

Step 1: Design for Scalability

- Leverage **Amazon EC2 Auto Scaling** to manage fluctuating workloads.
- Use **AWS Elastic Load Balancing** to distribute traffic across servers seamlessly.

Step 2: Prioritize Low Latency

- Deploy workloads using **AWS Wavelength** for edge computing on 5G networks.
- Use **Amazon CloudFront** for content delivery from globally distributed edge locations.

Step 3: Optimize Data Management

- Use **Amazon S3** and **Amazon FSx** for scalable, low-latency storage of 3D assets.
- Employ **AWS IoT Greengrass** for real-time data processing at the edge.

Step 4: Enhance Security

- Use **Amazon GuardDuty** for threat detection and **AWS Shield** for DDoS protection.
- Encrypt sensitive user data with AWS Key Management Service (KMS).

---

5. Metaverse Use Cases with AWS Networking

1. **Immersive Gaming**
   - Use **AWS GameLift** to host multiplayer sessions with real-time updates.
   - Deliver rich gaming experiences via **AWS Wavelength** and **CloudFront**.
2. **Virtual Commerce**
   - Deploy virtual storefronts with real-time payment processing using **Amazon CloudFront** and **AWS Lambda**.
   - Use **Amazon RDS** to manage transactional data securely.
3. **Remote Collaboration**
   - Support virtual offices and meetings with **AWS Local Zones** for low-latency communication.
   - Integrate AR/VR tools with real-time data streams for enhanced collaboration.
4. **Smart Cities in the Metaverse**
   - Process IoT sensor data in real-time with **AWS IoT Core**.
   - Use **Amazon Kinesis** to analyze live data streams for virtual city simulations.

---

6. Overcoming Networking Challenges in the Metaverse

AWS provides the tools necessary to address the most pressing challenges in the metaverse:

- **Latency Management**: Using edge computing services like **AWS Wavelength** to minimize delays.
- **Content Delivery**: Leveraging **Amazon CloudFront** for rapid asset distribution.
- **Interoperability**: Utilizing **Amazon API Gateway** to enable communication between disparate platforms.
- **Global User Access**: Building multi-region architectures with **AWS Global Accelerator**.

---

7. The Future of AWS in the Metaverse

AWS continues to innovate, driving the future of the metaverse:

- **Edge Computing Expansion**: More AWS Wavelength zones to enhance global coverage.
- **AI Integration**: Advanced machine learning models for creating intelligent virtual assistants.
- **Blockchain Integration**: Enhanced support for decentralized applications and digital assets.

Conclusion

The metaverse represents the next frontier in digital interaction, requiring robust networking, scalable compute, and secure data management. AWS's suite of services, including **CloudFront**, **Wavelength**, and **GameLift**, empowers businesses to build and scale metaverse applications effectively.

Preparing for Future Trends in Cloud Networking

As cloud computing continues to evolve, the landscape of networking within cloud environments is experiencing rapid innovation. Organizations leveraging cloud services like AWS must remain adaptable to future trends to ensure their networks remain scalable, secure, and aligned with emerging technologies. This chapter explores the key trends shaping the future of cloud networking and provides guidance on how to prepare for these advancements effectively.

---

1. The Evolution of Cloud Networking

Cloud networking is no longer just about connectivity; it now encompasses automation, optimization, and integration with cutting-edge technologies such as artificial intelligence (AI), edge computing, and blockchain. The following factors are driving the evolution of cloud networking:

- **Increasing Demand for Low-Latency Applications**: Real-time applications like gaming, augmented reality (AR), and virtual reality (VR) require high-performance, low-latency networks.
- **The Proliferation of IoT Devices**: Billions of interconnected devices necessitate robust networking solutions capable of managing massive data flows.
- **The Shift to Hybrid and Multi-Cloud Architectures**: Organizations are opting for hybrid cloud environments, requiring seamless integration and interoperability.

---

2. Emerging Trends in Cloud Networking

a. Edge Computing and Distributed Architectures

Edge computing brings compute, storage, and networking closer to end-users, reducing latency and bandwidth costs. AWS services like **AWS Local Zones**, **AWS Wavelength**, and **AWS IoT Core** are at the forefront of this trend.

b. 5G Integration

The rollout of 5G networks will transform cloud networking, enabling ultra-low latency and higher bandwidth. AWS is already exploring 5G integration through services like **AWS Wavelength**, which extends compute resources to the edge of 5G networks.

c. Artificial Intelligence and Machine Learning in Networking

AI and machine learning (ML) are becoming integral to network automation, security, and performance optimization. AWS tools like **Amazon SageMaker** and **Amazon Lookout for Metrics** can be utilized for predictive analytics and anomaly detection.

d. Enhanced Network Automation

The push for zero-touch networking and autonomous operations is increasing. AWS offers automation tools like **AWS CloudFormation**, **AWS CDK**, and **AWS CLI** to streamline configuration and management tasks.

e. Blockchain for Network Security

Blockchain technology is being explored for secure data sharing and verification in networking. AWS Blockchain Templates provide a foundation for building decentralized applications.

---

3. Preparing for Future Cloud Networking Trends

a. Invest in Education and Training

To stay ahead, organizations must prioritize upskilling their teams in emerging networking technologies:

- Enroll in AWS training programs focused on edge computing, 5G, and AI/ML.
- Gain certifications such as AWS Certified Networking – Specialty to stay competitive.

b. Design for Scalability and Flexibility

Future-proof your network by adopting scalable and flexible architectures:

- Use **AWS Auto Scaling** and **Elastic Load Balancing** to handle fluctuating workloads.
- Build multi-region architectures to ensure global coverage and disaster recovery.

c. Embrace Automation and Monitoring

Implement tools for automated network management and monitoring:

- Utilize **AWS CloudWatch** for real-time metrics and alerts.
- Automate repetitive tasks with **AWS Systems Manager** and **AWS Lambda**.

d. Leverage Edge Computing Services

Prepare for edge computing by adopting AWS services designed for distributed architectures:

- Deploy **AWS Outposts** for on-premises workloads that require low latency.
- Use **AWS IoT Core** to connect and manage IoT devices seamlessly.

e. Focus on Security

Stay proactive about security as networks grow more complex:

- Use **AWS Shield Advanced** and **Amazon GuardDuty** to protect against evolving threats.
- Implement robust encryption and key management strategies with AWS KMS.

---

4. The Role of AWS in Shaping Future Networking

AWS is a leader in cloud networking innovation, consistently introducing services and features that align with future trends. Key areas of focus include:

- **Sustainability Initiatives**: AWS is investing in green data centers and energy-efficient networks to support sustainability goals.
- **Enhanced AI/ML Capabilities**: AWS continues to expand its suite of AI-driven tools for network monitoring and optimization.
- **Global Expansion**: AWS is increasing its presence with new regions, availability zones, and edge locations to meet global demand.

---

5. Real-World Applications

a. Smart Cities

AWS-powered networks are enabling smart city initiatives by connecting IoT devices, processing real-time data, and ensuring secure communication.

b. Autonomous Vehicles

5G and edge computing will drive advancements in autonomous vehicle networks, with AWS supporting data processing and real-time decision-making.

c. Remote Work and Collaboration

AWS networking tools are facilitating seamless remote work and global collaboration through services like **Amazon WorkSpaces** and **Amazon Chime**.

Conclusion

Preparing for future trends in cloud networking requires a proactive approach to adopting new technologies, automating processes, and prioritizing security. AWS offers a comprehensive suite of services to address these challenges, enabling organizations to build resilient, future-ready networks.

By understanding and embracing emerging trends, businesses can leverage AWS to remain competitive in an increasingly digital world.

Appendices

Appendix A: Glossary of AWS Networking Terms

This glossary provides definitions for key terms used in AWS networking, serving as a quick reference for readers to understand complex concepts and terminologies introduced in the book.

A

- **Access Control List (ACL)**: A set of rules that control incoming and outgoing network traffic for a subnet. AWS offers Network ACLs to provide an additional layer of security for VPCs.
- **Amazon CloudFront**: A content delivery network (CDN) service that securely delivers data, videos, applications, and APIs to customers globally with low latency.
- **Amazon Route 53**: A highly available and scalable DNS web service for domain registration, routing traffic, and health checking.
- **AWS Auto Scaling**: A service that automatically adjusts compute capacity to maintain steady, predictable performance.
- **AWS Direct Connect**: A dedicated network connection between your premises and AWS for increased bandwidth and lower latency.
- **AWS Outposts**: Fully managed AWS infrastructure that extends AWS services to on-premises locations.

C

- **CloudFormation**: An AWS service that enables infrastructure as code by defining and provisioning AWS resources using templates.
- **CloudWatch**: A monitoring and observability service for AWS resources and applications, offering metrics, logs, and alarms.
- **Content Delivery Network (CDN)**: A distributed network of servers that delivers web content and media to users based on their geographic location.

D

- **Domain Name System (DNS)**: The system that translates domain names (like www.example.com) into IP addresses, enabling internet communication.
- **DDoS (Distributed Denial of Service)**: A type of cyberattack where multiple systems overwhelm a target with excessive traffic. AWS offers services like AWS Shield to mitigate such attacks.

E

- **Elastic Load Balancer (ELB)**: A service that automatically distributes incoming application traffic across multiple targets, such as EC2 instances or containers.
- **Elastic IP Address**: A static IPv4 address designed for dynamic cloud computing, allowing easy remapping to different instances.

- **Encryption**: The process of encoding data to protect its confidentiality and security.

I

- **IAM (Identity and Access Management)**: A service for securely controlling access to AWS resources, allowing fine-grained permission management.
- **Internet Gateway (IGW)**: A component that allows communication between instances in a VPC and the internet.

L

- **Latency**: The time it takes for data to travel from a source to a destination, often measured in milliseconds.
- **Load Balancer**: A networking device that distributes incoming network traffic across multiple servers to improve performance and reliability.

N

- **NAT Gateway**: A service that enables instances in a private subnet to access the internet or other AWS services without exposing the instances to incoming internet traffic.
- **Network Access Control List (NACL)**: A layer of security for your VPC that acts as a firewall for controlling traffic in and out of subnets.

P

- **Peering Connection**: A networking connection between two VPCs that allows them to route traffic privately.
- **PrivateLink**: A service that enables secure access to AWS services and applications over private connectivity.

R

- **Region**: A physical location around the world where AWS clusters data centers. Each region is isolated and contains multiple availability zones.
- **Route Table**: A set of rules, called routes, that determine where network traffic is directed.

S

- **Security Group**: A virtual firewall for controlling inbound and outbound traffic to and from AWS resources like EC2 instances.
- **Shared Responsibility Model**: The model that defines AWS's and the customer's responsibilities for security and compliance.

T

- **Transit Gateway**: A network transit hub that allows customers to connect their VPCs and on-premises networks to a single gateway.

V

- **Virtual Private Cloud (VPC)**: A logically isolated section of the AWS Cloud where you can launch AWS resources in a virtual network that you define.
- **VPN (Virtual Private Network)**: A secure connection that enables communication between your on-premises network and your AWS VPC over the internet.

Z

- **Zone**: Refers to an **Availability Zone (AZ)**, an isolated location within a region that provides redundancy and availability.

Appendix B: Key AWS Networking CLI Commands

This appendix serves as a comprehensive reference for essential AWS CLI commands used in managing and configuring AWS networking services. These commands help automate networking tasks, troubleshoot issues, and streamline workflows. For each command, its description and typical usage are provided.

General CLI Usage

- **aws configure:** Configures the AWS CLI with your credentials, default region, and output format.
  Example: `aws configure`
- **aws help:** Displays help information for AWS CLI commands.
  Example: `aws ec2 help`

Virtual Private Cloud (VPC)

- **Create a VPC:** Creates a VPC with a specified CIDR block.
  Example: `aws ec2 create-vpc --cidr-block 10.0.0.0/16`
- **Describe VPCs:** Lists all VPCs in your account.
  Example: `aws ec2 describe-vpcs`
- **Delete a VPC:** Deletes a specific VPC.
  Example: `aws ec2 delete-vpc --vpc-id vpc-0abc123def456`

Subnets

- **Create a Subnet:** Creates a subnet within a specified VPC and CIDR block.
  Example: `aws ec2 create-subnet --vpc-id vpc-0abc123def456 --cidr-block 10.0.1.0/24`
- **Describe Subnets:** Lists all subnets in your account.
  Example: `aws ec2 describe-subnets`
- **Delete a Subnet:** Deletes a specific subnet.
  Example: `aws ec2 delete-subnet --subnet-id subnet-0abc123def456`

Internet Gateway (IGW)

- **Create an Internet Gateway:** Creates an Internet Gateway for use with a VPC.
  Example: `aws ec2 create-internet-gateway`
- **Attach Internet Gateway:** Attaches an Internet Gateway to a specified VPC.
  Example: `aws ec2 attach-internet-gateway --internet-gateway-id igw-0abc123def456 --vpc-id vpc-0abc123def456`
- **Detach Internet Gateway:** Detaches an Internet Gateway from a VPC.
  Example: `aws ec2 detach-internet-gateway --internet-gateway-id igw-0abc123def456 --vpc-id vpc-0abc123def456`
- **Delete Internet Gateway:** Deletes a specific Internet Gateway.
  Example: `aws ec2 delete-internet-gateway --internet-gateway-id igw-0abc123def456`

Route Tables

- **Create a Route Table:** Creates a route table within a VPC.
  Example: `aws ec2 create-route-table --vpc-id vpc-0abc123def456`
- **Describe Route Tables:** Lists all route tables in your account.
  Example: `aws ec2 describe-route-tables`
- **Associate a Subnet with a Route Table:** Associates a subnet with a specific route table.
  Example: `aws ec2 associate-route-table --route-table-id rtb-0abc123def456 --subnet-id subnet-0abc123def456`
- **Create a Route:** Adds a route to a route table.
  Example: `aws ec2 create-route --route-table-id rtb-0abc123def456 --destination-cidr-block 0.0.0.0/0 --gateway-id igw-0abc123def456`

Security Groups

- **Create a Security Group:** Creates a security group within a VPC.
  Example: `aws ec2 create-security-group --group-name my-sg --description "My security group" --vpc-id vpc-0abc123def456`
- **Authorize Inbound Traffic:** Allows inbound traffic on a specific port.
  Example: `aws ec2 authorize-security-group-ingress --group-id sg-0abc123def456 --protocol tcp --port 80 --cidr 0.0.0.0/0`
- **Revoke Inbound Traffic:** Removes an inbound rule from a security group.
  Example: `aws ec2 revoke-security-group-ingress --group-id sg-0abc123def456 --protocol tcp --port 80 --cidr 0.0.0.0/0`

Elastic Load Balancer (ELB)

- **Create a Load Balancer:** Creates an Application Load Balancer.
  Example: `aws elbv2 create-load-balancer --name my-load-balancer --subnets subnet-0abc123 subnet-1def456`
- **Describe Load Balancers:** Lists all load balancers.
  Example: `aws elbv2 describe-load-balancers`
- **Delete a Load Balancer:** Deletes a specific load balancer.
  Example: `aws elbv2 delete-load-balancer --load-balancer-arn arn:aws:elasticloadbalancing:region:account-id:loadbalancer/app/my-load-balancer/50dc6c495c0c9188`

AWS Direct Connect

- **Describe Connections:** Lists all AWS Direct Connect connections.
  Example: `aws directconnect describe-connections`

VPN and Hybrid Networking

- **Create a VPN Connection:** Creates a VPN connection between your on-premises network and AWS.

Example: `aws ec2 create-vpn-connection --type ipsec.1 --customer-gateway-id cgw-0abc123def456 --vpn-gateway-id vgw-0abc123def456`

- **Describe VPN Connections:** Lists all VPN connections.
  Example: `aws ec2 describe-vpn-connections`

This appendix equips readers with the foundational AWS CLI commands necessary for configuring, monitoring, and managing AWS networking services effectively. Readers are encouraged to explore further CLI capabilities to automate complex workflows and enhance operational efficiency.

Appendix C: Comparison of AWS Networking Tools with Other Cloud Providers

This appendix provides an in-depth comparison of key AWS networking tools with their counterparts from other major cloud providers, including Microsoft Azure, Google Cloud Platform (GCP), and Oracle Cloud Infrastructure (OCI). Understanding these differences will help users select the right platform for their networking needs or better integrate multi-cloud strategies.

Virtual Networking

Feature	AWS	Azure	GCP	OCI
Virtual Network	Virtual Private Cloud (VPC)	Virtual Network (VNet)	Virtual Private Cloud (VPC)	Virtual Cloud Network (VCN)
Subnet Management	Fully customizable	Fully customizable	Fully customizable	Fully customizable
Regions & Zones	Regions, Availability Zones (AZs)	Regions, Availability Zones	Regions, Zones	Regions, Fault Domains
Multi-region Support	Transit Gateway	Global VNet Peering	VPC Network Peering	Dynamic Routing Gateway

Key Insights:

- AWS and GCP offer robust VPC peering options across regions.
- Azure provides a simpler global VNet peering mechanism without requiring additional gateways.
- OCI's dynamic routing gateway simplifies hybrid cloud connectivity.

Load Balancing

Feature	AWS	Azure	GCP	OCI
Basic Load Balancer	Elastic Load Balancer (ELB)	Azure Load Balancer	Network Load Balancer	Load Balancer
Advanced Load Balancer	Application Load Balancer (ALB)	Azure Application Gateway	HTTP(S) Load Balancer	Load Balancer (Layer 7 support)
Global Load Balancer	AWS Global Accelerator	Azure Traffic Manager	Cloud CDN + Global Load Balancer	Traffic Management Steering Policies
Scaling	Auto Scaling Groups with Load Balancer	Integrated Autoscale with Load Balancer	Managed Instance Groups	Autoscaling within Load Balancer Policy

Key Insights:

- AWS ALB provides superior support for containerized workloads with ECS/EKS.

- GCP's Global Load Balancer excels in performance for globally distributed applications.
- Azure Traffic Manager integrates DNS-based traffic routing but lacks direct load balancing capabilities.

Networking Security

Feature	AWS	Azure	GCP	OCI
Firewall Rules	Security Groups, NACLs	NSGs, Application Security Groups	Firewall Rules, VPC Network Firewall	Security Lists, NSGs
DDoS Protection	AWS Shield	Azure DDoS Protection	Cloud Armor	DDoS Protection
Encryption	KMS for Networking Traffic	Azure Key Vault	CMEK (Customer-Managed Encryption Keys)	Vault
Identity and Access	IAM	Azure AD	IAM	IAM

Key Insights:

- AWS Shield Advanced offers one of the most comprehensive DDoS protection solutions.
- Azure's integration with Active Directory simplifies identity management for hybrid environments.
- GCP's Cloud Armor is ideal for protecting web applications with preconfigured WAF rules.

Content Delivery Networks (CDNs)

Feature	AWS	Azure	GCP	OCI
CDN Service	Amazon CloudFront	Azure CDN	Cloud CDN	OCI Edge Services
Global Reach	450+ POPs worldwide	118+ POPs worldwide	140+ POPs worldwide	60+ POPs worldwide
Integration	Integrated with CloudFront	Azure Blob Storage	Cloud Storage	Object Storage
Cost Optimization	Savings Plans	Reserved Capacity	Sustained Use Discounts	Flexible Pricing

Key Insights:

- CloudFront provides the best integration with AWS-specific workloads.
- Azure's CDN offers versatile pricing tiers for small to large-scale deployments.
- GCP's CDN boasts low latency with edge caching closer to users globally.

Hybrid Networking

Feature	AWS	Azure	GCP	OCI
Direct Connectivity	AWS Direct Connect	ExpressRoute	Dedicated Interconnect	FastConnect
VPN Services	AWS Site-to-Site VPN	Azure VPN Gateway	Cloud VPN	VPN Connect
Hybrid Cloud Management	AWS Outposts	Azure Arc	Anthos	Oracle Roving Edge
Multi-cloud Networking	Transit Gateway + VPC Peering	Virtual WAN	Global Cloud Router	Service Gateway + Dynamic Routing

Key Insights:

- AWS Direct Connect integrates seamlessly with hybrid cloud environments.
- Azure ExpressRoute offers excellent low-latency connections for enterprise workloads.
- GCP Anthos is a leader in multi-cloud workload management.

Final Thoughts

AWS remains a leading cloud provider with powerful networking capabilities, particularly in areas such as hybrid networking, global reach, and security. However, Azure, GCP, and OCI each offer unique features that may be advantageous depending on the specific use case or organizational requirements. For organizations considering multi-cloud strategies, understanding these differences is key to leveraging the strengths of each platform effectively.

Appendix D: Troubleshooting Checklist for Common AWS Networking Issues

This appendix provides a comprehensive checklist to help you identify, diagnose, and resolve common networking issues in AWS environments. This step-by-step guide will ensure faster troubleshooting and minimize downtime in your cloud infrastructure.

---

1. General Connectivity Issues

- **Checklist:**
    1. Verify that the VPC, subnets, and route tables are correctly configured.
    2. Ensure the instance is assigned a public IP address if accessing it from the internet.
    3. Confirm that the security group allows inbound and outbound traffic for required ports and protocols.
    4. Check Network Access Control Lists (NACLs) for conflicting rules.
    5. Use **ping** or **telnet** commands to test connectivity between endpoints.
    6. Verify that Internet Gateways (IGWs) or NAT Gateways are attached to the correct VPC.

---

2. Instance Accessibility Issues

- **Checklist:**
    1. Confirm that the instance is in a running state and has the necessary IAM roles assigned.
    2. Check for an appropriate key pair and ensure the private key is accessible.
    3. Verify inbound rules in the instance's security group for SSH (port 22) or RDP (port 3389) access.
    4. Ensure the correct Elastic IP is associated with the instance, if applicable.
    5. Review VPC Flow Logs to analyze denied traffic.

---

3. Load Balancer Configuration Problems

- **Checklist:**
    1. Confirm that the Load Balancer is associated with the correct subnets and Availability Zones.
    2. Ensure that the target instances are healthy in the target group.
    3. Check security group rules for both the Load Balancer and the target instances.
    4. Review listener configurations for correct protocols (HTTP, HTTPS, TCP) and ports.
    5. Test connectivity using tools like **curl** or a browser to validate endpoint responses.

---

4. DNS Resolution Issues

- **Checklist:**
    1. Confirm that the Amazon Route 53 DNS configuration matches the required domain or subdomain.
    2. Validate the record set types (A, CNAME, etc.) for correct configurations.
    3. Use **nslookup** or **dig** to test DNS resolution.
    4. Check for missing or incorrect alias targets for Load Balancers or S3 buckets.
    5. Verify VPC DNS settings and ensure the DNS resolution feature is enabled.

5. NAT Gateway or Internet Gateway Issues

- **Checklist:**
    1. Ensure that the NAT Gateway is associated with a public subnet and has an Elastic IP assigned.
    2. Verify that private instances are configured to use the NAT Gateway in their route table.
    3. Confirm that the Internet Gateway is attached to the correct VPC.
    4. Test outbound connectivity using tools like **wget** or **curl** from private instances.

6. Hybrid Networking Issues

- **Checklist:**
    1. Confirm that AWS Direct Connect or VPN connections are properly established.
    2. Validate routing configurations on both the AWS and on-premises sides.
    3. Ensure that BGP settings are correctly configured for dynamic routing.
    4. Use **traceroute** or **ping** to check latency and packet loss between endpoints.
    5. Check AWS Transit Gateway settings if multiple VPCs are involved.

7. Security Group and Firewall Misconfigurations

- **Checklist:**
    1. Review inbound and outbound rules for any blocked ports or IPs.
    2. Ensure there are no overlapping or conflicting rules in NACLs and security groups.
    3. Validate firewall settings on EC2 instances, such as iptables or Windows Firewall.
    4. Use AWS Network Access Analyzer to identify misconfigurations.

8. High Latency or Network Performance Issues

- **Checklist:**
    1. Use **Amazon CloudWatch** metrics to monitor network traffic and instance performance.
    2. Enable **VPC Flow Logs** to identify bottlenecks or dropped packets.
    3. Test application performance with **AWS Global Accelerator** for low-latency routing.
    4. Check instance type and networking capabilities (e.g., Enhanced Networking).
    5. Ensure proper scaling configurations for traffic spikes.

9. Cross-Region or VPC Peering Problems

- **Checklist:**
    1. Confirm that VPC peering connections are in the "Active" state.
    2. Verify route table entries to allow traffic between peered VPCs.
    3. Ensure there is no overlapping CIDR range between VPCs.
    4. Test connectivity using private IP addresses between resources.
    5. Check that security group rules allow traffic from the peered VPC.

10. AWS Service-Specific Networking Issues

- **Checklist:**
  - ○ **S3 Bucket Access:** Ensure proper bucket policies and public access settings.
  - ○ **RDS Connectivity:** Confirm that RDS is in a publicly accessible or peered VPC.
  - ○ **EKS Networking:** Validate VPC CNI plugin configurations and subnet settings.
  - ○ **Elasticache Access:** Verify security group rules and cluster/subnet configurations.

---

11. Monitoring and Logging for Troubleshooting

- **Checklist:**
  1. Enable **VPC Flow Logs** to analyze traffic patterns.
  2. Use **CloudTrail** logs to trace API activity related to networking configurations.
  3. Leverage **Amazon CloudWatch Logs Insights** for in-depth analysis.
  4. Use **AWS Trusted Advisor** for automated recommendations.
  5. Monitor DNS logs with Route 53 Query Logging for domain-level issues.

Final Tips for Troubleshooting

- **Documentation:** Always refer to AWS documentation for service-specific troubleshooting steps.
- **Automation:** Use AWS CLI or SDKs to gather logs and automate remediation tasks.
- **Support:** Contact AWS Support if issues persist or require advanced troubleshooting.

This checklist provides a practical framework to address and resolve networking issues systematically in AWS environments. For complex issues, combining these steps with AWS support tools ensures quick recovery and efficient cloud operations.

Conclusion

As we conclude **"AWS Networking: Building Robust Cloud Networks"**, it's evident that mastering AWS networking is both a journey and a cornerstone of modern cloud architecture. The tools and techniques covered in this book empower you to design, implement, and optimize scalable, secure, and highly available networks in AWS environments.

Key Takeaways

- **Foundation of AWS Networking:** You have explored the core concepts, services, and components that underpin networking in AWS, from Virtual Private Clouds (VPCs) to routing and addressing mechanisms.
- **Security and Best Practices:** We delved into critical security aspects, including firewalls, identity management, and threat detection tools, equipping you with strategies to protect your cloud environment effectively.
- **Advanced Networking Capabilities:** The book covered advanced tools like Transit Gateway, Elastic Load Balancers, and AWS Global Accelerator, which facilitate seamless scaling and interconnectivity.
- **Performance and Monitoring:** Performance metrics, monitoring tools like CloudWatch, and optimization strategies ensure your AWS networks operate at their peak efficiency.
- **Real-World Applications:** Practical examples, from IoT integrations to big data workloads, showcased how AWS networking can be applied across diverse use cases.
- **Emerging Trends:** Lastly, we looked toward the future, highlighting AWS's pivotal role in technologies like 5G, edge computing, and the metaverse.

Embracing Continuous Learning

The dynamic nature of cloud computing requires staying updated with the latest AWS offerings and best practices. AWS consistently innovates, introducing new services and enhancements to meet evolving business needs. By leveraging AWS documentation, training resources, and community support, you can stay ahead in this ever-changing landscape.

The Bigger Picture

Networking is not an isolated discipline but a critical part of the larger cloud ecosystem. As you implement and refine your AWS networks, remember to align them with broader organizational goals—whether it's improving agility, ensuring compliance, or driving cost efficiencies.

Call to Action

Now that you are equipped with a deep understanding of AWS networking:

1. Apply the knowledge gained to build and optimize networks in your own projects.
2. Experiment with advanced tools and features to enhance your deployments.
3. Share your expertise and contribute to the AWS community by helping others navigate networking challenges.

AWS networking is the backbone of scalable and secure cloud solutions. By mastering these concepts and tools, you are well-positioned to lead the design and management of robust networks that power modern applications and services. Thank you for embarking on this journey, and here's to your continued success in AWS networking.